Introduction to futures and options

KEITH REDHEAD
Principal Lecturer in Economics
Coventry Polytechnic

Woodhead-Faulkner
NEW YORK LONDON TORONTO SYDNEY
TOKYO SINGAPORE

Published by Woodhead-Faulkner Limited,
Simon & Schuster International Group,
Fitzwilliam House, 32 Trumpington Street,
Cambridge CB2 1QY, England

First published 1990
Second impression 1992

British Library Cataloguing in Publication Data
Redhead, Keith, *1949–*
Introduction to financial futures and options.
1. Futures markets 2. Stock markets. Options
I. Title
332.644

ISBN 0-85941-624-0

Designed by Geoff Green
Typeset by Vision Typesetting, Manchester
Printed in Great Britain by BPCC Wheatons Ltd, Exeter

Contents

Contents

Preface

Whilst chief examiner for the financial futures and options paper on the securities industry examinations programme I became aware of the insufficiency of textbooks, in particular of books suitable for beginners. The shortage of suitable texts was also apparent when I took on the role of course leader of the City University course on financial futures and options. This book aims to fill that gap. It is a book that assumes no previous knowledge of financial futures and options but nevertheless takes the reader to a reasonably high level of sophistication in the subject. The book would therefore be read to advantage by both beginners and experienced market professionals.

The book is relatively non-mathematical: for the most part no more than a competence in arithmetic is required. Along with the provision of an intuitive understanding of the concepts and potential applications, there are numerous worked examples based on the sorts of problem that practitioners might face. It is to be emphasised that the suggested answers to these problems are not necessarily the only ones: there may be numerous possible solutions to any particular problem.

Each of Chapters 1–4 deals with one of the four classes of financial futures contract (currency futures, short-term interest rate futures, long-term interest rate futures and stock index futures). Each chapter considers the nature, the pricing and the potential uses of the respective instrument. Each class of financial futures contract has its own distinctive characteristics and it is therefore logical to treat each type of futures contract in turn.

Chapters 5–7 are concerned with options. These chapters are distinguished according to usage (hedging, trading and arbitrage) rather than according to type of option. The principles relating to the nature, pricing and use of options are largely common to all types of option contract. At any one point the concepts will be explained in relation to one type of option (currency, stock, stock index, bond or futures) but the reader should bear in mind that the principles involved relate equally to the other types of option.

Chapter 8 is on the use of futures and options in portfolio management. It is illustrative of a relatively well-developed area of usage and provides a good context in which to develop further the principles relating to the usage of these financial derivatives. Chapter 9 aims to provide the reader with a feel for approaches to the taxation of financial futures and options; any user of these instruments needs to be aware of the tax liabilities being incurred. Finally, Chapter 10 looks at possible future developments.

I should like to thank Mamie and Marjorie for the immense patience they have shown in the operation of word processors and typewriters on my behalf.

Introduction

Financial futures and options, alternatively known as financial derivatives, have emerged in response to price volatility in financial markets. Futures and options are means of managing risk with a view to reducing it – in other words, hedging. Futures markets for agricultural produce developed in Chicago in the mid-nineteenth century as a result of the substantial price fluctuations faced by the buyers and sellers of that produce. Agricultural futures allowed farmers to guarantee selling prices and merchants to guarantee buying prices so that both groups could be assured that they would not transact at loss-making prices.

Financial futures date from 1972, at which time currency futures emerged in response to the fluctuations in currency prices following the breakdown of the Bretton Woods fixed exchange rate system. Currency futures were followed by short-term interest rate futures, long-term interest rate (bond) futures and stock index futures. These developments in the financial futures markets were paralleled by innovations in options markets. Whereas a futures contract provides simultaneously the right and the obligation to buy/sell at a particular price in the future, an option provides the right but not the obligation to buy/sell at a specified price. Financial options are now available on currencies, stocks, bonds, interest rates, stock indices and futures.

Outsiders sometimes see financial futures and options markets as highly volatile speculative markets that contribute to instability in other financial markets. On the contrary, these markets arise in response to price instability in financial markets and are providers of means to reduce the risks associated with that instability. Futures and options provide a degree of certainty in an uncertain world.

This is not to suggest that there is no place for the more speculatively minded participants who seek to trade in financial futures and options in order to make profits rather than to reduce risks. Such traders are essential if the derivatives markets are to fulfil their function of providing means of hedging risks. It is unlikely that hedgers wishing to buy a particular contract are precisely matched by hedgers wanting to sell. Speculative traders will bring about a matching of buy and sell orders since they will sell when there is excess demand and buy when there is excess supply (the speculative traders would be responding to the respective price rises and price falls).

Financial futures and options provide fascinating opportunities for people wishing to trade in derivatives. For example, with futures it is possible to guarantee a selling price for something that you do not have and that you have no intention of ever delivering. Options provide the opportunity to buy or sell rights to buy or sell. Futures options (options on futures) allow one to buy or sell rights to buy or sell notional commitments to buy or sell.

Financial futures and options render possible a vast variety of strategies for managing financial risk.

The range of instruments for which there are financial futures and options contracts is indicated by Table I.1, which shows all the futures and options for which in excess of 100,000 contracts were traded during July 1989 (unless otherwise stated, futures contracts are being referred to). It is also suggestive of which exchanges are the most important.

Table I.1 Financial futures and options trading in excess of 100,000 contracts during July 1989

Contract	Exchange	July volume[1]	End of July open interest[2]
Stock indices			
XMI option	Amex	636,951	63,322
S & P 100 option	CBOE	4,977,829	676,203
S & P 500 option	CBOE	400,338	445,381
S & P 500	CME	751,267	122,096
S & P 500 option	CME	122,879	61,179
Dutch stock index option	EOE	151,414	89,952
FTSE 100 option	LTOM	162,995	76,568
NYSE composite	NYFE	123,768	6,305
Nikkei 225	Osaka	472,476	27,761
Swedish OMX index	SOM	278,706	68,225
Topix	TSE	292,844	30,709
Currencies			
D-mark 125,000	CME	594,387	66,181
D-mark 125,000 option	CME	236,143	164,977
Yen 12.5m	CME	638,838	56,683
Yen option	CME	244,290	155,827
BP £25,000	CME	186,322	26,345
SwFr 125,000	CME	420,754	39,847
D-mark 62,500 option	PHLX	427,791	290,961
Yen 6.25m option	PHLX	233,731	260,775
SwFr 62,500 option	PHLX	131,145	98,276
Interest rates			
US T-bond	CBOT	5,231,164	352,210
US T-bond option	CBOT	1,613,130	738,307
US T-note	CBOT	452,991	84,524
US T-note option	CBOT	109,909	85,022
US 5-yr T-note	CBOT	142,336	48,580
Eurodollar	CME	3,193,429	709,810
Eurodollar option	CME	393,694	349,798
Long gilt	Liffe	315,887	30,870
3-mnth sterling	Liffe	536,847	90,547
German Bund	Liffe	349,872	41,840
Eurodollar	Liffe	131,474	50,671
10-yr French gov. bond	Matif	806,280	95,034
10-yr French gov. bond option	Matif	633,038	341,254
Pibor	Matif	129,566	18,220
Eurodollar	Simex	284,009	42,088
10-yr Aus. gov. bond	SFE	200,264	42,129
90-day bank bills	SFE	467,558	130,212
10-yr Japanese gov. bond	TSE	1,741,548	218,315

Table I.1 (cont.)

Stock options	Contracts traded
Chicago Board Options Exchange	
IBM	598,500
Warner	404,600
Cyntex	271,000
NWA	252,140
Paramount	244,480
UAL	208,820
Avon	173,620
Honeywell	141,500
Wittman Corp	123,440
Eastman Kodak	122,640
Soffex	
Swiss Bank Corporation	171,226
European Options Exchange	
Philips	191,680
Kon. Ned. Hoogovens Staalfabr	147,471
Philadelphia Stock Exchange	
Time Incorporated	412,632
LIN Broadcasting Corp	141,711
American Stock Exchange	
USX Corp	315,808
Philip Morris	208,692
Union Carbide	139,926
Digital Equipment	139,843
Walt Disney	100,838

Notes:
1. Volume refers to the number of contracts traded during a period of time.
2. Open interest refers to the number of contracts held at a point in time (at the end of a business day).

Abbreviations:
Amex American Stock Exchange; CBOE Chicago Board Options Exchange; CBOT Chicago Board of Trade; CME Chicago Mercantile Exchange; EOE European Options Exchange; Liffe London International Financial Futures Exchange; LTOM London Traded Options Market; MATIF Marché à Terme International de France; NYFE New York Futures Exchange; Osaka Osaka Stock Exchange; PHLX Philadelphia Stock Exchange; SFE Sydney Futures Exchange; Simex Singapore International Monetary Exchange; Soffex Swiss Options and Financial Futures Exchange; SOM Stockholm Options Market; TSE Tokyo Stock Exchange.

Source: Futures and Options World, September 1989.

1

Currency futures

The nature of financial futures

A currency futures contract provides a simultaneous right and obligation to buy or sell on a specific future date a standard amount of a particular currency at a price that is known at the time of entering the contract. These commitments are tradable. A contract can be closed out (i.e. cancelled) by buying or selling an opposite contract. If someone has bought a futures contract, that contract can be closed out by means of selling another contract, the two contracts cancelling each other out.

It is desirable that the markets in such contracts are liquid so as to ensure easy trading conditions. Financial futures contracts are highly standardised so as to enhance the quantities of each contract and thereby generate market liquidity. The contracts traded on financial futures exchanges have a limited number of maturity dates each year. The contract sizes are also standard: for example, for sterling currency contracts they are £25,000 on the London International Financial Futures Exchange (LIFFE) and £62,500 on the Chicago Mercantile Exchange (CME). This standardisation limits the number of different contracts available and correspondingly increases the volume traded in each case.

Clearing houses are important to the operation of futures exchanges, performing two crucial functions. One of these functions is the registration and confirmation of all transactions in the market each day, thus providing an up-to-date record of the current futures positions taken by members. The other function is to become the counterparty to every futures position. Once two members have traded futures contracts with each other, the clearing house substitutes itself for both counterparties. This eliminates the possibility of a holder of a contract suffering from default by the counterparty. Thus buyers and sellers of contracts do not need to assess the creditworthiness of the other party to the deal. This allows the open outcry system to operate. Open outcry means that trades are solicited and agreed by means of dealers shouting and using hand signals. This process takes place in areas of the exchange known as pits. Open outcry trading could not proceed if counterparties needed to investigate each other's creditworthiness.

Hedging currency risk

The sterling futures will be discussed in the following exposition. Fluctuations in exchange rates produce risk. Suppose a UK exporter sells goods to a US importer and the transaction is priced in US dollars. The British exporter is thus due to receive a sum of US dollars some time after the transaction is agreed upon. The exporter is then exposed to foreign exchange risk. A fall in the value of the US dollar relative to the pound sterling would reduce the sterling value of the receipts. This would reduce the profitability of the exports, and perhaps even render them loss making. If the exporter wishes to avoid such a risk he can hedge. By hedging with financial futures he seeks to guarantee the rate of exchange at which he will buy the sterling. He wants to know in advance how much he will receive in terms of sterling. The guaranteed exchange rate might be less favourable than the current rate, but at least he is free of the risk that it might be so unfavourable as to render the sale unprofitable.

A hedger transfers his risk. If he buys futures, someone else must sell them: that is, his acquisition of the simultaneous right and obligation to buy currency on a specified date in the future at a price agreed upon in the present is matched by another user's right and obligation to sell that currency at that date and price. In the above example, the risk that the US dollar may fall in value is transferred to the seller of sterling futures. If the dollar falls (and hence sterling rises against the dollar) this seller finds that he has committed himself to selling sterling at a price that is lower than the spot rate available at the time that the currency actually changes hands. The seller of sterling futures would be either a hedger wanting to avoid the opposite risk – that is, a rise in the US dollar relative to sterling – or a futures trader willing to take on the risk in the expectation of making a profit.

If neither of the hedgers had undertaken the futures transaction, one would have made a windfall loss and the other a windfall gain (unless, of course, the exchange rate remained unchanged). By locking in the current exchange rate the two parties ensure that neither gains or loses. One avoids a windfall loss whilst the other forgoes a windfall gain. The essential point is that both have reduced the risk that the exchange rate might move to their disadvantage. (If the exchange rate at which futures are traded differs from the current rate, the buying or selling of futures is in order to guarantee a particular exchange rate gain or loss. The fact remains that the uncertainty as to what exchange rate will be received has been reduced: insurance against unforeseen exchange rate movements has been obtained.)

It will probably be the case that the value of the hedging required for one direction of exchange rate change is not perfectly matched by the amount of hedging required for the opposite change. So, for example, transactors wishing to avoid losses from a rise in sterling against the US dollar may not find sufficient hedgers wanting to avoid the risk of a fall in the value of sterling. This is where speculators fulfil the function of making the market. A speculator buys and sells futures in anticipation of making profits. If the futures price is above what he expects it to become, he will sell futures since he anticipates the opportunity of subsequently buying at a lower price. A futures price below his expectation would lead him to buy futures in the anticipation of being able to sell at a higher price later.

Such activities by speculators ensure that hedgers will be able to carry out their transactions. Suppose that hedgers in aggregate want to sell more sterling futures than they want to buy. That will tend to reduce the futures price. The fall in the futures price will entice speculators to buy. Hence speculators will take up the excess supply of sterling futures and thereby enable all exporters and importers to carry out their required hedging operations. By behaving in this way speculators render the futures market liquid: they ensure that desires to buy and sell futures can be realised. Speculators are often looked upon as unproductive and destabilising. The above analysis indicates that, on the contrary, they serve a useful purpose. By making the market for futures liquid they allow exporters and importers to hedge.

Closing out

Hedgers do not need to hold contracts until maturity. They may close out contracts prior to maturity whilst still having successfully hedged their risks. Suppose that the British exporter anticipated the receipt of US dollars four months hence and wanted to hedge against the possibility of a fall in the value of the dollar in terms of sterling. He could buy sterling futures with a six-month maturity with a view to closing out in four months. Indeed, since futures contracts relate to a small number of specific maturity dates in a year, it is unlikely that a futures maturity date coincides with the date on which the dollars are to be received. On 10 March the exporter may anticipate dollar receipts on 10 July and hedge by buying September sterling futures. If a rise in the value of sterling in terms of the US dollar by 10 July is matched by a rise in the price of September sterling futures, the hedge will be successful. The hedger can sell September futures on 10 July at a higher price than that for which he bought them in March. If he does so he will have made a profit from the purchase and subsequent sale of futures, a profit which offsets the loss on the US dollar receivables resulting from the exchange rate change. The hedger, by selling September futures in July, has closed out – that is, cancelled out – his long position in sterling futures. The clearing house, being the counterparty to both the long and short positions, deems them to negate each other, leaving the hedger with no outstanding position in futures arising from these contracts.

Basis

This manoeuvre will precisely offset the loss on the dollar receivables only if September futures prices move to exactly the same extent as spot prices. The price difference between the futures instrument and the cash instrument being hedged is known as basis. If September sterling futures have the same price in terms of dollars as spot sterling, basis is said to be zero. If basis were zero on 10 March and also on 10 July, the futures prices would have moved precisely in line with spot prices and the hedge would have been perfect. However, if on 10 July the September futures had not risen to the same extent as spot sterling, the profit on the futures transactions would have been insufficient to offset completely the loss on the dollar receipts. There would have been a change in basis. September futures prices would have risen less than spot prices and this change in basis would have rendered the hedge incomplete. The possibility of a change in basis is known as basis risk. Changes in basis may operate either to or against the hedger's advantage. A hedger could be said to have substituted basis risk for the outright risk from an open – that is, unhedged – position in foreign currency. Generally, basis risk is considerably less than outright risk.

Ticks

A tick is the smallest change in the price of a futures contract permitted by a futures exchange. Each tick has a specific money value: for example, sterling currency futures have a tick of $2.50 on LIFFE and $12.50 on

CME. These are based on \$0.0001 per £1 and \$0.0002 per £1 on LIFFE and CME respectively.

In the case of Deutschmark currency futures (which are distinct from the dollar–mark futures) the face value of a contract is DM125,000 and the tick size \$0.0001 per Deutschmark on both LIFFE and CME. This yields a tick value of \$12.50 (0.0001 × 125,000).

Hypothetical examples

The points covered thus far may be clarified by means of hypothetical examples. The case in which the hedger holds a contract until maturity and then takes delivery of, and parts with, currency is relatively straightforward and will not be illustrated by examples. The examples will deal exclusively with the more complex, and far more frequent, procedure which involves the hedger closing out contracts before they reach maturity.

In Example 1.1 it is assumed that a British exporter anticipates receipt of \$1 million on 1 May. The sale of goods is agreed upon on 3 February and the exporter wants to hedge against the risk that the dollar will depreciate against the pound before 1 May, thus reducing the sterling value of the dollar receipts. The exporter might actually anticipate a fall in the dollar or might simply want to insure against the possibility of a weakening of the dollar. In either case the exporter could hedge by buying sterling futures.

Example 1.1

Cash market	*Futures market*
3 February	
Exporter anticipates receipt of \$1 million on 1 May. The spot exchange rate is £1=\$1.50 (\$1 million=£666,666).	Buys twenty-six June sterling futures contracts, at £25,000 per contract, at an exchange rate of £1=\$1.50. Total value is £650,000, committing the exporter to a payment of \$975,000 for £650,000 if the contracts are held to maturity.
1 May	
The dollar has fallen so that the exchange rate stands at £1=\$1.60. The sterling value of the \$1 million is now £625,000.	Sells twenty-six June sterling futures contracts at £1=\$1.60. This gives the exporter the right to the receipt of \$1,040,000 (650,000

	× 1.60) in exchange for £650,000 upon maturity of the contracts.
Loss is £666,666 − £625,000 = £41,666 ($66,666).	Profit is $65,000.

The loss in the cash market, arising from the weakening of the dollar, is largely offset by the profit in the futures market. The offset is not perfect since the £666,666 in the cash market is coupled with only £650,000 in the futures market. Such a mismatch arises from the denomination of sterling futures contracts in units of £25,000 – perfect matching is impossible. Fortunately, there is no change in basis. The exchange rate in the futures market moves in line with that in the cash market, and is indeed equal to it.

The exchange rate for futures need not be equal to, or move to the same extent as, the spot exchange rate. If the spot and futures rates change by different amounts, there is a change in basis and a degree of imperfection enters the hedge. This possibility is illustrated by Example 1.2, which differs from Example 1.1 only in the assumption that the rate of exchange for the June sterling futures moves to £1 = $1.58 rather than £1 = $1.60. Basis thus changes from zero to $0.02 and as a result the hedge is imperfect.

Example 1.2

Cash market	*Futures market*
3 February	
Exporter anticipates receipt of $1 million on 1 May. The spot exchange rate is £1 = $1.50 ($1 million = £666,666).	Buys twenty-six June sterling futures contracts at an exchange rate of £1 = $1.50. $975,000 is due to be paid for £650,000 upon maturity.
1 May	
The dollar has fallen so that the exchange rate stands at £1 = $1.60. The sterling value of the $1 million is now $625,000.	Sells twenty-six June sterling futures contracts at £1 = $1.58. This yields $1,027,000 (650,000 × 1.58) in exchange for £650,000 upon maturity.
Loss is £666,666 − £625,000 = £41,666 ($66,666).	Profit is $52,000.

The change in basis results in a net loss of \$14,666 (\$66,666 – \$52,000). The hedge is only partially successful. The hedger replaces outright risk with basis risk and consequently replaces a loss of \$66,666 with a loss of \$14,666.

Margins

Clearing houses seek to avoid the risk of default by holders of contracts. They do this by means of margin requirements. When taking out a contract, whether as a buyer or a seller, it is necessary to deposit a sum of money with the clearing house. This money is known as initial margin. It is returned to the contract holder when the contract matures or is closed out. Money may be deposited or other assets may be used as security: for example, government stock might be lodged with the clearing house (but will continue to earn interest for the contract holder). If prices move to the disadvantage of a transactor, such that closing out would involve a loss, he must pay variation margin to the value of the loss. In this way, the contract holder must ensure that, after every business day, his margin account balance is at least equal to the initial margin. Price movements in a contract holder's favour lead to gains that are credited to his margin account and can be withdrawn from that account. Should a contract holder be unable to pay the requisite variation margin, the clearing house has the right to close out his position. Outstanding losses will then be made good from the initial margin. Initial margin is set at a level which is very unlikely to be exceeded by the loss arising from the price movement of one day. The clearing house thus seeks to ensure that it will not make financial losses through the default of contract holders. The process of revaluing all contracts on daily closing prices and paying or receiving variation margin payments is known as marking to market.

Interest rate parity

It is to be expected that the relationship between spot and futures prices will reflect the differential between the interest rates of the two currencies concerned. So, for example, if sterling interest rates exceed US dollar interest rates (on the eurocurrency markets) by 2 per cent p.a., the price of sterling futures should show a 2 per cent p.a. rate of depreciation of sterling against the dollar. Thus if the spot value of sterling is £1 = \$1.50, the futures price for a delivery date six months hence should be £1 = \$1.485, representing a 1 per cent depreciation over six months.

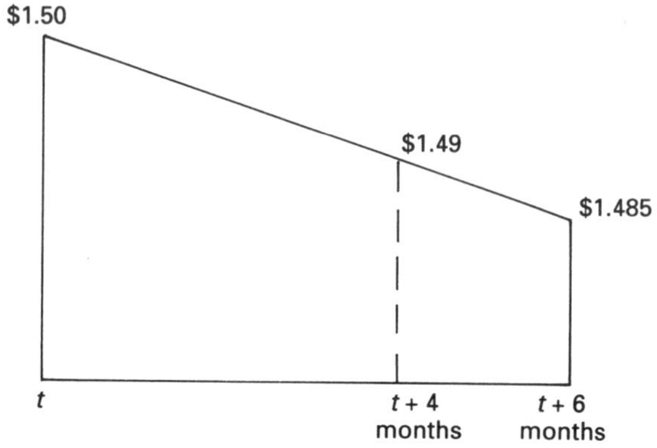

Figure 1.1 Variation of the effective exchange rate with time

The exchange rate that a hedger obtains will lie between the spot rate and the futures rate and will be dependent upon the timing of closing out. If the futures position is closed out immediately after being opened, the exchange rate obtained will be the spot rate, £1 = $1.50. If the contract is held to maturity, the rate obtained will be the futures rate ruling on the date of entering the contract, £1 = $1.485. Closing out on an intermediate date would attain an exchange rate between these two extremes, as indicated by Figure 1.1. The exchange rate obtained is a linear function of time. So, for example, if the futures contract is agreed at time *t* and closed out after 4 months, the exchange rate obtained would be £1 = $1.49.

The variation of the realised exchange rate with the passage of time can be explained in terms of changes in basis. Basis is initially $0.015 ($1.50 – $1.485) but after six months it will have eroded to zero: at maturity of a contract the futures and spot prices are identical. The difference between the spot and futures prices can be regarded as the rate of depreciation/appreciation required to offset the interest rate differential. As the time period shortens, the cash value of the interest rate differential falls proportionately and the corresponding depreciation/appreciation declines to match. So with just two months to maturity the cash value of a 2 per cent p.a. interest rate differential is one-third its level when six months remained and correspondingly the depreciation prior to maturity is $0.005 rather than the original $0.015.

As shown in Example 1.2, a change in basis renders a hedge imperfect. Figure 1.1 shows that basis changes over time, beginning at $0.015 and declining to zero. This change in basis renders hedging imperfect; and the greater the period of time that elapses, the more imperfect is the hedge. A contract that is closed out very quickly would entail little change in basis, the hedge would be nearly perfect and the exchange rate guaranteed would be very close to the spot rate when the contract was agreed. The more time that elapses before closing out, the greater is the change in basis and the larger is the divergence between the realised exchange rate and the spot rate ruling when the contract was entered into, as is illustrated by Figure 1.1.

Suppose, for example, that the spot exchange rate remained at \$1.50 for the whole six-month period. As the futures price converged towards the spot price, a buyer of the futures contract would receive variation margin payments. These receipts would be proportionate to the period of time that elapses, amounting to virtually zero after one day but to \$0.015 at expiry. Sterling would be purchased at \$1.50 but this would be offset by variation margin receipts varying from near zero after one day, so that the effective purchase price is \$1.50, to \$0.015 at expiry, so that the effective purchase price is \$1.485 (\$1.50 − \$0.015) (see Figure 1.2).

The foregoing might give the impression that if a hedger knows the date upon which the futures position will be closed out he knows by how much basis will have changed and can take this into account when designing the hedging strategy. He would appear to lock in a known profit or loss. However, basis would be deflected from the path suggested by the figures if the interest rate differential were to change. For example, if at the date $t+4$ months the interest rate differential had doubled to 4 per cent p.a. then the basis would be \$0.01 rather than \$0.005. So if basis risk were to be defined in terms of the possibility of unexpected (that is, excluding the predictable element) changes in basis, it can be seen to emanate from the

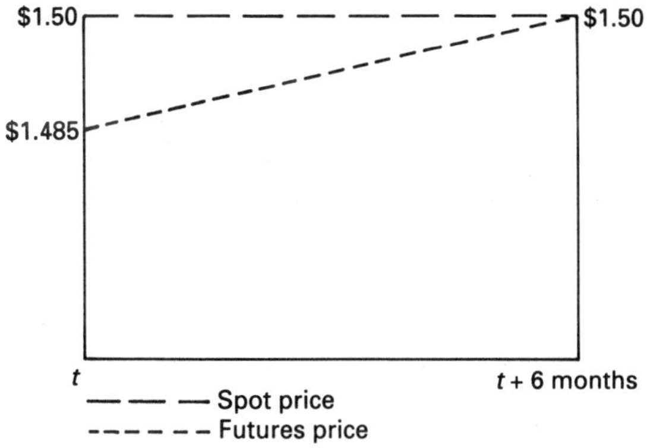

Figure 1.2 Variation of the effective purchase price with time

possibility of changes in the interest rate differential between the two currencies concerned.

Trading with currency futures

Traders play an important role in ensuring the liquidity of futures markets. There are long-term traders who hold contracts for days, weeks or even months in order to profit from price movements. There are day traders who may hold contracts for several hours but will always close out positions before the end of the business day. Finally, there are scalpers who keep positions open for merely seconds or minutes in order to make profits from small price movements occurring in short periods of time. If, for example, sales of March sterling currency futures contracts tend to outnumber purchases, there will be a tendency for the price of such contracts to fall. Traders seeing a divergence between the normal price and the weakened price will enter the market to buy such contracts. They will do so in the anticipation of making a profit when the price returns to normal. They buy at the lowered price with a view to selling when the price has risen to what they see as its normal level. Thus the excess supply of March sterling currency futures contracts is taken up by traders. In this way, other sellers (and buyers) of contracts can be assured of readily finding buyers (and sellers).

Trading can be divided into position trading and spread trading. Position trading involves buying or selling contracts in the anticipation of closing out at a profit when the price has moved in the expected direction. Position traders aim to make profits from changes in the prices of futures contracts. Spread traders seek to profit from changes in the relationships between the prices of futures contracts.

Spread trading

A spread is the purchase of one futures instrument coupled with the simultaneous sale of a different futures instrument. For example, short government bond futures contracts might be bought simultaneously with the sale of long government bond futures contracts. A straddle is a particular type of spread which involves contracts relating to the same underlying instrument but being for different maturity months. For example, a June sterling currency contract might be bought simultaneously with the sale of a September sterling currency contract.

Example 1.3

10 April
Buys a June sterling currency futures contract at £1 = $1.45.
Sells a September sterling currency futures contract at £1 = $1.47.

10 May
Closes out by selling June sterling currency futures contract at £1 = $1.46.
Closes out by buying a September sterling currency futures contract at £1 = $1.46.

Example 1.3 illustrates a straddle spread which is held by a trader who takes the view that the June sterling currency futures price will rise relative to that of the September contract. The trader makes a profit equal to 1 cent per £1 (100 ticks) on each of the two contracts. Since the contract size is £25,000, the profit is $250 on each of the two contracts. The trader took a view on the relative price of the June and September contracts. Any price movement common to both contracts would make no difference to the profitability of the trade.

Example 1.4

10 April
Buys a June sterling currency futures contract at £1 = $1.45.
Sells a September sterling currency futures contract at £1 = $1.47.

10 May
Closes out by selling a June sterling currency futures contract at £1 = $1.43.
Closes out by buying a September sterling currency futures contract at £1 = $1.43.

Example 1.4 differs from Example 1.3 in exhibiting a price movement common to both contracts. The trader makes a loss of 2 cents per £1 on the June contract and a profit of 4 cents per £1 on the September contract. A net profit of $500 is obtained as in Example 1.3. Despite the difference in the final exchange rates between the two examples, the profit is the same.

This is because both examples exhibit the same relative price change. It is the relative price change that affects profits; a price change common to both contracts has no effect on profits since a profit from one of the contracts would be offset by an equal loss on the other.

Spread positions, particularly straddle spreads, often display less volatility than pure open positions. In recognition of this, straddles on some exchanges involve lower initial margin requirements than pure open positions. The probability of large day-to-day common price movements is seen as being far higher than the probability of large day-to-day relative price movements.

A trader is said to buy a straddle when the nearest (earliest maturity) futures contract is the one being bought. If the nearest contract is being sold, the trader is said to be selling the straddle. The size of a straddle is the price of the first maturing futures contract minus the price of the later maturity contract.

If the size of the straddle becomes more positive or less negative, the spread is said to strengthen. Conversely, if it becomes less positive or more negative, it is weakening. If a straddle is expected to strengthen, it should be bought; if it is expected to weaken, selling is appropriate. In Examples 1.3 and 1.4 the straddle was expected to strengthen and was therefore bought. The subsequent strengthening of the straddle resulted in a profit for the trader.

Types of order

The most common type of order is the market order, which is an order to buy or sell at the best price available at the time. A trader might also provide his broker with limit orders. Limit orders can be used for the purpose of taking profits and limiting losses. A holder of a contract might give his broker a 'take profit' limit order to sell if the price rises to a particular level and a 'stop loss' limit order to sell if the price falls to a particular level. These orders reflect the need for discipline in trading. They are necessary for ensuring that profits are not removed through the price reversing direction and for avoiding very large losses.

Another form of limit order is the time limit. A day order is an order to buy or sell at a particular price that lasts for just one day. If by the end of the day the transaction has not been carried out, the order is cancelled. A 'fill or kill' (FOK) order involves an offer or bid at a specified price being made three times. If after the third attempt it has not been taken up, it is cancelled. A 'good till cancelled' (GTC) order specifies a price and remains in force until it is executed or countermanded. A 'market if touched' order turns into a market order as soon as there has been one transaction in the market at the price limit stipulated. 'Market on opening' and 'market on close' orders are for execution as market orders during the opening and closing periods.

2

Short-term interest rate futures

Basic principles

The basic principle of hedging with financial futures is that a futures position should be taken such that the feared interest rate change causes a profit on futures that compensates for the loss incurred on the assets or liabilities. Three-month sterling and three-month eurodollar futures contracts are notional commitments to borrow or lend for three months on specified future dates at interest rates agreed upon at the time of undertaking the contracts.

Both potential lenders and potential borrowers might find hedging desirable. Consider, for example, a company that anticipates receipts of £10 million two months hence and intends to lend this money. The company treasurer might expect that interest rates will fall over the next two months and would like a means of reducing the impact of that fall. Alternatively, he may simply want to avoid the risk that interest rates might fall. Either way he wants to hedge: that is, insure himself against the possibility of a fall in interest rates. On the other hand, a potential borrower could be worried about the possibility of an increase in interest rates by the time that the loan is actually taken out. He will want to avoid such a rise in interest rates: in other words, he desires to hedge against the possibility that interest rates will increase.

Buying a June three-month sterling interest rate futures contract notionally commits the buyer to the deposit of £500,000, for three months from the June maturity date, at an interest rate determined in the present. The seller is simultaneously notionally committed to borrowing for that period and is also guaranteed that interest rate.

In Example 2.1, for the three months commencing 1 February the interest cost on the loan would be £50,000 more than would have been the case had the interest rate remained at 10 per cent p.a. However, there is an

Example 2.1

Cash market	*Futures market*
2 January Treasurer intends to borrow £10 million on 1 February. Fears that interest rate will rise above the current 10% p.a.	Sells twenty March futures contracts, thereby notionally guaranteeing that £10 million will be borrowed at 10% p.a. on the March maturity date.
1 February Borrows £10 million at an interest rate of 12% p.a.	Buys twenty March futures contracts, thereby entering a notional commitment to lend £10 million at 12% p.a. on the March maturity date.

offsetting gain from the futures position. For a future three-month period the hedger is committed to lending at 12 per cent p.a. and borrowing at 10 per cent p.a. This provides a gain equal to 2 per cent p.a. on £10 million for three months, namely £50,000.

As with other futures contracts, the vast majority of short-term interest rate futures contracts are closed out prior to the maturity date. By the time that closing out occurs, the hedger should have received, or paid, variation margin that offsets movements in the interest rate. A potential borrower, for example, having to pay more because of increased interest rates should have received a sum of money to compensate for the higher interest payments. If a contract is held to maturity, there will be a final cash settlement based on the exchange delivery settlement price.

Pricing

Short-term interest rate futures contracts are quoted on an index basis. The index is equal to 100 minus the annualised interest rate: for example, a three-month interest rate of 3 per cent, giving an annualised rate of 12 per cent, would mean that the contract would be priced at 88. It is to be emphasised that such prices are merely indices that are used in ascertaining profits and losses from futures trading and do not represent the money payable for contracts.

A tick is the smallest price movement recognised and recorded by an exchange. In the case of most short-term interest rate contracts, it is 0·0025 per cent of the face value of a contract. The eurodollar contracts each have a face value of $1 million and the value of a tick is $25, on both CME and LIFFE. In terms of the pricing system outlined above, each tick is depicted by 0·01. So a price change from 88 to 88·05 represents an increase of 5 ticks, amounting to $125. The difference between the 0·0025 per cent and the 0·01 arises because the index used for pricing is based on annualised interest rates, whereas the interest actually payable is a quarterly one, so the annual interest rate must be divided by four.

Suppose that a hedger buys, in December, a June three-month eurodollar interest rate contract at a price of 90 (annualised interest rate of 10 per cent). The following day the price rises by one tick to 90·01 (annualised interest rate of 9·99 per cent). Upon buying the contract, the hedger guaranteed the receipt of 2·5 per cent over three months from the June maturity date on a eurodollar deposit of $1 million. A contract bought a day later would have guaranteed merely 2·4975 per cent (9·99/4). Thus the hedger has guaranteed the receipt of $25,000, whereas one day later he would have guaranteed only $24,975. On the day following his purchase he would close out his position by selling a contract and receive the value of one tick, $25, as his profit. By selling a contract the hedger acquires the notional right to borrow. The interest receivable from the long contract is $25,000 whilst the interest payable on the short contract would be $24,975. In the absence of closing out, the $25 would be paid to him as variation margin. Example 2·1 can now be rewritten as in Example 2.2, using the pricing convention outlined above.

Example 2.2

Cash market	*Futures market*
2 January	
Treasurer intends to borrow £10 million on 1 February. Fears that interest rate will rise above the current 10% p.a.	Sells twenty March three-month sterling interest rate futures contracts at a price of 90.
1 February	
Borrows £10 million at an interest rate of 12% p.a.	Closes out by buying twenty March three-month sterling interest rate futures contracts at a price of 88.

Loss is 2% p.a. on £10 million for three months, £50,000.	Profit is 200 ticks at £12.50 per tick on each of twenty contracts, £50,000.

The transactions in the futures market have provided a perfect hedge to the cash market transaction. The possibility that futures interest rates might change by different amounts than cash market interest rates produces basis risk. Such incomplete matching of interest rate changes can render hedging imperfect. This is illustrated by Example 2.3, which differs from Example 2.2 in that the futures interest rate rises by less than the cash market interest rate. Basis has changed from zero (90 − 90) to −0·5 (88·00 − 88·50) and as a consequence the gain on futures trading is insufficient to offset completely the loss from cash market transactions. The hedge is imperfect. Of course, if basis had changed such that futures interest rates were greater than cash market rates, the gain from futures trading would have been more than that required to offset the cash market loss.

Example 2.3

Cash market	*Futures market*
2 January	
Treasurer intends to borrow £10 million on 1 February. Fears that interest rate will rise above the current 10% p.a.	Sells twenty March three-month sterling interest rate futures contracts at a price of 90.
1 February	
Borrows £10 million at an interest rate of 12% p.a.	Closes out by buying twenty March three-month sterling interest rate futures contracts at a price of 88·50.
Loss is 2% p.a. on £10 million for three months, £50,000.	Gain is 150 ticks at £12.50 per tick on each of twenty contracts, £37,500.

Basis risk will be greater in the case of cross hedging. Cross hedging involves hedging a cash market position in one financial instrument with a futures market position in a different financial instrument. For example, if a cash position in American T-bills were hedged by a futures position in three-month eurodollars, the basis risk would be greater than in the case of hedging cash market eurodollar deposits with eurodollar futures. Cross hedging that takes the form of using three-month interest rate futures to hedge risk on instruments of different terms – for example, six-month deposits – requires an appropriate adjustment in the number of futures contracts bought or sold. In the example of the six-month deposits, losses from a particular interest rate change would be twice as great as those suffered on three-month deposits. Hence twice as many futures contracts would be required for the hedging.

The determination of futures prices

The prices of short-term interest rate futures are influenced, for the nearer maturities at least, by arbitrage based on forward/forward calculations. Suppose that the three-month interest rate is 14 per cent p.a. whilst the six-month rate is 15 per cent p.a. A trader could borrow for three months and lend for six and thereby guarantee a profit from the 1 per cent margin during the first three months. However, he is at risk from a rise in the three-month interest rate by the commencement of the second three-month period. There is a three-month rate for the second period above which the loss on the second period will push the whole operation into a loss. That is the forward/forward rate. Suppose that the trader lends £1 million for six months at 15 per cent p.a. and borrows it for three months at 14 per cent p.a. He will receive £1,072,380.50 at the end of the six-month period. Meanwhile he must pay £1,033,299·50 at the end of the first three months and must borrow £1,033,299·50 in order to repay the debt. A £39,081 interest payment on this second loan would mean that the trader breaks even on the exercise, since the second debt could be repaid with the £1,072,380·50 from the £1 million originally lent. On a three-month loan of £1,033,299·50, £39,081 corresponds to a rate of interest of 16·01 per cent p.a.

This is the forward/forward rate and arbitrage tends to ensure that the futures rate approximates closely to it. If the futures rate were significantly below the forward/forward rate, arbitrageurs would lend long and borrow short, using the futures market to guarantee future short-term interest rates. This would involve selling futures (commitments to future borrowing) and the increased sales would push down their prices. The fall in futures prices corresponds to a rise in futures interest rates. This increase in futures interest rates will tend to eliminate the scope for further arbitrage profits.

CALCULATION OF A FORWARD/FORWARD RATE

The figure of x per cent p.a. is the three-month forward rate that renders two successive three-month periods equivalent to one six-month period in terms of interest payments.

6 months at 10% p.a.

3 months at 9% p.a. | 3 months at x% p.a.

$$(1+0{\cdot}1)^{\frac{1}{2}} = (1+0{\cdot}09)^{\frac{1}{4}}\,(1+x/100)^{\frac{1}{4}}$$

$$\frac{(1+0{\cdot}1)^{\frac{1}{2}}}{(1+0{\cdot}09)^{\frac{1}{4}}} = (1+x/100)^{\frac{1}{4}}$$

$$\frac{(1+0{\cdot}1)^{2}}{(1+0{\cdot}09)} = (1+x/100)$$ Taking both sides to the power of 4.

$$\frac{(1{\cdot}1)^{2}}{(1{\cdot}09)} - 1 = x/100$$

$$\left[\frac{(1{\cdot}1)^{2}}{1{\cdot}09} - 1\right] \times 100 = x$$

$$x = 11{\cdot}01\%$$

Note: As an alternative to

$$(1+0{\cdot}1)^{\frac{1}{2}} = (1+0{\cdot}09)^{\frac{1}{4}}\,(1+x/100)^{\frac{1}{4}}$$

one could use

$$(1+0{\cdot}1)^{\frac{182}{365}} = (1+0{\cdot}09)^{\frac{91}{365}}\,(1+x/100)^{\frac{91}{365}}$$

which replaces the fractions with the number of days to which the interest rate applies divided by the number of days in the year. This alternative is particularly attractive when dealing with periods that cannot be described in terms of a number of whole months.

The preceding formulae are not the only ones that could be used. A popular formula for ascertaining forward/forward rates is as follows:

3-month forward/forward

$$= \left\{\left[\frac{1+(R_1 \times T_1/360)}{1+(R_2 \times T_2/360)}\right] - 1\right\} \times \frac{360}{T_1 - T_2}$$

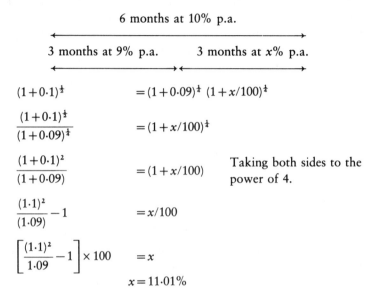

where

R_1 = interest rate to the far end of the forward/forward period
R_2 = interest rate to the near end of the forward/forward period
T_1 = days to the far end of the forward/forward period
T_2 = days to the near end of the forward/forward period

Here 360 has been used rather than 365. This is the convention in the cases of currencies other than sterling. The interest rates used in the formula are likely to be mid-point rates. Futures prices are based on offer rates (100 − LIBOR).

Using this approach to the calculation of the forward/forward rate in the preceding two cases would give the following results:

Lends at 15 per cent p.a. for six months and borrows for three months at 14 per cent p.a.: forward/forward mid-point rate = 15·64 per cent p.a.
Lends at 10 per cent p.a. for six months and borrows for three months at 9 per cent p.a.: forward/forward mid-point rate = 10·94 per cent p.a.

These calculations have been based on mid-point interest rates. For the purposes of ascertaining arbitrage possibilites *vis-à-vis* futures prices, it is necessary to calculate both forward/forward borrowing rates and forward/forward lending rates taking account of the bid/offer spreads. The difference between the borrowing and lending rates constitutes a price channel that is considerably wider than the usual $\frac{1}{8}$ bid/offer spread. Arbitrage opportunities would require futures prices to fall outside the price channel (note that futures prices are based on offer rates: 100 minus LIBOR).

With reference to the 15 per cent/14 per cent example,

$$\left\{\left[\frac{1+(0{\cdot}150625\times 182/360)}{1+(0{\cdot}139375\times 91/360)}\right]-1\right\}\times\frac{360}{91}=0{\cdot}1564\ (15{\cdot}64\%\ \text{p.a.})$$

using mid-point rates

$$\left\{\left[\frac{1+(0{\cdot}15\times 182/360)}{1+(0{\cdot}14\times 91/360)}\right]-1\right\}\times\frac{360}{91}=0{\cdot}1545\ \ (15{\cdot}45\%\ \ \text{p.a.})$$

lending for six months at 15 per cent p.a. and borrowing for three months at 14 per cent p.a.

$$\left\{\left[\frac{1+(0{\cdot}15125\times 182/360)}{1+(0{\cdot}13875\times 91/360)}\right]-1\right\}\times\frac{360}{91}=0{\cdot}1582\ (15{\cdot}82\%\ \text{p.a.})$$

borrowing for six months at 15·125 per cent p.a. and lending for three months at 13·875 per cent p.a.

The channel is between 15·45 per cent p.a. and 15·82 per cent p.a. Futures prices above 84·55 (100 – 15·45) would provide a possibility of arbitrage taking short futures positions, whilst prices below 84·05 (100 – 15·82 – 0·125) might provide arbitrage opportunities using long futures positions (depending upon the size of commissions). In other words, if it is possible to lock in a borrowing rate, with futures, of less than 15·45 per cent (the forward/forward lending rate) there may be scope for arbitrage profit. Similarly, if it is possible to lock in a lending rate, with futures, of greater than 15·82 per cent p.a. (the forward/forward borrowing rate) there may also be scope for arbitrage profit (a bid rate of 15·82 per cent p.a. requires an offer rate of about 15·95 per cent and hence a futures price of about 84·05).

The yield curve and basis risk

In the foregoing example futures prices stood at a discount to cash prices. This is generally the case with upward-sloping yield curves (longer-term interest rates higher than shorter-term ones). Downward-sloping yield curves would involve futures prices standing at a premium to cash prices. It follows that changes in the slope of the yield curve alter basis and are thus a source of basis risk.

Example 2.4 illustrates a situation in which futures prices move from being at a premium to being at a discount with respect to cash prices (futures interest rates move from being lower to being higher than spot three-month rates). In this example basis changes by one percentage point. From a cash market interest rate 0·5 per cent above the futures rate there is a change to a cash market rate 0·5 per cent below the futures rate. As a result the overall loss is $25,000 and the attempt to hedge fails completely. Indeed, a fall in the futures price would have rendered the effects of the hedging attempt perverse: for example, a fall in the futures price to 90 on 10 April would have added a $12,500 futures loss to the $25,000 cash market loss.

It is worth bearing in mind that basis always reaches zero at maturity. This observation can influence the choice of maturity date when buying or selling futures contracts. If basis is close to zero at the time of buying or selling, seeking the nearest possible maturity date would make sense. Maturity dates should fall after the date on which the risk to be hedged disappears (i.e. the date on which a deposit is made or loan taken out)

Example 2.4

Cash market	*Futures market*
10 February	
Company plans to deposit $10 million on 10 April. Current rate of interest on three-month eurodollar deposits is 10% p.a.	Buys ten June three-month eurodollar interest rate futures contracts at a price of 90.5.
10 April	
Company deposits $10 million at an interest rate of 9% p.a.	Sells ten June three-month eurodollar interest rate futures contracts at a price of 90·5.
Loss equals 1% on $10 million for three months = $25,000 (0·01 × 10 million × 0·25).	There is no gain since the price is unchanged at 90·5.

otherwise there would be a period during which hedging is absent. Using the earliest possible maturity date after the disappearance of the risk increases the probability that basis will be close to zero when the contract is closed out. If basis were close to zero when the contract was bought or sold, this procedure would minimise the likelihood of basis changing between entering and closing out contracts. In any event, the tendency for basis to converge towards zero as a contract approaches maturity implies that the closer a contract is to its maturity date the less susceptible it is to changes in basis arising from yield curve movements. For this reason it is advisable to choose futures contracts that mature early after the risk being hedged has passed.

It is to be emphasised that cash and futures prices typically do exhibit reasonably close correlation so that basis risk tends to be much less than the outright risk of unhedged positions (so long as the instrument being hedged is not very different to the futures instrument).

The fact that basis always reaches zero at maturity suggests that basis could be regarded as an element of loss (or profit) that cannot be hedged. If a contract is held to maturity, the basis can be seen as representing an interest rate change that cannot be avoided but is at least known at the outset. If a contract is held to maturity, the futures price when the contract was bought or sold is the locked-in price and this differs from the spot price (rate) on the date of buying or selling the contract by the value of the basis. In the absence of basis risk from other sources, the flow of variation margin would provide the hedger with an interest rate between the spot rate and the futures rate ruling at the time of entering the contract. Early closing out would provide a rate close to the original spot rate, whereas closing out near to the maturity of the futures contract would provide a rate close to the futures rate. The actual rate obtained could be treated as a linear function of time.

Figure 2.1 is based on the simplifying assumption that the spot three-month interest rate remains unchanged until the delivery date of the futures contract. It illustrates the convergence of the futures price towards the spot price. A hedger or trader who buys a futures contract today would receive variation margin payments as the futures price rises. The amount received would be approximately proportional to the time that elapses. The effective interest rate is the spot rate adjusted for the variation margin receipts. In Figure 2.1 the potential lender receives the spot rate of interest plus the variation margin receipts, which generates an effective interest rate in excess of the spot rate. The excess of the effective rate over the spot rate is dependent upon the time that elapses and is greatest if the futures contract is held to its delivery date. (It is to be noted that movements in the spot price that are paralleled by movements in the futures price would lead to mutually offsetting profits and losses, effectively leaving the situation as indicated by Figure 2.1.)

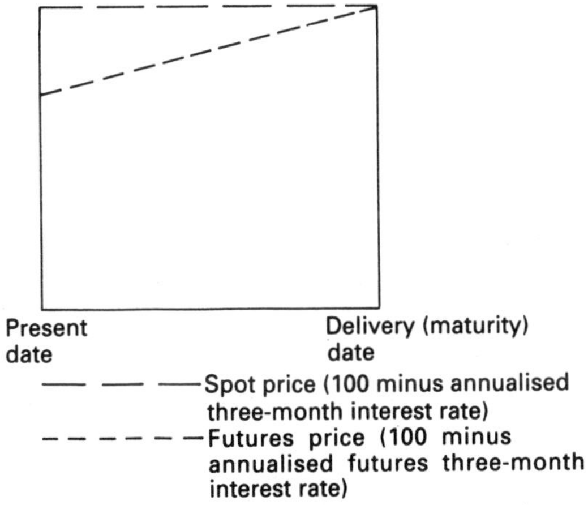

Figure 2.1 Convergence of futures and spot prices

Speculation

Risk may be transferred to a speculator rather than to another hedger. The speculator will accept the risk in the hope of making a profit. A speculator who believes that interest rates will probably rise would be prepared to sell futures in the anticipation of being able to buy at a lower price when interest rates have risen. If, for example, there is insufficient demand by hedgers for December three-month eurodollar futures contracts, some of the would-be sellers could find themselves unable to carry out the futures transactions required for hedging. The excess supply would cause a fall in the futures prices. Futures interest rates would increase. Such a rise in interest rates would cause some speculators to expect a fall back to what they consider to be a normal level. Expecting a rise in futures prices, such speculators become ready to buy in anticipation of being able to sell at a higher price later. In this way, speculators will fill any gap between futures sales and futures purchases.

Strips, rolls and spreads

Hitherto only simple hedges have been considered. In the examples short-term risk has been covered by a single futures position in each case. Borrowers and lenders may have longer-term anxieties.

Consider a roll-over loan on which the interest is reassessed every three months. The borrower may face revisions of the interest rate on 1 May and 1 August. A strip hedge would involve taking out June and September futures contracts. This could prove difficult if there is inadequate liquidity in the more distant contract. Alternatively, a rolling hedge could be employed. Rolling hedges always use the nearest futures contract (subject to the maturity date of the contract falling after the earliest interest rate reassessment date). A simple rolling hedge involves hedging only the earliest interest rate change. The borrower sells June futures contracts sufficient to match the value of the loan in order to hedge the interest rate risk of 1 May. This leaves the 1 August risk, and any subsequent risks, unhedged. A piled-up roll involves hedging more than one future interest rate change by using the nearest contract. The face value of the contracts would be a multiple of the value of the loan: for instance, hedging for two interest rate reassessment dates would involve selling contracts with an aggregate face value of twice the value of the loan. On 1 May, at which date the contracts would have been closed out, September contracts are sold in order to hedge the 1 August risk (effectively replacing previously held contracts that hedged the 1 August risk). The advantage of piled-up rolls is that they avoid the liquidity problems that may arise from dealing in distant contracts, whilst hedging risk on more than one future interest rate reassessment date. The disadvantages of piled-up rolls are that they involve a relatively large number of contracts and hence greater commission charges, and that they leave the hedger exposed to changes in the slope of the yield curve. Hedging distant interest rate changes with nearby futures contracts is effective if far and near rates move in line with each other, but if the near–far differential changes (i.e. the slope of the yield curve changes) then the effectiveness of the hedge may be reduced.

When hedging for periods that exceed three months, it may be desirable to use more than one maturity of futures contract. For example, when hedging an interest rate risk for the period 1 June to 1 December equal numbers of June and September delivery date contracts would be appropriate. The six-month interest rate can be looked upon as being based on a three-month interest rate (June–September) compounded with a following three-month interest rate (September–December). A change in the six-month rate might be due to expectations of a higher rate for September–December which is not matched by a higher June–September rate. September three-month interest rate futures prices would respond to the expected change in the September–December rate, whereas the June futures prices would not.

Exercise 2.1

Question
It is 12 August and the following information is available:

US$/£ spot 1·5795–1·5805

A UK corporate treasurer has a $5,000,000 liability with interest fixed at LIBOR + 3/4% p.a. on a six-monthly basis, the roll-over dates being 1 November and 1 May.
The treasurer wishes to hedge both the interest rate and currency risks. How can this be done, using futures, for the next two roll-over dates if liquidity is poor beyond the next two delivery dates? What sources of uncertainty would remain?

Answer
A possible approach would be the use of a piled-up roll. Initially 20 December eurodollar futures contracts should be sold.

$$\frac{\text{Liability}}{\text{Contract size}} = \frac{\$5,000,000}{\$1,000,000} = 5$$

Twelve months from 1 November is to be hedged. So the number of contracts needs to be multiplied by

$$\frac{\text{Period hedged}}{\text{Period to which contract relates}} = \frac{12 \text{ months}}{3 \text{ months}} = 4$$

December sterling currency futures can be sold, the number of contracts being

$$\frac{\$5{,}000{,}000}{\text{Spot rate} \times £25{,}000} = 126{\cdot}62, \text{ i.e. } 126 \text{ or } 127 \text{ contracts}$$

Only half the original number of eurodollar futures contracts would be required after 1 November, and that half might better be replaced with March contracts prior to 1 November. More distant (up to June) eurodollar and currency futures should replace the earlier ones when liquidity in more distant maturities becomes adequate.

Remaining sources of uncertainty include basis risk and a vulnerability to changes in the slope of the yield curve.

Using futures straddles to hedge against yield curve slope changes

In some circumstances it may be possible to hedge against adverse changes in the slope of the yield curve. If a borrower seeks protection from a rise in the slope of the yield curve, he can buy a futures straddle.

Suppose it is March and a corporate treasurer has a roll-over loan whose interest rate is reassessed six monthly on 1 June and 1 December. A strip hedge to protect him from rising interest rates would involve selling June and December interest rate futures contracts. However, liquidity may be inadequate beyond the September contract. Protection against the 1 December risk can be obtained by selling September contracts with a view to closing out the September contracts and replacing them with December contracts when liquidity in the latter becomes adequate.

While the 1 December risk is being protected by September contracts, the treasurer is vulnerable to an increase in the slope of the yield curve. September interest rates would rise by less than December interest rates and hence September contracts would give incomplete protection. To offset this the treasurer might take a futures position that would yield a profit in the event of the yield curve becoming more positively sloped. A more positively sloped yield curve involves September futures prices falling relative to June futures prices. So the hedger sells September contracts and buys June contracts. In other words, he buys a futures straddle. (Since both June and September contracts are being sold in order to hedge the interest rate risk, the purchase of the straddle effectively involves raising the number of September contracts sold and reducing the number of June contracts sold.)

Other currencies

Three-month interest rate futures contracts in sterling, eurodollars, Deutschmarks and yen are traded. Synthetic three-month interest rate contracts on other currencies can be constructed, where they are not otherwise available, by means of combining three-month interest rate contracts with currency futures straddles. In the cases of currencies for which three-month interest rate contracts are available, the possibility of constructing parallel contracts synthetically might provide opportunities for profitable arbitrage. The following shows how such synthetics can be created, using Deutschmarks as the example.

A change in, say, Deutschmark interest rates could be broken down into two components: firstly, the change that is matched by eurodollar rates; and secondly, the variation in the differential between eurodollar and Deutschmark interest rates. The first component can be hedged with eurodollar futures and the second can be hedged by means of a futures straddle or forward swap. A futures straddle involves buying futures for one delivery month and selling for another, both in the same instrument. Buying a Deutschmark currency straddle involves buying Deutschmark futures contracts and simultaneously selling the same number of Deutschmark futures contracts for a later delivery month. There would be a premium or discount between the two delivery months: that is, the two futures prices would imply an appreciation or depreciation of the Deutschmark against the US dollar during the period between the two delivery dates. Selling the straddle entails selling contracts for the earlier delivery month and buying for the later delivery month.

Interest rate parity suggests that the rate of appreciation/depreciation implied by the futures prices represents the difference between dollar and Deutschmark interest rates between the two delivery months. Buying or selling a straddle thus provides a means of hedging changes in the interest rate differential.

Exercise 2.2

Question

It is 17 March and delivery into June sterling currency futures is due on 17 June. The spot price of sterling is $1·6000–1·6010.

The June sterling currency futures price is \$1·5848.
The 3-month sterling interest rate (interbank) is $9\frac{7}{16}-9\frac{9}{16}$.
The 3-month eurodollar interest rate is $6\frac{3}{8}-6\frac{1}{2}$.
Are there arbitrage opportunities? Provide details of your analysis.

Answer
Borrow sterling, sell sterling (buy dollars), deposit dollars, buy sterling futures.
Rate of interest on sterling debt = 9·5625% p.a.
Rate of interest on dollar deposit = 6·3750% p.a.
Interest rate differential = 3·1875% p.a.
Rate of premium on dollars =

$$\frac{1{\cdot}6000}{1{\cdot}5848} = 1{\cdot}0096$$

This implies a rate of return of 3·8957%, on an annualised basis, from the dollar premium. (3·8957% is based on continuous compounding; multiplying the quarterly rate of premium by four gives 3·84% p.a.) This more than compensates for the excess of the sterling interest rate over the eurodollar interest rate. So this is a profitable arbitrage strategy. (Alternatively, the theoretical futures price could be calculated and compared with the actual futures price.)

Exercise 2.3

Question
It is 15 March and the information shown in Tables 2.1 and 2.2 is available. Are there opportunities for arbitrage between CME and LIFFE futures contracts?

Answer
The annualised interest rate differential implied by CME sterling currency futures is

$$\frac{1{\cdot}8405 - 1{\cdot}8320}{1{\cdot}8405} \times 4 \times 100 = 1{\cdot}847\%$$

(Since futures annualised interest rates are not based on continuous compounding, it would appear to be inappropriate to annualise interest rate differentials using continuous compounding.)
The 3-month eurodollar interest rates implied by CME June eurodollar futures are 100 − 92·86 = 7·14% p.a.
The 3-month sterling interest rates implied by CME contracts are thus 7·14 + 1·85 = 8·99%.
The 3-month sterling interest rate implied by LIFFE June futures is 100 − 91·16 = 8·84%.
There could be a profitable arbitrage from a short position in LIFFE 3-month sterling interest rate futures and a synthetic long from CME contracts. The synthetic long would involve a long 3-month eurodollar interest rate position together with selling a June–September sterling futures straddle.

Table 2.1 Chicago Mercantile Exchange futures prices

	Sterling currency
June	1.8405
September	1.8320
	Eurodollar
June	92.86
September	92.58

Table 2.2 LIFFE sterling interest rate futures

June	91.16
September	90.96

Thus if a hedger needs to synthesise the sale of three-month Deutschmark futures so as to guarantee a Deutschmark borrowing rate, he could sell eurodollar futures contracts, buy Deutschmark currency contracts for the maturity date of the eurodollar futures contracts and sell Deutschmark currency futures contracts for the following maturity date.

In effect, the hedger is committing himself to borrowing eurodollars and converting them into Deutschmarks in the near maturity month, and then selling Deutschmarks in order to obtain the eurodollars required to pay off the eurodollar debt in the following maturity month. The Deutschmark interest rate obtained is equal to the eurodollar rate minus the rate at which the dollar declines relative to the Deutschmark, as embodied in the two Deutschmark currency futures prices. From the Deutschmark perspective the interest rate is the rate at which the eurodollar debt rises minus the rate at which dollars become cheaper.

The transactions involved are depicted in Figure 2.2. The relationship between the number of Deutschmarks to be sold in order to repay the eurodollar debt, DM_2, and the number obtained from selling the dollars borrowed, DM_1, provides the effective rate of interest on the synthesised Deutschmark borrowing.

Figure 2.3 illustrates a synthetic Deutschmark deposit. The relationship between the number of Deutschmarks received at the end of the three-month period and the number sold at the beginning of the period indicates the effective rate of interest on the synthetic Deutschmark deposit.

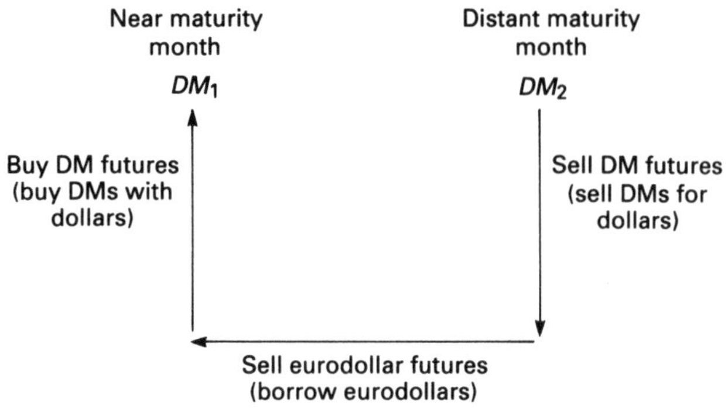

Figure 2.2 Constructing a synthetic Deutschmark borrowing

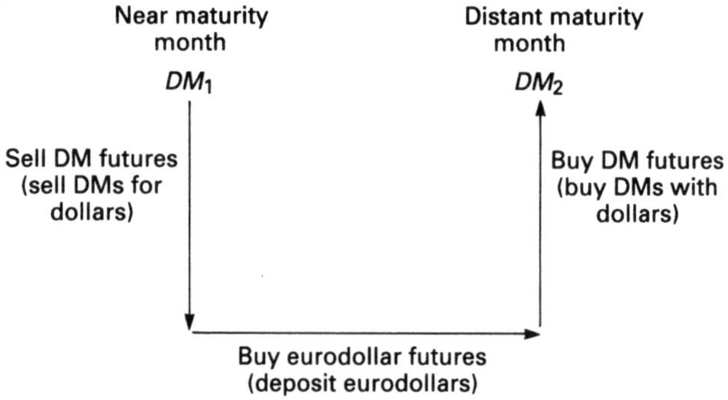

Figure 2.3 Constructing a synthetic Deutschmark deposit

Exercise 2.4

Question

It is 12 August and the information shown in Table 2.3 is available.
The bid–offer spread in the underlying deposit markets is 1/8.
What Deutschmark interest rates could be locked in for the September–March period?

Answer

The interest rate for a borrower would be (selling eurodollar futures and buying DM currency straddles):

$$7{\cdot}12-2{\cdot}64=4{\cdot}48\% \text{ p.a.}$$

Table 2.3

	Eurodollar futures	Deutschmark currency futures
September	92.88	0.5301–98
December	92.42	0.5339–36
March	92.07	0.5378–75

for September–December, and

$$7{\cdot}58 - 2{\cdot}70 = 4{\cdot}88\% \text{ p.a.}$$

for December–March. This implies a September–March borrowing rate of about 4·68% p.a.

The interest rate for a lender would be (buying eurodollar futures and selling DM currency straddles):

$$7{\cdot}12 - 0{\cdot}125 - 3{\cdot}10 = 3{\cdot}9\% \text{ p.a.}$$

for September–December, and

$$7{\cdot}58 - 0{\cdot}125 - 3{\cdot}15 = 4{\cdot}31\% \text{ p.a.}$$

for December–March. This implies a September–March lending rate of 4·11% p.a.

Alternatively, one might roll over eurodollar futures and use September–March DM currency straddles.

EXAMPLE

On 28 June a corporate treasurer considers the next quarterly roll-over of a Deutschmark loan of DM20 million due for 1 September. Fearing a rise in Deutschmark interest rates, the treasurer decides to hedge the Deutschmark interest rate exposure by selling September three-month eurodollar contracts and buying September–December Deutschmark currency straddles. The transactions that might be involved on 28 June are indicated in Figure 2.4.

Figure 2.4 highlights one of the practical difficulties that arise when this type of strategy is pursued: the currency futures values do not precisely dovetail with the interest rate futures values. The $11 million on the September maturity date corresponds to DM19,869,942, when the exchange rate is $0·5536/DM, and this corresponds to 158·96 Deutschmark currency contracts. Therefore 159 is merely an approximation to the appropriate number. Similarly, the notional repayment of $11,211,615 at

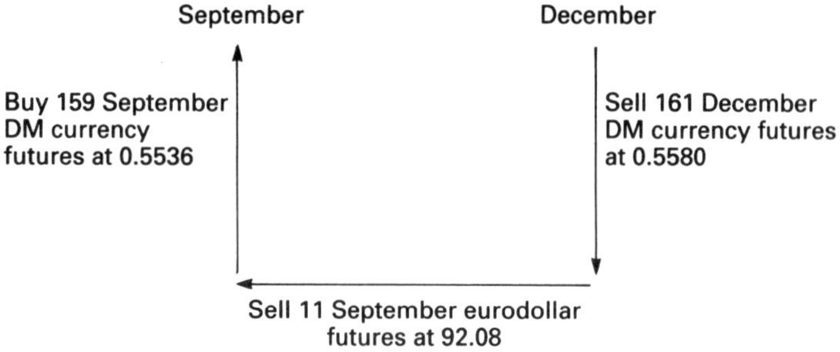

Figure 2.4

an exchange rate of \$0·5580/DM requires DM20,092,500, which corresponds to 160·74 Deutschmark currency futures contracts. So 161 is again merely an approximation to the ideal number of contracts.

The numbers of contracts calculated above take no account of variation margin leverage. Compensation for adverse movements in Deutschmark interest rates is received in the form of variation margin which can be invested at a rate of interest. (Deutschmark interest rate changes which reflect those on eurodollars would lead to variation margin receipts from the eurodollar contracts, whereas Deutschmark interest rate movements relative to eurodollar rates would produce variation margin receipts from the currency contracts.) Similarly, advantageous movements in Deutschmark interest rates would be offset by variation margin payments, and interest would be foregone (or paid) on the funds used. Interest on variation margin reduces the number of futures contracts required to produce the requisite cash flows. The numbers of futures contracts calculated above need to be ratioed down. The ratio is known as the variation margin leverage.

Assuming a dollar interest rate of 8 per cent p.a., the variation margin leverage applicable to the present example would be calculated as follows (on the basis of there being 63 days between 28 June and 1 September, and 92 days between 1 September and 1 December):

$$1 + 0{\cdot}08\ (31{\cdot}5 + 92)/360 = 1{\cdot}027$$

This method assumes that variation margin cash flows occur at a constant rate. If this assumption is correct, the interest receipts (or payments) arising from variation margin during the 28 June to 1 September period can be approximated by multiplying the annualised interest rate (0·08) by the average number of days that the money is held (63/2 = 31·5) expressed as a fraction of a year (31·5/360). Since the interest on the loan being hedged is due on 1 December, the variation margin receipts (or payments) will be held (or forgone) for a further 92 days after the futures positions are closed out on 1 September. The interest rate applicable to this latter period is equal to the annualised rate multiplied by 92 expressed as a fraction of a year $(0{\cdot}08 \times 92/360)$.

Typically the numbers of futures contracts calculated without consideration of the variation margin leverage would be in excess of the numbers actually needed. In order to take account of the interest on variation margin, the number of futures contracts should be divided by the variation margin leverage.

In the example illustrated by Figure 2.4, the effect of the appropriate ratioing is to suggest the following numbers of futures contracts:

September Deutschmark currency	158·96/1·027 = 154·78
September eurodollar	11/1·027 = 10·71
December Deutschmark currency	160·74/1·027 = 156·51

Rounding to discrete numbers of contracts provides the revised numbers of 155, 11 and 157 in the place of the previously calculated 159, 11 and 161.

The fact that the ideal numbers of contracts are not discrete implies that there must be a degree of approximation in the hedging process. The approximate nature of the process is further exacerbated by the relationship between the futures contracts and the loan being hedged. The effective rate of interest to be paid is not the rate implied by the futures contracts. The futures contracts merely provide compensation for movements in the interest rate on the underlying Deutschmark loan. Indeed, the compensation may fail to match precisely the change in interest cost on the underlying loan for two further reasons. Firstly, changes in the loan rate on the one hand may not correspond with movements in the eurodollar rate adjusted by the implied currency appreciation/depreciation (implied by the currency futures prices) on the other hand. Secondly, futures prices may not maintain a constant relationship with the prices of their underlying instruments: in other words, basis may change. So the hedging process involves a degree of approximation and some elements of risk remain.

Butterfly spreads

A complex type of spread is the butterfly. Whereas in the case of the spread described in the previous chapter the trader takes a view on the relationship between two prices, in the case of butterfly spreads the view is on the relationship between two spreads. A butterfly is a spread of spreads.

Table 2.4

June	September	December
92.00	90.50	90.00

Table 2.5 Prices on 5 July

September	December	March
90.50	90.00	89.00

Table 2.6 Prices on 25 July

September	December	March
90.50	89.75	89.00

Suppose that three-month eurodollar futures contracts have the prices shown in Table 2.4 for the next three maturity months. The value of a spread is obtained by subtracting the farther price from the nearer price. Within the butterfly the nearby spread is 150 ticks, whilst the deferred spread is 50 ticks. The value of the butterfly spread is therefore 100 ticks (150 – 50).

The rule of thumb for butterfly spreads is the same as that for ordinary spreads. If the butterfly spread is expected to strengthen (more positive/less negative), the butterfly spread is bought; in the opposite case, the butterfly is sold. Example 2.5 illustrates a case in which the expectation of a strengthening of a butterfly spread leads a trader to buy that spread. It is based on three-month eurodollar futures.

Example 2.5

On 5 July (see Table 2.5) the nearby spread is 50 ticks and the deferred spread is 100 ticks. So the value of the butterfly is –50 ticks. The trader expects that the nearby spread will increase relative to the deferred spread. In other words, the butterfly spread is expected to strengthen. On 5 July he buys a butterfly spread.

Buy 1 September contract at	90·50
Sell 2 December contracts at	90·00
Buy 1 March contract at	89·00

On 25 July (see Table 2.6) he closes out by selling that butterfly spread. Selling a butterfly spread involves selling the nearby spread and buying the deferred spread.

Sell 1 September contract at	90·50
Buy 2 December contracts at	89·75
Sell 1 March contract at	89·00

There is a profit of 25 ticks on each of the two December contracts, which at $25 per tick is a profit of $1,250. The trader was correct in expecting that the butterfly spread would strengthen. The nearby spread increased from 50 to 75 ticks and the deferred spread fell from 100 to 75. So the butterfly strengthened from −50 to zero.

Intercontract spreads

Intercontract spreads involve the simultaneous purchase and sale of futures contracts relating to different underlying instruments. The underlying instruments need not even be on the same exchange: for example, the spread might involve the three-month eurodollar interest rate contract on LIFFE and the domestic certificate of deposit contract on the International Monetary Market (IMM) in Chicago. It is possible for the contracts being bought and sold to have the same maturity months in the case of intercontract spreads.

Intercontract spreads are subject to greater risk than straddle spreads. There is greater likelihood of divergent price movements, and the more unrelated are the two instruments, the larger is the risk. A LIFFE three-month eurodollar straddle is less risky than an intercontract spread between LIFFE three-month eurodollar and IMM domestic certificate of deposit contracts. The risk on the latter would in turn be less than that between LIFFE three-month eurodollar and Chicago Board of Trade (CBOT) US treasury bond contracts. Since intercontract spreads are riskier than straddles, all the contracts involved in an intercontract spread normally require payment of the full initial margin: there may be no reduced initial margin as might occur in the case of straddles.

Euro-rate differential futures

The Chicago Mercantile Exchange has introduced futures based on three-month euro-rate differentials (DIFFs). These DIFFs allow users to lock in an interest rate differential between eurodollars on the one hand and eurosterling, eurodeutschmarks or euroyen on the other. DIFFs lock in the interest rate spreads for a three-month period commencing on the maturity date of the futures contract (the third Wednesday of the futures expiration month).

They are priced on an index basis parallel to that used for eurodollar futures. If eurodollar LIBOR exceeds LIBOR for the other eurocurrency, the DIFF is priced as 100 minus the interest rate differential. If the eurodollar rate is the lower one, the price of the DIFF is 100 plus the interest rate difference. The nominal contract size is $1 million and the minimum price change is one basis point (worth $25).

The question arises as to what these contracts might be used for. Since the ultimate purpose of any futures contract must be the provision of a means of managing risk with a view to reducing it – in other words, hedging (the functions of traders and arbitrageurs are those of bringing liquidity, efficiency and stability to the market) – ascertaining potential uses largely involves identifying hedging possibilities. Four such possibilities are (a) hedging non-dollar eurocurrency interest rates, (b) offsetting risks incurred by the providers of currency forward contracts, (c) banks funding loans in one currency with money borrowed in a different currency, and (d) currency swap counterparties.

As far as eurosterling and eurodeutschmark interest rates are concerned, the three-month sterling and eurodeutschmark contracts available on LIFFE would seem to be the most efficient hedging vehicle. The DIFFs would need to be bolted on to three-month eurodollar contracts. Apart from the increased transactions costs arising from using twice as many contracts, and the possible difficulties of simultaneous execution, there is the problem that variation margin flows would be in US dollars rather than in the relevant currency. An exchange rate risk would be involved.

The other three possible hedging uses would not have competition from other exchange traded instruments, although there are over-the-counter (OTC) alternatives. A provider of a forward contract would need a means of ascertaining the appropriate premium/discount. This would be calculated from the difference between the interest rates on the two currencies. Forward contract providers who might prefer to deal in three-month cash markets or who face requests for broken date forward contracts would find DIFFs a useful source of information upon which to base quoted premiums/discounts and a useful vehicle for covering their positions.

A bank funding a loan in one currency with money borrowed in another currency faces both exchange rate and interest rate risks. DIFFs provide a means of covering the interest rate risks. A party to a currency swap may be in a situation in which the foreign currency liability acquired via the swap involves floating interest rate charges that are not to be financed from returns on the foreign currency asset that is matched by the acquired liability. The interest costs may need to be met from base currency sources. There is an exposure to changes in the relationship between base currency interest rates and foreign currency rates. DIFFs provide a means of hedging that exposure.

There are OTC alternatives to DIFFs for hedging these types of risk. These alternatives are ERAs, FSAs and FXAs. ERAs (exchange rate agreements) are forward contracts on premiums/discounts in the forward exchange markets. FSAs (forward spread agreements) are instruments for locking in future interest rate differentials between currencies. FXAs (forward exchange agreements) fix forward exchange rates for future dates.

3

Long-term interest rate futures

The contracts available include futures based on UK gilts, US treasury notes, US treasury bonds, and Australian, French, German and Japanese government bonds. General principles relate to all of them and will, for the most part, be explained with reference to just one, leaving the reader to extend the analysis to the others.

Government bond futures are commitments to buy or sell government bonds during specified future months. There is a limited number of bonds eligible for delivery in fulfilment of a futures contract and the seller has the choice as to the specific bond. Contracts are commonly not held until maturity but are closed out by means of the holder taking out an opposite contract: for example, a buyer can close out by selling bond futures in an amount and for a delivery month corresponding to those of the contracts previously bought. There are cash flows by way of variation margin to reflect the change in futures prices between the dates of buying and selling.

Those using these financial futures for hedging may wish to safeguard either the value of securities or the cash flow arising from them.

Hedging the value of a portfolio

A portfolio manager may fear an increase in long-term interest rates, an occurrence that would reduce the prices of bonds held in a portfolio. He could attempt to avoid this effect on the value of the portfolio by taking a position in futures that would provide an offsetting gain from a fall in bond prices. To achieve this he would sell futures contracts. A fall in bond prices should be accompanied by a fall in the prices of bond futures. If a loss was made from a decline in the value of bonds, the portfolio manager would be compensated by profits from the futures position. He would be able to buy bond futures at a lower price than that at which he sold.

This process is illustrated by Example 3.1, which needs to be preceded by details of the specification of a particular (hypothetical) long-term interest rate futures contract. This German government bond futures contract has a nominal value of DM250,000 and the prices of contracts are expressed as Deutschmarks per DM100 nominal value. The price of the notional bond (upon which the futures are based) would be 100 when the long-run interest rate is 6 per cent p.a. but would rise above 100 when the interest rate is lower; the converse applies for higher rates. The tick, the minimum price movement, is DM0·01 for these bond futures.

Example 3.1

Cash market	*Futures market*
2 January The 20-year interest rate is 6% p.a. The DM1 million bond portfolio is vulnerable to an increase in long-term interest rates.	Sells four March German government bond futures contracts. Futures price is 100, reflecting a 6% p.a. interest rate.
15 February The 20-year interest rate has risen to $7\frac{1}{2}$% p.a. Correspondingly, the value of the bond portfolio has fallen to DM865,000 (this figure could be anywhere between DM800,000 and DM1 million depending upon the maturities of the bonds held).	Closes out by buying four March German government bond futures contracts. The price of the contracts has fallen to 82.22, reflecting a $7\frac{1}{2}$% p.a. futures interest rate.
There is a loss of DM135,000 in the value of the bond portfolio.	There is a profit of DM177,800 from the futures position.

In Example 3.1 a portfolio manager with bonds worth DM1 million on 2 January is anxious about the possibility that interest rates might rise and thereby reduce the value of his bonds. He hedges by selling four bond futures contracts and is more than successful in offsetting the fall in the value of his bonds. The reason for this over-compensation is the fact that the average maturity of the bonds in his portfolio is less than twenty years (this German government bond futures contract is based on a notional bond with a twenty-year maturity). The value of a portfolio responds less to interest rate changes as the average maturity declines. In the light of this he could have chosen to hedge with fewer than four futures contracts; three might seem appropriate, particularly when it is borne in mind that with four contracts a fall in interest rates would have entailed a futures loss greater than the increase in the value of the bond portfolio.

Anxiety about the volatility of interest rates may not be specific to a particular period. It is possible that a portfolio manager is consistently nervous about the instability of interest rates and the possibility that it might involve a fall in the value of his bond portfolio. The holding of futures positions, to hedge against changes in the value of a portfolio, could thus be permanent with new futures positions being entered into as old ones are closed out.

Hedging cash flow

Example 3.2 is that of a corporate treasurer intending to raise money by the sale of securities with a fixed coupon yield. His anxiety is that interest rates might rise before the sale is made with the result that the raising of a particular sum of money would then entail a greater future cash flow commitment to the security holders.

The treasurer could use the DM355,600 futures profit to reduce his borrowing requirement from DM2 million to DM1,644,400 and hence reduce the annual servicing cost to DM123,330. A perfect hedge would have provided a futures profit of DM400,000 so that the cash flow required to service the debt returned to DM120,000 p.a. The futures gain was less than DM400,000 because the notional bond (on which the futures are based) is of a twenty-year maturity and only the price of an irredeemable bond responds proportionately to interest rate changes. A more effective hedge would have been obtained by using nine contracts, which would have provided a futures profit of DM400,050.

In both of the examples, the hedger would be able to ascertain the appropriate number of futures contracts required – three and nine respectively – before selling the contracts. The ratio of the nominal value of futures contracts required to the sum of assets or liabilities to be hedged is known as the hedge ratio. Even with the correct hedge ratio, hedging may not be perfect. Imperfections would arise if the cash market and futures interest rates did not change to the same extent. However, this basis risk tends to be much less than the outright risk of unhedged positions since the difference between cash and futures interest rates fluctuates less than cash market rates.

Example 3.2

Cash market	*Futures market*
2 January The corporation intends to raise DM2 million on 15 February by the sale of irredeemable bonds. The interest rate on undated bonds is 6% p.a. The treasurer wants to ensure that the cost of servicing the debt will be limited to DM120,000 p.a.	Sells eight March German government bond futures contracts. Futures price is 100, reflecting a 6% p.a. interest rate.
15 February The interest rate on undated stock has risen to $7\frac{1}{2}$% p.a.	Closes out by buying eight March German government bond futures contracts. Futures price is 82·22 reflecting a $7\frac{1}{2}$% p.a. futures interest rate.
The cost of servicing a DM2 million debt would now be DM150,000 p.a.	There is a profit of DM355,600 from the futures position.

Delivery

In most cases the months during which government bonds may be delivered in settlement of futures contracts are March, June, September and December. The seller chooses the day of the month on which delivery takes place. The seller also chooses which bond to deliver, subject to the bond meeting certain criteria concerning maturity.

Price (conversion) factor

The price factor will be described in relation to the long gilt futures contract (long gilts are British government bonds with relatively distant maturities); the description can be readily extended to the other long-term interest rate contracts.

The long gilt futures contracts each have a nominal value of £50,000. Likewise the gilts delivered when a contract matures must amount to £50,000 in nominal value. Gilts with the same nominal value may, however, have differing market values despite identical nominal values. A £50,000 bond issued when the market rate was 12 per cent p.a. would provide a coupon of £6,000 p.a., whereas a £50,000 bond issued at a rate of 10 per cent p.a. would yield £5,000 p.a. The market value of bonds will vary according to the size of the coupon yield. A bond yielding £6,000 p.a. is worth more than one with a coupon of just £5,000 p.a. If the seller delivers high coupon gilts, he expects to receive more money than if he delivers lower coupon gilts. To ensure that this happens, price factors are used in the calculation of the sums for which buyers are invoiced, the relevant adjustment being made by means of multiplying the futures price by the price factor.

To obtain the price factor for a long gilt, its price if it were to have a gross redemption yield of 9 per cent p.a. is ascertained. This price is then divided by the nominal value of the gilt and the result is the price factor. Higher coupon yields are reflected in higher price factors.

If the bonds were perpetuities, the price factor would equal the ratio of the percentage yields. The price factor for an $11\frac{1}{4}$ per cent p.a. bond would be 1·25 since an $11\frac{1}{4}$ per cent p.a. yield into perpetuity would render the bond 25 per cent more valuable than one yielding a perpetual 9 per cent p.a. However, most long gilts have maturity dates (as does the notional gilt upon which futures contracts are based). Since the bonds are not perpetuities, the price factor tends to differ from the ratio of the percentage yields, with the factor approaching 1 as the period to maturity declines towards zero.

DETERMINING THE CONVERSION FACTOR

The determination of the conversion factor will be illustrated by means of the Chicago Board of Trade treasury bond futures contract.

The treasury bond contract is based on a notional bond with an 8 per cent coupon and a maturity of at least fifteen years. The conversion factor is designed to put all eligible bonds on an equivalent basis for delivery purposes. If the bond delivered has a coupon greater than 8 per cent, the conversion factor will be greater than 1. The invoice amount will therefore be greater than that for an 8 per cent coupon bond. The converse applies for bonds with coupons of less than 8 per cent.

In calculating the conversion factor, the first step is to ascertain the remaining period to the maturity of the bond (in the case of a callable bond the first call date is used instead of the maturity date), dating from the first day of the delivery (expiration) month. The period is rounded down to the nearest period expressable in three-month units: for example, 17 years, 10 months and 25 days would be rounded down to 17 years, 9 months.

Time is divided into six-month periods and the coupon expressed as a six-monthly percentage:

$$F=(C/2)\left(\frac{1-(1{\cdot}04)^{-T}}{0{\cdot}04}\right)+(1{\cdot}04)^{-T}$$

where F is the conversion factor, C is the coupon of the bond and T is the time to maturity expressed as a number of six-month periods.

Some understanding of how the expression works can be obtained by considering specific values. If the coupon on the treasury bond were 8 per cent, the value of F arrived at would be 1:

$$F=0{\cdot}04\left(\frac{1-(1{\cdot}04)^{-T}}{0{\cdot}04}\right)+(1{\cdot}04)^{-T}$$

$$F=1-(1{\cdot}04)^{-T}+(1{\cdot}04)^{-T}=1$$

This result is unaffected by the time to maturity. However, with coupons other than 8 per cent the time to maturity becomes significant. Consider a bond with a coupon of 10 per cent. The computation becomes as follows:

$$F=0{\cdot}05\left(\frac{1-(1{\cdot}04)^{-T}}{0{\cdot}04}\right)+(1{\cdot}04)^{-T}$$

$$F=0{\cdot}01\left(\frac{1-(1{\cdot}04)^{-T}}{0{\cdot}04}\right)+0{\cdot}04\left(\frac{1-(1{\cdot}04)^{-T}}{0{\cdot}04}\right)+(1{\cdot}04)^{-T}$$

$$F=0{\cdot}01\left(\frac{1-(1{\cdot}04)^{-T}}{0{\cdot}04}\right)+1$$

$$F=0{\cdot}25\ (1-(1{\cdot}04)^{-T})+1$$

If T is infinity (which would be the case if the bond were undated), the computation provides a value of 1·25 for F. So when T is infinity, the conversion factor is proportional to the coupon. For values of T less than infinity, the relationship between the coupon and the conversion factor is less than proportional. The responsiveness of the conversion factor to variations in coupon declines as T diminishes. If T were, for example, 40 (corresponding to a maturity of twenty years) then

$$F = 0{\cdot}25\ (1 - (1{\cdot}04)^{-40}) + 1$$
$$F = 1{\cdot}19793$$

and for $T = 30$, F would equal 1·17292.

Invoice amount

The futures price upon which the invoice amount is based might be referred to as the settlement price, which is the market price of futures contracts at a specific point in time prior to delivery. The principal invoice amount is the settlement price multiplied by the price factor and by the nominal value of the futures contract divided by 100:

$$\text{Principal invoice amount} = \text{Settlement price} \times \text{Price factor} \times \frac{\text{Nominal amount of a contract}}{100}$$

The sum for which the buyer is invoiced is equal to the principal invoice amount plus accrued interest on the bonds. The resulting invoice amounts would normally differ from the market values of the corresponding bonds.

The cheapest-to-deliver bonds

The seller chooses which bond to deliver in fulfilment of the contract. It is in the interests of the seller to deliver the bond whose invoice amount exceeds the market price by the largest margin (or whose invoice amount falls short of the market price by the smallest margin). This is the cheapest-to-deliver (CTD) bond.

Cash-and-carry arbitrage

This refers to the process of simultaneously buying bonds spot and selling futures contracts. If the invoicing amount, inclusive of accrued interest, at maturity exceeds the sum of the purchase price and financing cost, then arbitrage profits are available. Arbitrageurs can buy spot and simultaneously guarantee a profitable future selling price by selling futures contracts. Buying spot and selling futures raises the spot price, lowers the futures price and thus tends to remove the scope for arbitrage profits. The arbitrage activity will bring about a situation in which the capital gain (loss) is equal to the excess (shortfall) of the cost of financing the long bond position over the running yield on the bond. If the yield on the bond falls short of the financing cost of holding that bond, the spot price will be lower than the futures price since some capital gain will be necessary to offset the excess financing cost. The benefits from holding a bond, in terms of running yield and capital gain, should equal the cost of financing the holding of the bond in terms of the interest payable on money borrowed in order to finance the purchase of the bond.

Thus cash-and-carry arbitrage serves to keep spot and futures prices close to each other, with the relationship between them being dependent upon the financing costs. Since the arbitrageurs would gain most by using the cheapest-to-deliver bond, it is this bond whose value is reflected by the invoicing amount for maturing futures contracts. This implies that the futures price itself is based on the cheapest-to-deliver bond. It is to be expected that the bond which is cheapest to deliver is the bond most accurately hedged by the futures contract. Changes in spot bond prices may, however, change the cheapest-to-deliver bond.

Basis

The market price of a bond has two components: the clean price and the accrued interest. The latter refers to the right to interest receipts accumulated since the last interest payment date. A purchaser of a bond realises the interest receipts that accumulated while the seller was holding the bond. The price paid for the bond will include compensation for the accrued interest unrealised by the seller. The remainder of the price is known as the clean price.

Division of the clean price, per £100 nominal, by the price factor renders the price comparable with the futures price. The difference between the price thus obtained and the futures price is known as the basis. In the case of the cheapest-to-deliver bond, basis is determined by the difference between the yield on the bond and the interest paid (or forgone) on the money required to finance the purchase of the bond. Basis converges to zero as the maturity date of the futures contract is approached. As maturity is approached, the period over which interest is paid and received shortens and hence the monetary value of the interest differential declines towards zero.

Suppose that it is 2 October and a December futures contract has been sold as part of a cash-and-carry arbitrage operation. The cost of financing the holding of the bond exceeds the running yield obtained from the bond. This implies that the arbitrageur will choose to deliver (the seller chooses

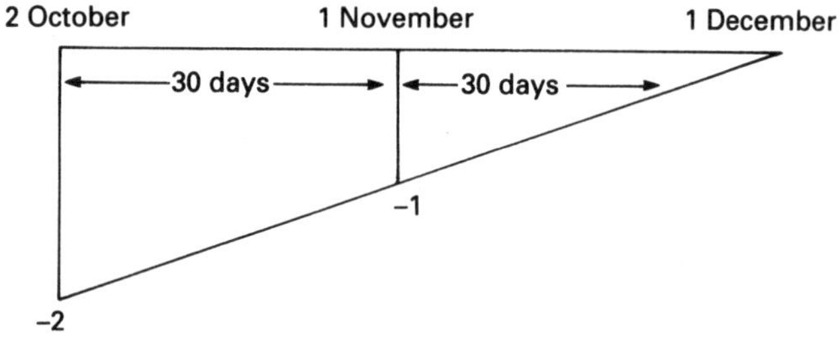

Figure 3.1 Erosion of basis over time

the delivery date) at the earliest possible date (1 December) since there is a net loss to be expected from holding the bond after that date. It also implies that the futures price is at a premium to the spot price.

If the clean price of the cheapest-to-deliver bond is 121-00 and the price factor is 1·1 whilst the futures price is 112-00 then basis is obtained as follows:

$$\text{Basis} = \frac{121}{1{\cdot}1} - 112 = -2$$

Figure 3.1 illustrates the expected erosion of the basis over time.

The fact that basis is expected to change over time means that the price that a hedger seeks to guarantee may differ from the spot price at the time of taking out the futures contracts. The greater the time lapse between agreeing the contracts and closing out, the higher will be the expected guaranteed price. Closing out soon after 2 October tends to provide an effective price close to the 2 October spot price, whereas closing out shortly before 1 December gives a price close to the futures price at which the contract was agreed.

If the risk being hedged occurs halfway between the present and the maturity date, the locked-in price will be the average of the present spot price and the price implied by the futures price. If it occurs after only a quarter of the time has elapsed, the price guaranteed would equal three-quarters of the initial spot price plus a quarter of the price implied by the futures price, and so on.

A holder of a futures contract may hold it to maturity. By so doing he guarantees being able to buy or sell the cheapest-to-deliver bond at the price implied by the price of the futures contract bought or sold. In most cases, contracts are not held to maturity. This might be because the risk being hedged does not fall in a delivery month or because the bond (or other instrument) being hedged is not the cheapest-to-deliver bond.

Table 3.1

	Clean price	Price factor	Next coupon
$13\frac{1}{2}$% Treasury 2004/08	156	1.1083271	26 September

In the case of a bond other than the cheapest to deliver, its value relative to that of the cheapest to deliver also affects basis. Variations in the relative values of the two bonds would cause movements in basis.

Exercise 3.1

Question
It is 14 April and the information shown in Table 3.1 is available.
Money market rates to 2 June are $9\frac{1}{4}$% p.a., and to 30 June are $9\frac{1}{4}$% p.a.
The June long gilt futures price is 140-28.
If the $13\frac{1}{2}$% Treasury 2004/08 is the cheapest-to-deliver gilt, are arbitrage profits available?

Answer
First ascertain whether delivery will be on 2 or 30 June. The annualised rate of return on the bond is

$$(13{\cdot}5/157{\cdot}8) = 0{\cdot}0856 \text{ gives } 8{\cdot}56\% \text{ p.a.}$$

where 157·8 equals 156 plus interest accrued between 14 April and 2 June. The accrued interest is $13{\cdot}5 \times (49/365) = 1{\cdot}8$ (when rounded to one decimal place). (Effectively 8·56% p.a. is obtained by dividing the interest to be accrued during June by the clean price plus interest accrued prior to June and then multiplying by twelve in order to annualise the result.) The financing cost exceeds the return on the bond, so the bond will be delivered on 2 June.

A transaction on 14 April would lead to the delivery of the bond on 15 April. Nineteen days would have elapsed since the last coupon date; forty-nine days remain to 2 June. Price (inclusive of accrued interest) on 14 April is

$$156 + (19/365)13{\cdot}5 = 156{\cdot}703$$

Financing cost is

$$156{\cdot}703 \times 0{\cdot}0925 \ (49/365) = 1{\cdot}946$$

(i.e. £1·946 per £100 nominal; £156·703 being the price per £100 nominal).
Accrued interest from 15 April to 2 June is

$$13{\cdot}5 \times (49/365) = 1{\cdot}812$$

(i.e. £1·812 per £100 nominal).

Excess of financing cost over accrued interest = 0·134.

$$\frac{0{\cdot}134}{1{\cdot}1083271} = 0{\cdot}121$$

(Both the financing cost and accrued interest need to be divided by the price factor since the CTD has a high price and high yield when compared with the notional bond upon which the futures contract is based. Division of the difference between the financing cost and the accrued interest by the price factor achieves this end.) Expected futures price is

$$140{\cdot}753 + 0{\cdot}121 = 140{\cdot}874$$

where 140·753 is obtained by dividing 156 by the price factor. This is virtually equal to the observed futures price ($140\frac{28}{32}$) and so there are no arbitrage profits available.

Cash flows

It is useful to consider what type of cash flows might be involved in producing an effective price of the cheapest-to-deliver bond. Consider two extreme possibilities. Firstly, suppose that the futures price corresponds to the expected price and that expectations prove to be correct. In such a case, the sum paid for the bond will change over time, whilst the futures price remains unchanged.

Secondly, suppose that the spot price remains constant. Whenever the contract is closed out, the same price is paid for the bonds. However, the futures price moves towards the spot price at a constant rate over time, becoming equal to it at maturity (the constancy of the rate depends upon financing costs remaining unchanged). This involves the payment (or receipt) of variation margin spread evenly over time. The spot price plus variation margin paid (or received) equals the price implied by the original spot and futures prices: that is, the price that lies between the initial spot and futures prices and which draws closer to the futures price as the maturity (delivery) date of the contract is approached. So if the contract were held to maturity, for example, the difference between the initial futures price and the unchanged spot price would have been paid (or received) in the form of variation margin.

Basis risk

As mentioned above, basis, the difference between the futures price and the adjusted spot price (clean spot price divided by the price factor), reflects the financing cost relative to the yield on the bond. A change in the interest rate on money borrowed to finance the purchase of a bond in cash-and-carry arbitrage would alter the basis. Such a change in basis introduces a degree of imperfection into the hedge, departing from the profile suggested by Figure 3.1. This possibility is known as basis risk. Fortunately, basis risk is likely to be low when the cheapest-to-deliver bond is being hedged. As the characteristics of the instrument being hedged diverge further and further from those of the cheapest deliverable bond, basis risk progressively increases. To the basis risk arising from the possibility of changes in financing costs must be added the basis risk from possible changes in the relative prices of the cheapest-to-deliver bond and the instrument being hedged. The greater the difference between the cheapest deliverable bond and the bond (or other instrument) being hedged, the greater the basis risk arising from this latter source. When basis risk is so large that there is not a close relationship between changes in the futures price and changes in the price of the instrument being hedged, the futures contract does not provide a suitable means of hedging.

Hedge design

The hedger must decide upon the number of contracts required to accomplish the desired hedge. This calculation is simplest when hedging the cheapest-to-deliver bond.

$$\text{Number of contracts} = \frac{\text{Nominal value of position}}{\text{Nominal value of a contract}} \times \text{Price factor}$$

The multiplication by the price factor is necessary to adjust for the price difference between the cheapest-to-deliver bond and the notional bond on which the futures price is based. A high coupon yield bond has a higher value to be hedged than a low coupon yield bond and will require a correspondingly larger number of contracts for the hedging (this difference will be greater the more distant are the maturity dates of the bonds).

Suppose that for the December 19XX contract month the cheapest-to-deliver short gilt was the Exchequer 12½% 1990, whose price factor was 1·0858888. If the hedger wished to hedge £10 million nominal of this short gilt, the requisite number of contracts would have been calculated thus:

$$\text{Number of contracts} = \frac{£10{,}000{,}000}{£100{,}000} \times 1{\cdot}0858888 = 108{\cdot}58888$$

The hedger would have used either 108 or 109 short gilt futures contracts to hedge the position. (Note that the contract size for short gilt futures is £100,000.)

When hedging bonds other than the cheapest to deliver, account must be taken of the relative volatility of the bonds. Relative volatility can be measured in terms of the money value of a (say) 1 per cent yield change per \$100 nominal. If the bond being hedged is more volatile than the cheapest to deliver, a correspondingly greater number of contracts will be required for the hedge (and vice versa for less volatile bonds). In this way, the larger price movements of relatively volatile bonds are handled. The formula becomes as follows:

$$\text{Number of contracts} = \frac{\text{Nominal value of position}}{\text{Nominal value of a contract}} \times \begin{matrix}\text{Price factor of cheapest}\\ \text{to deliver}\end{matrix} \times \begin{matrix}\text{Relative}\\ \text{volatility}\end{matrix}$$

Thus if the money value of a 1 per cent yield change per £100 nominal were £5 for the gilt being hedged and £3·50 for the cheapest-to-deliver gilt, then the number of contracts necessary to hedge £10 million nominal of the gilts, in an example parallel to the previous one, would be as follows:

$$\begin{matrix}\text{Number of}\\ \text{contracts}\end{matrix} = \frac{£10{,}000{,}000}{£100{,}000} \times 1{\cdot}0858888 \times \frac{5}{3{\cdot}5} = 155{\cdot}13$$

The appropriate number of short gilt futures contracts is 155. A large number of futures contracts is necessary so that the profits/losses on futures succeed in offsetting the relatively large losses/profits on the gilt being hedged. Without adjusting for relative volatility only £3·50 of every £5 price change would be offset. (Note that the difference between the price factor of the hedged gilt and that of the cheapest to deliver is reflected in the relative volatility: a relatively high price factor indicates a relatively expensive gilt – per £100 nominal – and this is reflected in a correspondingly larger price movement for each 1 per cent change in interest rates. The converse applies for a low price factor gilt.)

Fixed interest securities other than government bonds can be hedged with government bond futures; however, it must be borne in mind that the more dissimilar are the cheapest-to-deliver bond and the instrument being hedged, the less effective is the hedge likely to be.

The definition of volatility used above is known as perturbation. This uses the impacts of a specific interest rate change (e.g. 1 per cent) on the prices of the bond to be hedged and the cheapest deliverable.

There are other approaches to generating the hedge ratio. One is to use the price factor of the bond being hedged:

$$\text{Number of contracts} = \frac{\text{Nominal value of position}}{\text{Nominal value of a contract}} \times \text{Price factor of hedged bond}$$

This reflects the fact that relative volatility and relative price factors both emanate from particular characteristics of the bonds, in particular coupon yield and maturity.

A popular approach is to use duration. The duration of a bond is a measure of the sensitivity of the price of the bond to changes in the rate of interest. To be more specific, duration is the relationship between the proportionate (or percentage) change in the value of the bond and the proportionate (percentage) change in $(1+r)$ that caused it, where r is the redemption yield. Although the percentage change in $(1+r)$ is closely related to the change in the percentage rate of interest, the two are not identical.

Relative duration might be used as the relative volatility in the hedge ratio. It is more likely, however, that duration is rendered closer to the concept of perturbation when it is used in the calculation of a hedge ratio. In particular, the following expression might be used to convert relative duration into a form approximating to relative perturbation.

$$\frac{\left[1+\begin{matrix}\text{Redemption yield}\\ \text{of cheapest to deliver}\end{matrix}\right]}{\left[1+\begin{matrix}\text{Redemption yield}\\ \text{of hedged bond}\end{matrix}\right]} \times \frac{\left[\begin{matrix}\text{Clean price}\\ \text{of hedged bond}\end{matrix}\right]}{\left[\begin{matrix}\text{Clean price of}\\ \text{cheapest to deliver}\end{matrix}\right]} \times \frac{\left[\begin{matrix}\text{Duration of}\\ \text{hedged bond}\end{matrix}\right]}{\left[\begin{matrix}\text{Duration of}\\ \text{cheapest to deliver}\end{matrix}\right]}$$

The first term in this expression effectively changes the formulation

$$\frac{\text{Proportionate change in price}}{\text{Proportionate change in } (1+r)}$$

into

$$\frac{\text{Proportionate change in price}}{\text{Absolute change in } (1+r)}$$

The second term in the expression converts proportionate changes in price into absolute changes in price. In these ways duration is turned into the expression

$$\frac{\text{Change in price}}{\text{Change in } (1+r)}$$

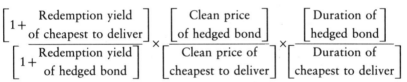

which differs from perturbation in using the change in (1 + redemption yield) rather than change in interest rate as the denominator.

Spread trading

Example 3.3 illustrates the case in which a trader sells a straddle based on a bond futures contract since he expects the spread to weaken. (A futures straddle involves selling/buying a contract relating to one delivery month whilst buying/selling a contract relating to another delivery month.)

Example 3.3

10 April	
Sells a June futures contract at	91·00
Buys a September futures contract at	90·00
10 May	
Closes out by buying a June futures contract at	92·00
Closes out by selling a September futures contract at	92·00

The spread does weaken as expected. There is a loss of 1·0 on the contract sold on 10 April and a profit of 2·0 from the contract bought on 10 April. There is thus a net profit of 1·0, which amounts to $1 per $100 nominal (totalling $1.000 on a US T-bond future with a nominal value of $100,000), from selling the spread and subsequently closing out by buying the spread.

Price limits

Many long-term interest rate futures contracts have price limits. When a price limit is reached, trading in the contract ceases. For example, US treasury bond futures contracts on the Chicago Board of Trade (CBOT) which have a face value of $100,000 have a price limit of 3 points ($3,000) per contract above or below the previous day's settlement price, and the Japanese government bond futures traded on LIFFE have a price limit of Y1 million (on a unit of trading of Y100 million) from the Tokyo Stock Exchange closing price. Hitting a price limit does not necessarily cause the cessation of trading for the remainder of the business day: for example, in the case of LIFFE's Japanese government bond futures, trading resumes one hour after the limit has been hit, with no limit in force for the remainder of the trading day.

The wild card option

Chicago Board of Trade treasury bond and treasury note futures contracts provide those holding short positions with a form of put option (the right to sell bonds at a particular price) during the delivery months. Futures trading ceases at 3 p.m. and the settlement price upon which the invoice amount is based is established at that time. However, trading in the treasury bonds and notes themselves continues until 5 p.m. The holder of the short position can initiate delivery at the day's settlement price up to 9 p.m.

So if the prices of treasury bonds or notes fall significantly between 3 p.m. and 5 p.m., holders of short futures positions can deliver at a profit. They deliver at the relatively high price that is determined by reference to the 3 p.m. futures settlement price, whilst buying the bonds or notes to be delivered at a relatively low price. In effect, those with short futures positions hold, during the delivery month, put options whose exercise prices (the price at which the holder of a put option has the right to sell bonds) are related to the 3 p.m. futures settlement prices. The potential losers, the effective writers of these options, are the holders of long futures positions.

As with any other, this wild card option has to be paid for. The payment is implicit in the futures price. The futures price is lowered so that, in the absence of the option being exercised, the invoice amount for the delivered bonds or notes falls short of the purchase price of the bonds or notes.

4

Stock index futures

Basic principles

When using stock index futures to reduce stock market risk, the anticipation is that any losses arising from movements in stock (equity) prices are offset by gains from parallel movements in futures prices. An investor might be anxious about the possibility that the prices of his stocks (equities) might fall. He could reduce the risk of a reduction in the value of his portfolio by taking a position in the futures market that would provide him with a gain in the event of a fall in stock prices. In such a case, the investor would take a short position in stock index futures contracts. By taking a short position he guarantees a notional selling price of a quantity of stock for a specific date in the future. Should stock prices fall and stock index futures behave in a corresponding fashion, the notional buying price for that date would be less than the predetermined notional selling price. The investor could close out his short position in futures by taking a long position in the same number of contracts. The excess of the selling price over the buying price is paid to the investor in cash in the form of variation margin. This gain on the futures contracts is received on a daily basis as the futures price moves (a procedure known as marking to market). Had the prices of stocks risen, the investor would have gained from his portfolio but lost on his futures dealings. In either case, the investor has succeeded in reducing the extent to which the value of his portfolio fluctuates.

A stock index futures contract is a notional commitment to buy or sell a given quantity of stock on a specified future date at a price determined at the time of taking out the contract. The quantity of stock is a basket of shares. Two examples of stock index futures are the Standard & Poor's (S & P) 500 on the CME and the Financial Times Stock Exchange (FTSE) 100 on LIFFE. The S & P 500 futures are valued at $500 per index point and the FTSE 100 futures have a contract size equal to £25 per index point. In both cases there are just four delivery dates each year, following a March, June, September and December sequence. The contracts do not involve delivery of stock if they are held to the 'delivery' day. There would be a final settlement in cash on the delivery day, which together with the variation margin flows that would already have occurred provides compensation for any difference between the stock index ruling on the last trading day and the futures index when the contract was entered into. A tick is the smallest price movement allowed by an exchange; its size for the S & P 500 futures is 0·05 index points ($25) and for the FTSE 100 futures it is 0·5 index points (£12·50).

The use of futures to hedge the risk of a fall in stock prices does not require any alteration of the original portfolio. It is thus preferable to any form of hedging that involves changing the composition of the portfolio: for example, liquidating part of the portfolio.

Hypothetical examples

In Example 4.1 the portfolio holder fears a generalised fall in stock prices and wishes to avoid a fall in the value of his portfolio. By 10 May the portfolio holder feels that the fall in stock prices is complete and chooses to close out his futures position. Should he wish to insure against adverse market movements on a permanent basis, he could maintain a permanently open futures position, rolling over contracts as they reach maturity. Of course, this strategy is one that reduces variations in the value of the portfolio holder's assets. If, in Example 4.1, the FTSE 100 index had risen, there would have been a cash market gain offset by a futures market loss.

Example 4.1

Cash market	*Futures market*
5 April	
Holds a balanced portfolio of UK shares valued at £1 million but fears a fall in its value. The current FTSE 100 index is 2000.	Sells twenty June FTSE 100 contracts at a price of 2000 each. He has thus committed himself to the notional sale of £1 million of stock on the June delivery date at the level of equity prices implied by the futures price on 5 April.

10 May The FTSE 100 index has fallen to 1900. Correspondingly the value of the portfolio has declined to £950,000.	Closes out the futures position by buying twenty June FTSE 100 contracts at a price of 1900. The notional buying price of each contract is thus 100 below the notional selling price. There is a gain of 200 ticks on each of the twenty contracts.
Loss on the portfolio =£50,000.	Gain from futures trading =£50,000 (200 × 20 × £12·50).

Example 4.2 shows how a long position in futures can be used as a hedge. In this case a fund manager anticipates receipt of $1 million on 10 January and intends to use it to buy a balanced portfolio of US common stock. He fears, one month earlier, that stock prices will rise before the money is received.

Example 4.2

Cash market	*Futures market*
10 December Anticipates receipt of $1 million on 10 January. Current S & P 500 index is 400. Fears a rise in the index.	Buys five March S & P 500 futures contracts at a price of 400. He thereby notionally commits himself to paying $1 million (5 × 400 × $500) for stock on the maturity date of the contracts.
10 January The new S & P 500 index is 420.	Closes out by selling five March S & P 500 futures contracts at a price of 416. He notionally guarantees a receipt of $1,040,000 (5 × 416 × $500) upon maturity of the contracts.

Requires an additional $50,000 in order to buy the quantity of stock that $1 million would have bought on 10 December.	Profit from futures of $40,000.

In Example 4.2 futures prices did not move precisely in line with the S & P 500 index and as a result the hedge was imperfect. In other words, there was a change in basis, which had initially been zero. Of course, if basis had changed so as to establish futures prices in excess of cash market prices, the fund manager could have gained more from the futures market than he needed for the hedge.

Cross hedging

Cross hedges involve hedging risk on one instrument with futures in another. For example, three-month certificates of deposit might be hedged with three-month interest rate futures, or movements of a single stock price might be hedged by using stock index futures. Cross hedging is subject to greater basis risk and there is a level beyond which basis risk becomes unacceptable. Basis risk can be measured by correlating the changes in the relevant cash market and futures prices. The nearer the correlation to 1, the closer are the movements of the two instruments. A correlation coefficient of 1 indicates that the cash and futures instruments have moved precisely in line with each other, so that changes in the price of the cash market instrument could have been hedged perfectly by the futures instrument. The correlation coefficient of 1 indicates an absence of basis risk in the past and that bodes well for the future. A correlation coefficient of zero indicates that the two instruments have moved in completely unrelated ways in the past and therefore basis risk is high. Low values of the correlation coefficient suggest that the futures instrument is unlikely to be suitable for hedging risk on the cash instrument. A rule of thumb might be that a correlation coefficient of at least 0·6 is required to suggest that the hedging would be reasonably successful: a correlation coefficient of 0·6 indicates that the proportion of the risk eliminated is 0·36, i.e. $(0{\cdot}6)^2$.

The more dissimilar the cash market instrument and the instrument upon which the futures are based, the lower will be the correlation coefficient and the higher the basis risk. Three-month certificates of deposit (CDs) and three-month deposits are very similar and hence futures on the latter (i.e. three-month interest rate futures) could safely be used to hedge risk on the former. There is less similarity between, say, a portfolio of shares in the stocks of financial companies and the portfolio represented by a general stock index, so it may be expected that the correlation coefficient is lower and basis risk higher. Reasonable effectiveness of the hedge would be less certain.

Hedge ratios

Hedge ratios become necessary when the volatility of the futures contract is likely to differ from that of the instrument to be hedged. If the instrument to be hedged shows relatively large variations, it is appropriate to use more futures contracts than in the case of a more stable instrument. It is unlikely that a portfolio of stocks for which hedging is required precisely corresponds to the composition of the stock index. It is thus probable that it will show more or less volatility than the index.

The beta factor of a stock is a measure of the extent to which it has moved in line with stock prices in general. A balanced portfolio is likely to have a beta factor of about 1. A stock with only half the movement of the market as a whole will have a factor of 0·5, whilst one with double the degree of change has a factor of 2. The beta factor of a portfolio of stocks is the weighted average of the beta factors of the stocks that constitute the portfolio.

If the calculation indicates a beta factor of 1·2, the portfolio tends to change by 20 per cent more than balanced portfolios of stocks. Hedging the portfolio would require the value of the stock index futures contracts used to exceed the portfolio value by 20 per cent. The relatively large losses (or profits) arising from the high volatility require correspondingly large offsetting profits (or losses) from futures contracts, and this necessitates a relatively large number of futures contracts.

Determination of futures prices

In the chapters on currency and interest rate futures, the prices of futures contracts were seen as being determined by arbitrage: covered interest arbitrage to establish interest rate parity in the case of currency futures, arbitrage based on forward/forward rates in the case of short-term interest rate futures, and cash-and-carry arbitrage in the case of long-term interest rate futures.

Stock index futures prices are also affected by cash-and-carry arbitrage.

This arbitrage activity tends to produce futures prices that are at a premium/discount (against spot cash market prices) that is dependent upon the yield on stocks relative to the financing cost of holding shares of those stocks. However, it is to be expected that this arbitrage effect will be weaker in the case of stock index futures than in the case of long-term interest rate futures because of the expense of acquiring balanced portfolios of stocks: whilst the gilt arbitrageur needs to acquire only the cheapest-to-deliver gilt, the stock index arbitrageur needs to purchase a weighted portfolio of stocks.

Thus factors other than arbitrage acquire significant influence in determining the prices of stock index futures. Expectations of future stock prices are likely to be important. If traders expect stock prices to be higher than those suggested by futures prices, they will buy futures so as to make profits when futures prices rise into line with the expected stock prices. These purchases of futures contracts will tend to pull futures prices up towards the expected levels. Conversely, if stock prices are expected to be lower than those implied by futures prices, trading for the purpose of obtaining speculative profits would tend to pull down futures prices (futures contracts would be sold with a view to closing out by buying at lower prices). Thus there will be some tendency for stock index futures prices to reflect expected stock prices.

Indeed, expectations of future cash market prices are likely to have some influence in the determination of the prices of other futures contracts. This is likely to be the case for the more distant delivery months. Arbitrage opportunities may be more fully taken in the nearer contracts than in the more distant ones, so that the prices of the latter become more influenced by expectations of cash market prices. In fact, futures prices are often used as indicators of market expectations (this is sometimes known as the price discovery function of futures).

Arbitrage and expectations cannot provide a complete explanation of futures prices. Futures prices are established by demand and supply (offers to buy and sell in the pit). Arbitrage and trading based on expectations influence prices by way of their impacts on demand and supply. Anything that impacts on offers to buy and sell will affect prices.

Speculators and arbitrageurs

These types of transactor serve to render the market liquid and stable. It is unlikely that hedgers' demand for contracts will exactly equal hedgers' supply of contracts for a particular delivery month. Speculators and arbitrageurs fill the gap between demand and supply, thereby ensuring the marketability of the contracts and reducing the price fluctuations that result from imbalance between demand and supply.

If there is a temporary excess demand for the contracts of a particular delivery month, there will be tendency for the price of those contracts to rise. The speculator would take a short position in those contracts in anticipation of closing out by taking a long position when the price has fallen back to its normal level. He thus sells at the higher price and buys at the lower price. In so doing he fills the gap between the long and short positions desired by hedgers. Speculators thus help to ensure that hedgers can take the positions required and simultaneously prevent the abrupt price movements that might otherwise result from mismatching of desired short and long positions.

Arbitrageurs may operate between the futures market and the market for the underlying financial instrument. In this way, they help to create liquidity in the futures market and dampen excessive divergences between futures prices and the prices of the underlying financial instruments. Thus if hedgers sought to take a net long position for a particular delivery month, there would be a tendency for the price of the contract to rise. The arbitrageur could sell futures and buy stocks with a view to subsequently closing both positions and making a profit. Such might be the case if the premium of the futures price over the cash market price gave a return greater than the excess of the financing cost of holding shares of a stock over the running yield of those shares. Thus tendencies for futures prices to diverge too far from the underlying stock prices will be tempered by arbitrage. This means that arbitrage reduces basis risk.

This arbitrage process is likely to be less than complete for several reasons. Firstly, the arbitrageur faces uncertainty in the stock market. He may incur costs represented by the difference between interest paid on money borrowed to finance the stock purchases and the return on the stocks, which takes the form of dividend receipts. These costs are subject to considerable uncertainty arising from the possibility of unexpected changes in dividends. The arbitrageur would therefore look for a risk premium. Secondly, buying a portfolio of stocks that correlates strongly with the stock index is likely to prove expensive since a large number of individual purchases would be involved. Furthermore, it is unlikely that they could all be purchased simultaneously with the sale of the futures contracts. The arbitrageur faces the risk of price movements whilst making his purchases. An arbitrageur seeking to take a long position in the futures market and a short position in the cash market faces the additional problem of how to sell something that he does not have. So arbitrage might operate only weakly in the opposite direction.

PROGRAM TRADING

Cash-and-carry arbitrage with stock index futures is often carried out by computer. Computers are programmed to identify arbitrage opportunities and to initiate immediately the transactions required to make the arbitrage profits. This can cause sudden movements in stock indices as numerous computers simultaneously initiate buy or sell orders (see Appendix I for discussion of this process in the stock market crash of October 1987). This process renders prices in stock and futures markets consistent with one another. For example, the identification of overpriced futures should lead to purchases of stocks and sales of stock index futures. Stock prices rise and futures prices fall until the relationship between them is such that arbitrage profits are no longer available.

It may be the case that large numbers of arbitrageurs seek to unwind their arbitrage positions when the futures contracts expire. This leads to heavy buying or selling in the stock markets and can cause sharp price movements. In the United States stock index futures, stock index options and options on stock index futures expire simultaneously. The last trading hour on the common expiry day is often referred to as the Triple Witching Hour. The transactions in stocks corresponding to the closing out of the futures and options positions can cause dramatic movements in stock prices.

5

Hedging with options

Call options

A call option gives the buyer of that option the right, but not the obligation, to buy stock at a particular price. That price is known as the exercise, or strike, price. At the time of buying the option there would be a range of exercise prices available to choose from. For example, when the price of XYZ stock was $236 on 12 November 19XX, the available option exercise prices were $220, $240 and $260. If the holder of a call option decides to exercise it, he will buy 100 shares at the strike price chosen when buying the option. (This example relates to a US stock option whose price is expressed in dollars per share and which relates to 100 shares. United Kingdom equity options have prices quoted in pence (£0·01) per share and typically relate to 1,000 shares. In other countries there are different specifications.)

It will be profitable to exercise a call option if the market price of the stock turns out to be higher than the strike price. In the event of the market price being lower than the strike price, the option holder is not obliged to exercise it, and presumably would not do so since exercising it would realise a loss. The buyer of an option thus has potential for profit without the risk of a loss. For this favourable situation the buyer of an option pays a premium. Continuing the previous example, the premiums for XYZ call options, at the close of trading on 12 November 19XX, were as shown in Table 5.1. November, December and January were expiry months. The expiry month of an option is the month in which it ceases to be exercisable. Premiums are normally payable at the time the option is bought. The premium for the December $240 XYZ call is $17 which, since this is the premium per share, amounts to $1,700 for an option to buy 100 shares of the stock.

Table 5.1

Exercise price	Premium		
	November	December	January
220	19	30	39
240	5	17	27
260	1	11	18

THE PROFIT/LOSS PROFILE AT EXPIRY

Since an option buyer is not obliged to exercise an option, he has the right simply to disregard it. In such an event the premium paid is lost but there would be no further loss. The premium paid is the maximum loss that can be incurred. On the other hand, the profit potential is subject to no limits. There is no upper limit to the stock price and hence no upper limit to the potential profit. Figure 5.1 shows the profit/loss profile of a call option at expiry.

The option used for the illustration is the December 240 XYZ call whose premium is 17. If the buyer holds the option to the expiry date and the stock price turns out to be 240 or less, there is no point in exercising the option. There is no benefit from exercising an option to buy stock at 240 when that stock can be bought at the same, or a lower, price in the market.

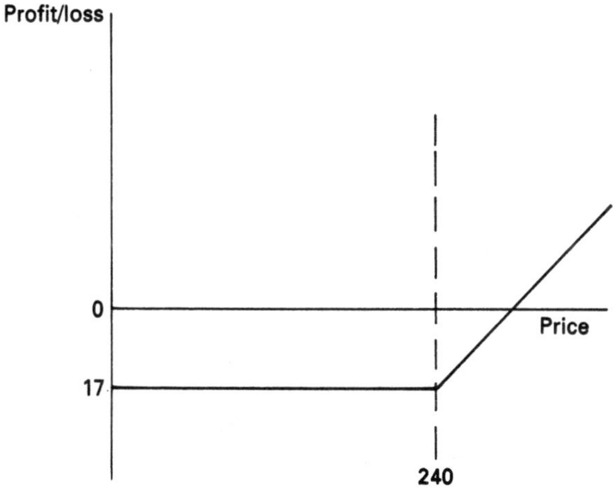

Figure 5.1 Profit/loss profile of a call option at expiry

In such a situation the option buyer makes a net loss because of the payment of the 17 premium, which is non-returnable. This is shown in Figure 5.1, which depicts a loss of 17 at all prices up to 240.

If the price of the stock turns out to be greater than 240 it will be worthwhile to exercise the option. The option holder could choose to exercise the option to buy at 240 and then immediately sell the stock at the higher price, thereby realising a profit. At a stock price of 257 this profit would exactly offset the premium paid. Hence 257 is the break-even price at which net profit is zero. At prices above 257 the gross profit exceeds the premium so that there is a net profit.

The gross profit referred to is alternatively known as the intrinsic value of the option. Intrinsic value can be defined as the profit to be obtained by immediately exercising the option (disregarding the premium) and is equal to the difference between the exercise price and the market price when the option is in the money.

An in-the-money call option is one whose exercise price is less than the market price, and which therefore offers an immediate gross profit. An at-the-money option is one whose exercise price is equal to the market price. An out-of-the-money call option is one whose exercise price is greater than the market price. Only in-the-money options have intrinsic value.

THE PROFIT/LOSS PROFILE PRIOR TO EXPIRY

At the time that a traded option expires, its price (premium) will be equal to its intrinsic value. Prior to expiry the premium would normally exceed the intrinsic value. This excess of the price of the option over the intrinsic value is known as the time value. When an option is exercised, only the intrinsic value is realised. The seller of an option will obtain a price that incorporates some time value as well as the intrinsic value. When account is taken of the time value, the profit/loss profile of an option differs from the at-expiry profile depicted in Figure 5.1. A prior-to-expiry profile is shown by the broken line in Figure 5.2. Time value is indicated by the vertical distance between the two profiles.

Time value is at its highest when the option is at the money. Time value declines as the option moves either into or out of the money and will approach zero as the market price of the stock diverges substantially from the exercise price. The broken line indicates the market price of the option minus the initial premium paid (17 in this case). When an option is purchased, the premium paid will be the market price and the profit/loss

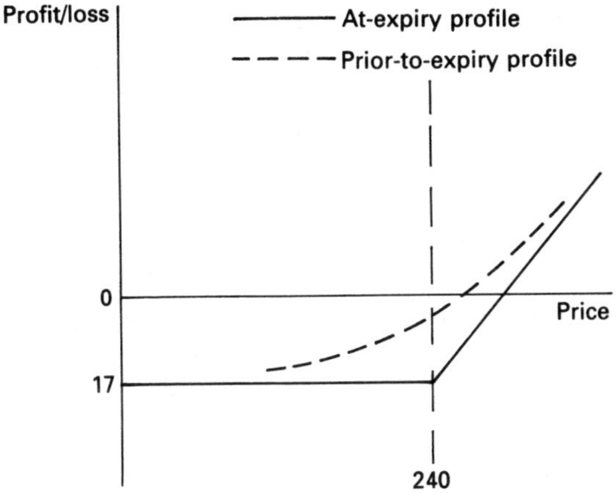

Figure 5.2 Profit/loss profile of a call option prior to expiry

profile (broken line) will intersect the horizontal axis indicating zero net profit at the ruling market price. (This is equivalent to saying that at the moment of purchase the value of the option is equal to the price paid for it.) As time passes and the stock price changes, the net profit will cease to be zero. The net profit shown by the prior-to-expiry profile is the price that the trader could sell the option for minus the price (premium) that he paid for it.

Below the exercise price (240 in this case) the price of the option consists of time value only, but above the exercise price the price consists of both time and intrinsic value. This ensures that the gradient of the prior-to-expiry profile increases as the stock price rises. This gradient is known as the option delta and can alternatively be expressed as the change in the price of the option as a proportion of the change in the price of the stock. The delta approaches zero as the option becomes deeply out of the money and approaches 1 when it is deeply in the money. The delta is approximately 0·5 when the option is at the money.

DETERMINANTS OF THE PREMIUM

The explanation of an option premium subdivides into ascertaining intrinsic value and assessing the influences on time value. The intrinsic value of a call option is equal to the stock price minus the exercise price of the option, with zero being the minimum intrinsic value. In principle, the option premium cannot fall below the intrinsic value. If the option premium were below the intrinsic value, there would be a guaranteed profit from buying and immediately exercising the option. It would be irrational for anyone to sell an option for a price that was less than its intrinsic value.

The determination of time value is more complex. Major influences on time value are the expected volatility of the stock price, the length of the period remaining to the expiry date, and the extent to which the option is in or out of the money.

The higher the expected volatility, the greater will be the premiums. An option on a volatile share has a strong chance of acquiring intrinsic value at some stage prior to expiry. Similarly, the probability of an option acquiring intrinsic value prior to expiry rises with the length of time remaining to the expiry date. It can be seen from Table 5.1 that the options with the more distant expiry dates have the higher premiums.

Time value is at its peak when the option is at the money and declines as the option moves either into or out of the money. Out-of-the-money options have less time value than at-the-money options because the stock price has further to move before intrinsic value is acquired. In-the-money options have less time value than at-the-money options since their prices contain intrinsic value which is vulnerable to a fall in the stock price, whereas at-the-money option premiums contain no intrinsic value. The risk that existing intrinsic value might be lost reduces the attractiveness of the option and lowers its price.

Put options

A put option gives its holder the right, but not the obligation, to sell stock at a specified price at any time prior to the expiry date of the option. The holder of an option can exercise it, sell it or allow it to expire. It is worthwhile exercising an option – that is, exercising the right to sell stock at the strike price – only if the market price of the stock turns out to be lower than the strike price. If the strike price is greater than the market price, the option is said to have intrinsic value. The intrinsic value would be equal to the excess of the strike price over the market price. An option without intrinsic value might simply be allowed to expire since its holder is not obliged to exercise it, and presumably would not if the strike price were below the market price of the stock.

The buyer of an option pays a premium, which is the price of the option. The premium consists of the intrinsic value, if there is any, plus time value. It is likely that the holder of an option would choose to sell it in preference

Table 5.2

Strike price	Premium		
	November	December	January
220	$1\frac{1}{2}$	7	12
240	9	14	22
260	25	28	32

to exercising it or allowing it to expire. By selling the option he would receive the time value as well as any intrinsic value.

Table 5.2 shows the premiums of XYZ put options at the close of trading on 12 November 19XX. The price of XYZ stock was $236. The months referred to in Table 5.2 are expiry months. All the option contracts in the table belong to one class, namely XYZ puts. Within that class there are nine series. Each series is characterised by a strike price and an expiry date, e.g. $220 November, $260 January. When an expiry date is reached, options with a new expiry date are introduced. Substantial movements of the stock price will invoke the introduction of new strike prices, so that there are strike prices either side of the stock price.

THE PROFIT/LOSS PROFILE AT EXPIRY

Since the option buyer is not obliged to exercise the option, and presumably would not do so if it involved selling at a loss relative to the market price of the stock, the premium paid is the maximum loss that the buyer of the option can incur. So, for example, a buyer of XYZ November 240 puts faces a maximum loss of $9 per share, which amounts to $900 per contract since each put option contract is for the sale of 100 shares of the stock.

The maximum profit is limited only by the fact that stock prices cannot fall below zero. Since it is conceivable that a stock price can fall to zero, the net gain from a put option can, in principle, be as much as the strike price minus the premium paid. The buyer of XYZ November 240 puts stands to gain as much as 240 − 9 per share. This amounts to $23,100 per option contract. The option holder could buy shares at zero and, by exercising the option, sell them at 240.

Figure 5.3 shows the profit/loss profile of XYZ November 240 puts at expiry: that is, on the day in November upon which the option ceases to be capable of being exercised. If the share price is 240 or higher when the

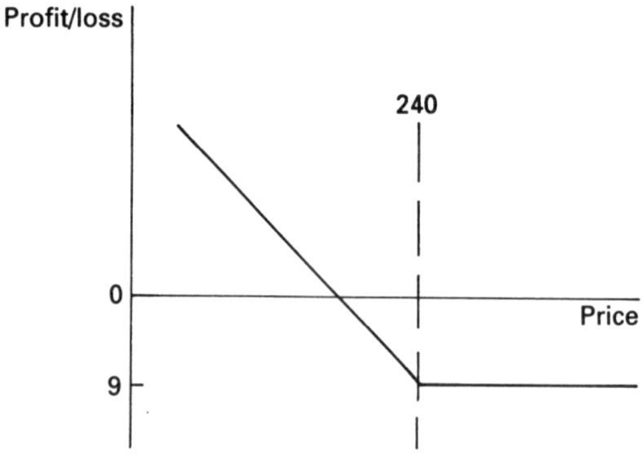

Figure 5.3 Profit/loss profile of a put option at expiry

option expires, the holder of the option records a net loss of 9 per share ($900 per option contract). If the stock price turns out to be less than 240 there is a profit to be made by exercising the option. Exercising the option would allow the option holder to sell shares at 240 whilst buying them at a lower price. The profit from exercising the option minus the premium paid is the net profit. If the share price lies between 231 and 240 there is a net loss, whereas below the break-even price of 231 there is a net profit.

THE PROFIT/LOSS PROFILE PRIOR TO EXPIRY

At expiry an option would have only intrinsic value, which could be equal to zero. Prior to expiry the option would have time value as well as intrinsic value. The profit/loss profile of Figure 5.3 is based on intrinsic value only. Since intrinsic value is the profit to be made from exercising the option, it will be zero at or above the strike price of 240, whereas below 240 it will be equal to the difference between the market price and the strike price. The net profit or loss at expiry is equal to the intrinsic value minus the premium paid.

Prior to expiry the price of an option will exceed the intrinsic value. This excess is the time value and is shown in Figure 5.4 by the vertical distance between the at-expiry profile and the prior-to-expiry profile indicated by the broken line. The prior-to-expiry profile indicates the current market price of the option minus the price that the present holder paid for it. As time passes, the prior-to-expiry profile will tend to converge on the at-expiry profile, with the convergence becoming complete as expiry is reached.

This convergence reflects the tendency for the time value of an option to decline with the passage of time. This erosion of time value can be explained in terms of the decreasing likelihood of a substantial increase in intrinsic value as the time available for the requisite stock price movement declines. A second factor affecting time value is the expected volatility of the stock price. With high volatility there is a relatively high chance of substantial gains in intrinsic value at some stage prior to expiry. So the greater the expected volatility of a stock, the greater will the time value of an option on that stock tend to be.

A third factor affecting time value is the relationship between the stock price and the strike price of the option. Time value is at its highest when the stock price is equal to the strike price. When the stock price is equal to the strike price, the option is said to be at the money. As the stock price and strike price diverge, in either direction, time value declines.

When the stock price exceeds the strike price, the put option is said to be out of the money. A better price can be obtained by selling the stock in the market than by exercising the option. Time value declines as the option moves further out of the money (in other words, as the stock price rises), reflecting the decreasing likelihood of the stock price declining sufficiently to cause exercise of the option to become profitable.

When the stock price is lower than the strike price, the put option is said to be in the money. A better price can be obtained by exercising the option than by selling the stock in the market. It is possible to make a profit by buying stock at the market price and selling it at the price guaranteed by the option contract. Time value declines as the option becomes deeper in the money (that is, as the stock price falls). This can be understood in terms of there being an increasing amount of intrinsic value that is at risk of

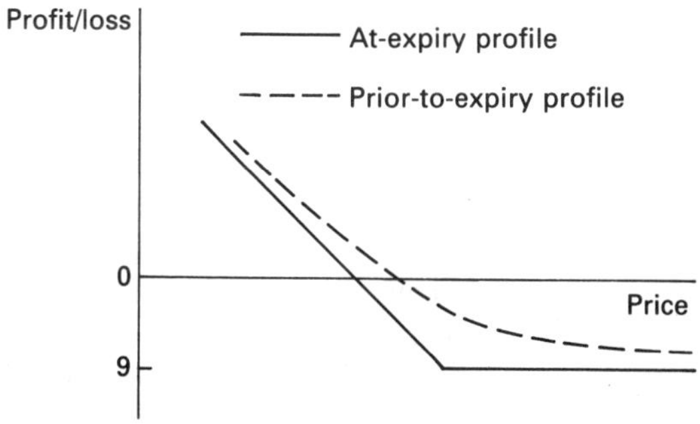

Figure 5.4 Profit/loss profile of a put option prior to expiry

being lost. The price of an in-the-money option contains the intrinsic value of that option. Part, or all, of the intrinsic value of a put option would be destroyed by a rise in the stock price. The buyer of an in-the-money option bears this risk, whereas the buyer of an at-the-money option does not. The risk borne rises as the option becomes deeper in the money. This risk is reflected in the time value. The buyer of an at-the-money option pays a higher price for time value than the buyer of an in-the-money option, with the price paid declining as the option becomes deeper in the money.

The gradient of the prior-to-expiry profile is known as the delta and represents the ratio between the change in the price of the option and the change in the stock price. In the case of put options, deltas are negative. The delta increases in absolute value as the option moves deeper in the money (as the stock price falls). As the option becomes increasingly deep in the money, the prior-to-expiry profile approaches the 45° line of the at-expiry profile because of the decline in time value. This means that the delta approaches −1 when a put option becomes very deep in the money.

The delta decreases in absolute value as the option moves further out of the money. The prior-to-expiry profile approaches the horizontal line of the at-expiry profile since time value diminishes as the stock price moves away from the strike price of the option. The delta tends towards zero as the option becomes very deeply out of the money.

Using call options

Options may be used to either reduce or increase risk. Reducing risk could be regarded as hedging and increasing risk as speculating.

HEDGING ANTICIPATED PURCHASES

Options can be used to hedge intended purchases of stocks. Suppose it is 12 November 19XX and that a portfolio manager intends to buy XYZ stock with funds expected to become available at the end of November. The current price of XYZ stock is $236 and the portfolio manager wishes to avoid the risks of having to pay a much higher price in December. The prices of XYZ call options are found to be as shown in Table 5.3.

The portfolio manager could buy December 240 call options at 17. Each option contract provides the right, but not the obligation, to buy 100 XYZ shares at a price of 240 per share. The price of the option is 17 per share, which amounts to $1,700 ($17 × 100) per option contract.

If when the stock was purchased in December the price were 260, the

Table 5.3

Exercise price	Premium		
	November	December	January
220	19	30	39
240	5	17	27
260	1	11	18

portfolio manager could exercise the option and thereby buy stock at 240. This represents a saving of 20 per share at a premium cost of 17 per share: a net profit of 3 per share.

By exercising the option the hedger obtains its intrinsic value. If instead he sold the option, he would receive the time value as well as the intrinsic value. The time value might be 10 and hence the sale price of the option would be 30. The portfolio manager would have bought options for 17 and sold them for 30. There would have been a net profit of 13 per share rather than the 3 obtained from exercising the option. The 13 per share profit from the option partially offsets the increased price of the stock, whose effective price becomes 247 (260 – 13).

If the stock price were 240 or less at the time the stock was purchased, the options held would have no intrinsic value and therefore could not be profitably exercised. However, they would still have time value. For example, if the share price were still 236, the December 240 call options might be selling at 13. The options would have been bought for 17 and sold for 11 (assuming a bid–offer spread of 2). The net cost of 6 (that is, $600 per contract covering 100 shares) compares favourably with the net cost of 17 ($1,700) incurred if the option is allowed to expire unexercised.

DELTA HEDGING

In the previous example the hedger did not obtain full cover for the proposed stock purchase. The stock price rose by 24 whilst the net profit per share obtained from the options was only 13. Delta hedging provides a means of obtaining full compensation for the adverse stock price movement.

The delta of an option is the ratio of the change in the price of that option to the change in the price of the underlying stock. Delta hedging involves buying more than one option for each block of 100 shares covered. If, for example, the delta were 0·5, the hedger would buy two options for each block of 100 shares covered. When the option price changes by half as much as the stock price, twice as many options are bought (since each call option represents the right to purchase 100 shares, this implies two options per block of 100 shares covered). By using the appropriate ratio of options to shares, the extra cost of the stock to be purchased can be exactly offset by a profit from a rise in the price of the options.

In the previous example, the stock price rose by 24 whereas the option price rose by 13. This implies that the average delta of the option was 0·54 (13/24) over the share price range 236–260. Approximately 1·85 (i.e. 1/0·54) options per 100 shares would have provided full cover against the stock price movement. The requisite number of options per 100 shares is the reciprocal of the delta.

A difficulty that arises with delta hedging is the tendency for the delta to change as the stock price moves. In the example, the delta would have been less than 0·5 at the stock price of 236 and greater than 0·5 at the stock price of 260. The requisite number of option contracts per 100 shares would have moved from above two to below two. This suggests the need to adjust constantly the number of options held as the stock price moves. This is problematical not only because of the time and expense involved in constantly monitoring and adjusting option holdings, but also because option contracts are indivisible. Since fractions of contracts cannot be bought, precise cover cannot be achieved.

The lack of divisibility is not a significant drawback when large blocks of shares are to be purchased, but it can be very inconvenient when small blocks, such as 100 shares, are to be bought. Nevertheless a hedger covering an anticipated purchase of 100 shares would have achieved a much better hedge with two option contracts (the number that would have been approximately the quantity indicated by the delta when the share price was 236p) than with the simple one option per 100 shares strategy.

HIGHLY GEARED POSITION TAKING

Call options can be used for obtaining much higher percentage returns than those available from holding the stocks to which the options relate. However, this is at the risk of much higher percentage losses. Options allow exposure to the movements of the stock price with an outlay equal to the premium rather than the stock price.

Consider the example used hitherto. A trader expecting a rise in the price of XYZ stock and wishing to profit from that rise could either buy the stock or buy call options. If the stock were purchased at 236 and subsequently sold for 260 the profit would have been 10·2 per cent. Alternatively, the trader could have bought December 240 calls at 17 and subsequently sold them for 30, thereby making a 76·5 per cent profit.

Although taking advantage of the high gearing offered by options can produce high percentage profits, it can also lead to heavy percentage losses. Suppose that instead of rising by 24 the stock price fell by 24, to 212. In such a circumstance the option price might have fallen to 9. There would have been a 47·1 per cent loss compared to the 10·2 per cent loss from buying and selling the stock itself.

Options, unlike stock, have expiry dates. When that date has passed, the option has no value (it ceases to exist). So if the stock price remains at 236 until the expiry date there would be a 100 per cent loss on an option held to that date, whereas there would have been neither profit nor loss from holding the stock (disregarding any dividends). Since the passage of time erodes time value, there would be a tendency for profits to decline, and losses to increase, as time passes. An option that expires unexercised would provide its holder with a 100 per cent loss.

GOING LIQUID WHILST REMAINING EXPOSED

A trader who fears a sharp fall in stock prices, or who wishes to take profits following a market rise but who wishes to profit from any further upward movement, can use the 90/10 strategy. This involves the investor selling his stock and holding most of the proceeds as deposits whilst using a small proportion to buy call options. For example, 100 shares of XYZ stock might be sold for $23,600, of which $1,700 is used to buy a December 240 call. Should there be a sharp fall in the price of the stock, the investor still retains at least $21,900 ($23,600 – $1,700). The investor's capital cannot fall below $21,900. At the same time, the investor would benefit in the event of a rise in the stock price because of the call option held. However, the ability to profit from a rise in the stock price is only temporary. After the December expiry date there is no exposure to the market, unless part of the $21,900 is used to buy another call option with a more distant expiry date.

Using put options

Options can be used to fine-tune the amount of risk that an investor faces. A holder of stock may use them either to reduce or to increase the exposure of the value of the stockholding to movements of the stock price.

Table 5.4

Strike price	Premium		
	November	December	January
220	$1\frac{1}{2}$	7	12
240	9	14	22
260	25	28	32

HEDGING THE VALUE OF A STOCKHOLDING

A put option guarantees a minimum selling price for a block of 100 shares (1,000 shares in the United Kingdom). Table 5.4 shows the premiums of XYZ put options at the close of trading on 12 November 19XX, at which time the price of XYZ stock was $236.

A holder of 500 XYZ shares would be able to ensure that the value of the stockholding could not fall below $110,000 (500 × $220) by buying five 220 put options. These options would provide the right to sell 500 XYZ shares at 220. The option prices are expressed in dollars per share, so the cost of providing such protection until the December expiry date would be $3,500 (500 × $7). Of course, should the stock price remain in excess of 220, the shareholder would not exercise the right to sell at 220.

Although the stockholder has the right to exercise the option and thereby sell stock at 220, he is more likely to sell, rather than exercise, the option. This can be understood by considering the elements that make up an option premium. The premium (that is, the price) of an option can be subdivided into its intrinsic value and its time value. The intrinsic value represents the profit that could be obtained by immediately exercising the option. For example, a November 240 put option has an intrinsic value of 4 when the stock price is 236 since, by exercising the option, shares can be sold at 4 more than the price at which they are bought. The difference between the option premium and the intrinsic value is termed time value, which is 5 in the case of the November 240 put options. Time value can be regarded as a payment for the possibility that intrinsic value will increase prior to the date on which the option expires: that is, the date beyond which it cannot be exercised. If a stockholder exercises an option, only the intrinsic value is received; whereas if the option is sold, both the intrinsic and time values are obtained. It thus makes sense to sell an option in preference to exercising it.

In Table 5.4 the 220 puts have exercise prices below the market value of the stock. Therefore they cannot be exercised at a profit and have zero intrinsic value. Their price consists entirely of time value. Put options with exercise prices below the market price of the stock are said to be out of the money. When the stock price is equal to the exercise price, the option is said to be at the money. Put options with exercise prices above the stock price (the only ones with intrinsic value) are termed in the money.

Time value is at its highest when the option is at the money and declines as the stock price moves away from the exercise price (in either direction). If the stockholder bought December 220 put options at 7 on 12 November and saw the stock price fall by 20 the following day, he would simultaneously have seen the price of his options rise. A new option price of 14 would seem plausible (an intrinsic value of 4 plus time value raised from 7 to 10).

Faced with the choice between exercising the options and thereby selling stock at the exercise price of 220 and following the alternative route of selling stock at the new market price of 216 and simultaneously selling the options at 14, the investor will clearly favour the latter procedure. The $14 premium would include time value of 10, the receipt of which via selling the options gives an effective share price of 230 (223 after taking account of the original cost of the options) instead of the 220 from exercising the option ($213 after deducting the $7 original cost).

Had the stock price fallen to a more modest extent, say to 224, there would have been no benefit from exercising the options. However, there would have been some time value; 10 is plausible. Selling the stock at 224 and simultaneously selling the options at 10 gives an effective selling price of 234 ($227 allowing for the initial $7 premium paid).

Exercise 5.1

Question

On 12 April a treasurer is considering the possibility of borrowing $2 million for six months, beginning on 10 June. The borrowing, the need for which is uncertain, would be at a spread of 0·75% over LIBOR.

The June eurodollar interest rate futures price is 93·72.

The September eurodollar interest rate futures price is 93·71.

The current LIBOR for both three- and six-month eurodollars is $6\frac{5}{16}$%.

The eurodollar options are as shown in Table 5.5.

Suggest three alternative hedging strategies, pointing out any remaining sources of uncertainty. In each instance state the worst-case outcome (in the sense of the highest possible interest rate). Indicate the relative merits of the three strategies.

Table 5.5

	Calls		Puts	
	June	September	June	September
93.00	0.75	0.78	0.03	0.07
93.25	0.54	0.58	0.07	0.12
93.50	0.36	0.40	0.14	0.19
93.75	0.21	0.26	0.24	0.30
94.00	0.11	0.16	0.39	0.45
94.25	0.05	0.08	0.58	0.62
94.50	0.01	0.04	0.79	0.83

Answer

A possible strategy would involve the purchase of June 93·75 puts. If the puts were exercised on 10 June, the interest rate achieved would be in the region of

$6{\cdot}25+0{\cdot}24+0{\cdot}75=7{\cdot}24\%$ p.a. (which can be regarded as the worst-case outcome)

i.e. (100 − futures price) + premium + spread

The actual interest rate is likely to differ slightly from this because (a) if the puts are sold rather than exercised there may be some time value obtained, and (b) there would be some basis risk. These are two sources of uncertainty as to the interest rate to be obtained. Four contracts would be appropriate since each contract relates to $1 million for three months, and the cover is for $2 million over six months.

An alternative strategy would be that of buying two June and two September puts. The advantage of this strategy relative to the previous one is that it would provide protection against unexpected changes in the slope of the yield curve. Disadvantages would include higher basis risk through having to sell September contracts long before the maturity date of the underlying futures contracts and the greater risk that arises if the markets for contracts with distant expiry dates are illiquid. If, in the case of this second strategy, 93·75 puts were purchased, the worst-case outcome would be the average of

$$6{\cdot}25+0{\cdot}24+0{\cdot}75=7{\cdot}24\% \text{ p.a.}$$

and

$$6{\cdot}25+0{\cdot}30+0{\cdot}75=7{\cdot}30\% \text{ p.a.}$$

which is 7·27% p.a. The sources of uncertainty mentioned in relation to the first strategy would be present (and more strongly so) in the second strategy.

A third strategy might use 93·50 puts. The hedger would be accepting a greater degree of risk but the premium payments would be less. The worst-case outcome from the purchase of four 93·50 June puts would be

$$6{\cdot}50+0{\cdot}14+0{\cdot}75=7{\cdot}39\% \text{ p.a.}$$

The previously mentioned sources of uncertainty would also be present in the case of the third strategy. The basis risk arises from the relationship between the futures price and the interest rates in the cash market. The remaining time value provides exposure to uncertainty arising from possible changes in market expectations of volatility; this is often referred to as volatility risk.

DELTA HEDGING

In neither of the foregoing two cases did the stockholder succeed in maintaining the value of his stockholding. The effective stock prices were 223 and 227, after deducting the original premium, even when the options were sold rather than exercised.

Delta hedging provides a technique for maintaining the original value of the stockholding. In other words, it can ensure that the stock price plus profit on the options equals 236 per share. This is achieved by factoring up the number of options contracts purchased.

The delta of an option is a measure of the responsiveness of the option price to movements in the underlying stock price. It is the change in the options price divided by the change in the stock price. Put options have negative deltas because they become more valuable as the stock price falls. Deep out-of-the-money options have deltas close to zero, at-the-money options have deltas close to −0·5, and deep in-the-money options have deltas that approach −1.

An option buyer can be regarded as having acquired an asset. Delta hedging involves ensuring that increases in the value of one asset, the options, offset declines in the value of another asset, the stockholding.

Referring again to Table 5.4, it can be seen that the 240 put options are slightly in the money. December 240 put option deltas might plausibly be −0·625. Delta hedging involves factoring up the number of option contracts by the reciprocal of the delta, in this case 1·6 (i.e. 1/0·625). The hedger wishing to protect the value of 500 XYZ shares at $118,000 (500 × $236) can do so by purchasing eight (5 × 1·6) December 240 put options at 14. The initial cost of the options would be $11,200 (800 × $14). A $1 fall in the stock price would be accompanied by a $0·625 rise in the option price. So the $500 (500 × $1) loss on the value of the shares would be accompanied by a $500 (800 × $0·625) profit on the options.

Unfortunately, the movement of the stock price would tend to change the value of the delta. So a delta hedge would need to be constantly monitored and the number of options increased or decreased in the light of changed circumstances. These circumstances include not only the

Table 5.6

	Price factor	Relative volatility
£2,000,000 Treasury $8\frac{3}{4}$ 2003–07	0.9797593	0.99
£2,000,000 Treasury 7 2007	0.7504174	0.76
£2,000,000 Treasury $10\frac{1}{2}$ 2004–08	1.1129495	1.13

underlying stock price, but also the time remaining to the expiry date of the option and the expected volatility of the stock price.

This need for monitoring and rebalancing the number of options contracts is a significant drawback of delta hedging, as is the possibility that the requisite number of options might not be a whole number. Options are indivisible and so perfect hedging is impossible when something other than a whole number of contracts is required. For a holder of a diversified portfolio, stock index options might be an attractive

---

Exercise 5.2

Question

It is 3 March and a bond portfolio manager is concerned about the possibility of a rise in interest rates. His portfolio consists of the assets shown in Table 5.6. (The relative volatility is between the listed bond and the cheapest to deliver.)
The June government bond futures price is 119-58 (pricing in 1/64ths).
Government bond futures options prices are (deltas in brackets, pricing in 1/64ths) as shown in Table 5.7.
The price factor of the cheapest-to-deliver bond is 0·98327.
Describe three possible hedging strategies, indicating the number of contracts involved in each instance. Highlight their relative merits. (Assume that the contract sizes are £50,000.)

Answer

Possible strategies include the following:

(a) A short position in futures.

$$(£2{,}000{,}000/£50{,}000) \times 0{\cdot}98327 \times 0{\cdot}99 = 38{\cdot}94$$
$$(£2{,}000{,}000/£50{,}000) \times 0{\cdot}98327 \times 0{\cdot}76 = 29{\cdot}89$$
$$(£2{,}000{,}000/£50{,}000) \times 0{\cdot}98327 \times 1{\cdot}13 = 44{\cdot}44$$

Total number of contracts 113·27

Sell 113 June government bond futures contracts.

Table 5.7

	Calls		Puts	
	June	September	June	September
116	4-49 (0.83)	5-35 (0.79)	0-55 (−0.17)	1-51 (−0.21)
118	3-18 (0.65)	4-20 (0.61)	1-24 (−0.35)	2-36 (−0.39)
120	2-18 (0.45)	3-18 (0.46)	2-24 (−0.55)	3-34 (−0.54)
122	1-22 (0.23)	2-27 (0.28)	3-28 (−0.77)	4-43 (−0.72)
124	0-52 (0.09)	1-48 (0.13)	4-58 (−0.91)	6-00 (−0.87)

(b) Buy June 120 futures options puts with a view to using a fixed hedge. There would need to be as many option contracts as futures contracts indicated in (a).

(c) Use futures options puts in delta hedging. June 120 futures options puts might be bought. The appropriate number of contracts is (using the calculations in (a))

$$113{\cdot}27 \times 1/0{\cdot}55 = 205{\cdot}95$$

Buy 206 June 120 futures options puts.

Relative merits would include factors such as the absence of premiums with futures hedges, the facility of gaining from favourable price movements with options in a fixed hedge and the need for constant monitoring and rebalancing in the case of delta hedges (the hedger is unlikely to use delta hedging with options if there is adequate liquidity in a corresponding futures market).

alternative to hedging individual stocks with their corresponding option contracts because the problem of indivisibility becomes proportionately smaller when larger numbers of shares are being hedged.

TAKING A SHORT POSITION

Put options, unlike shares, provide a means of making profits from a fall in stock prices. If a trader in options believes that the price of a particular stock will fall, that trader can seek to profit from such a fall by buying put options.

In the example used above, the trader, expecting a fall in the price of XYZ stock, could buy December 220 put options at 7 on 12 November. The following day the stock price falls to 216 and the price of the options rises to 14. Put options provide a right to sell at a particular price and that right becomes more valuable as the stock price falls.

In this context it is worth noting that, whereas in-the-money and at-the-money options will give the higher absolute profits (because of the enhancement of intrinsic value), out-of-the-money options could provide the higher percentage returns because of the lower initial premiums.

Market practices and terms

All the call options on a particular underlying stock together constitute a *class* of options. Similarly, all the puts on the same underlying stock would together comprise another class. Within each class there will be a number of series. An option series is specific to a particular exercise price and a particular expiry month as well as to a particular stock and call/put categorisation. So, for example, $50 December calls and $60 January calls on the stock of ABC are two different series within the same class (the class being ABC call options).

An opening purchase is a transaction whereby the buyer of an option becomes its *holder*; a closing purchase is a transaction in which a writer (seller) of an option buys an option identical to the one previously written, whereupon the two positions are deemed to cancel each other out. An opening sale is a transaction in which the seller of an option becomes its *writer*; a closing sale involves the cancellation of a previously purchased option.

Premiums in respect of traded options are normally payable via the broker to the clearing house on the morning following the day of the trade. Payment to the writer of the option would come from the clearing house, which usually acts as a registrar for all open contracts. If the holder of an option exercises it, the clearing house, using a random selection process, chooses a writer who is then assigned to sell (in the case of calls) or buy (in the case of puts) to or from the holder at the exercise price.

There are often position limits to the number of options in any one class that can be held or written by any one individual or organisation. For example, in the case of equity options traded on the London Traded Options Market, the position limits are 5,000, 10,000 or 20,000 contracts depending upon the market capitalisation of the company to whose shares the options relate.

Using currency options

The nature of currency options parallels that of stock options; however, the analysis of their potential for hedging involves some different considerations.

Forwards and futures are techniques for guaranteeing a specific exchange rate for a future date or for obtaining compensation for deviations of actual rates from target rates. A currency manager using a forward or futures position avoids losing from adverse movements on currencies but also fails to gain from advantageous movements. An option is a suitable tool for the currency manager who has a view as to future exchange rate movements but is not absolutely certain that the direction of change will be as he anticipates and wishes to reduce the losses arising in the event of his forecast being incorrect.

Suppose that a UK corporate treasurer anticipates US dollar receivables. If he forecasts an appreciation of the dollar against sterling, he may wish to back his forecast. Forwards and futures hedging would deny the treasurer the anticipated gains from an appreciating dollar. The purchase of sterling call options would allow the treasurer to benefit from an appreciating dollar (depreciating sterling) whilst providing protection against the opposite movement. Options provide maximum buying prices or minimum selling prices without compelling users to trade at those prices if more favourable ones are available.

Options may be more appropriate than forwards or futures when it is possible that competitors are not hedging. If an importer locks in a particular exchange rate whilst his competitors do not, either because they do not hedge at all or because they hedge with options, he will suffer a competitive disadvantage in the event of the exchange rate moving to his competitors' advantage. By hedging with options he too can gain from a favourable currency movement and hence avoid the competitive disadvantage.

Suppose, for example, that a UK importer invoiced in US dollars buys a put option for the sale of sterling for US dollars at an exercise price of £1=$1·70. An increase in the value of the US dollar, say to £1=$1·50, would provide the option holder with a gain of $0·20 per £1 at the expense of the option writer. The option holder would be in the position of selling sterling at the price of $1·70 instead of $1·50. On the other hand, should the foreign exchange value of the US dollar fall below $1·70, the option holder would not exercise the option to buy at $1·70 but would buy at the lower price. A user of futures or forwards could not benefit from such a fall in the US dollar and could lose out to unhedged competitors.

Options are ideal for hedging tenders since if the tender is unsuccessful the option need not be exercised. A UK exporter tendering for a contract in US dollars faces exchange risk from the date of making the tender. A weakening of the US dollar relative to sterling would undermine the profitability of the trade. Although the purchase of options would be primarily for the purpose of hedging exchange rate risk, it is unlikely that, in the event of the tender being unsuccessful, the exporter would simply allow an option to expire if the exercise or sale of the option would produce a profit. If sterling had strengthened by the date on which the tender was rejected, a call option to buy sterling could be exercised and the sterling thus purchased in turn sold to give a profit. In the case of traded options, the intrinsic value of the options would give them a high sale value.

A distinction to be drawn is between 'European-type' and 'American-type' options. The former can be exercised on one date only, the expiry date. The latter may be exercised on any business day up to the expiry date. American-type options provide greater flexibility and the choice of date increases the likelihood of a profit being made. Correspondingly, it is to be expected that an American-type option would involve a higher premium than that required in the case of a European-type option.

The profit/loss profile arising from the purchase of a call option is illustrated by Figure 5.5. It is assumed that the chosen exercise price is £1=$1·40 whilst the exchange rate at the time of buying the option is £1=$1·39. The premium payable is $0·02 (2 cents) per £1.

If the price of sterling is less than $1·40 per £1 on the date that the option would be exercised, or when it expires, the option holder would choose not to exercise the option but instead would buy sterling at the cheaper price. In such an event the option buyer would make a net loss equal to the value of the premium paid, namely 2 cents. This is the maximum loss that

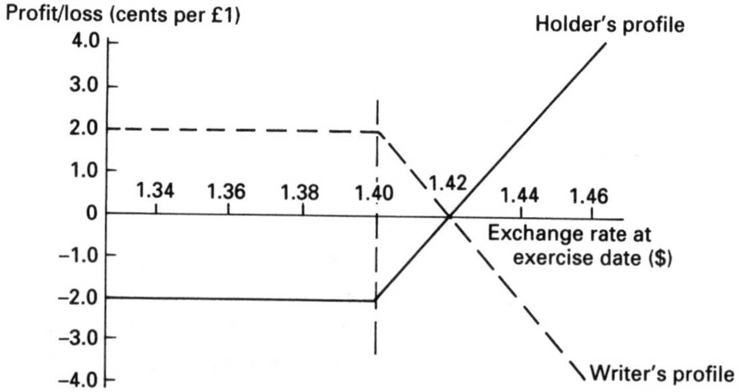

Figure 5.5 Holder's and writer's profiles on a call option

the option holder can incur. On the other hand, should the price of sterling be greater than $1·40 when the option is to be exercised, there would be a profit from exercising the option. It pays the option holder to exercise the right to buy at $1·40 if the price of sterling is greater. If the exchange rate is £1 = $1·42 there would be a gain of 2 cents per £1 from the exercise of the option. This would exactly offset the 2 cent premium paid, so $1·42 is the break-even price. At prices below $1·42 a net loss is incurred, whilst at higher rates there is a net profit. The possible extent of gain is unlimited since the price of sterling could conceivably be at any level. The option holder is thus in a position in which the extent of possible loss is limited to the premium paid whilst the potential profit is unlimited.

The writer of the option faces the opposite situation. His maximum profit is the premium, this profit being fully realised in the event of the option not being exercised. The writer's scope for loss is unlimited. A very high price for sterling would put the writer in the position of paying a high price for sterling which he is obliged to sell at a mere $1·40 per £1. The writer's profit/loss profile is a mirror image of the holder's profile.

The buyer of the option guarantees a maximum price of sterling of $1·40 per £1 at the cost of a premium of $0·02 per £1. Taking account of the premium, the exchange rate is effectively limited to £1 = $1·42.

Hedging and trading are not always distinct activities. The exporter mentioned above is more likely to hedge against an increase in the dollar price of sterling if he expects sterling to appreciate than if he expects a fall in its value. When the decisions as to whether to hedge, and how to hedge, are influenced by the view taken as to future exchange rate movements, the hedging is effectively mixed with trading. A pure hedge would be unaffected by expectations.

A hedger buying an option is faced with a decision as to what exercise price to choose. This choice determines the profit/loss profile and is made in the light of the buyer's tolerance of risk and his view as to future exchange rate movements. This view encompasses not only the direction of change but also its extent, speed and probability of occurrence. Figure 5.6 shows hypothetical call option profit/loss profiles at three exercise prices. It is assumed that the exchange rate is currently £1 = $1·39.

Buying a call option to buy sterling at £1 = $1·45 involves the greatest risk in terms of potential adverse exchange rate movements since a hedger would be unprotected against a rise in the dollar price of sterling between $1·39 and $1·45 per £1. However, at 0·5 cents per £1 the premium cost is the lowest. This approach would be favoured by a hedger willing to bear a high degree of risk and/or feeling that it is unlikely that sterling would

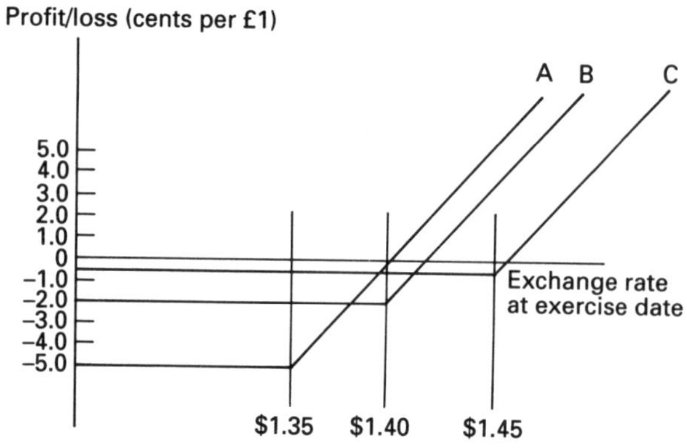

Figure 5.6 Selecting an exercise price

strengthen. If the hedger anticipates that it is likely that sterling will weaken or rise by only a very modest amount he would be reluctant to pay a high premium (such as 2 cents for a $1·40 call) to hedge against the possibility of sterling appreciation. A hedger with such a view as to future exchange rate movements might prefer merely to insure against an extreme appreciation of sterling (beyond $1·45) and correspondingly economise on the premium paid. A hedger with a firmly held view that there will be an appreciation of sterling might be more likely to choose the $1·35 call option. This option provides the greatest absolute benefit in the event of an increase in the dollar price of sterling (the $1·35 call allows a profit to be made between $1·39 and $1·40; also the 4 cents intrinsic value at $1·39 will cost less than 4 cents in premium and hence the $1·35 call would be attractive if the buyer believes that sterling will not fall below $1·39).

Although the exposition thus far has concentrated on the buying of call options, similar analyses apply to the purchase of put options. A British importer needing to make a future payment in US dollars may be anxious about the possibility that sterling will depreciate against the dollar and hence render the necessary dollars more expensive. He could buy sterling put options and thereby obtain the right to sell pounds at a particular dollar exercise price. If the dollar price of sterling fell below this exercise price the importer could exercise the option to exchange sterling for dollars at that exercise price. The importer would thus have successfully hedged against a sterling depreciation by setting a lower limit to the dollar value of sterling (and hence an upper limit to the sterling value of the dollar). This is illustrated by Example 5.1.

Table 5.8

March	June	September
1.8240	1.8165	1.8100

Table 5.9

March	June	September
0.6168	0.6228	0.6293

Example 5.1

UK importer invoiced in US$ needs to obtain $1,500,000.
Buys £ puts at an exercise price of £1 = $1·50 and thereby acquires the right to sell £1,000,000 for $1,500,000.
Spot exchange rate is £1 = $1·50 and premium is 2·5 cents/£ = $25,000.
Outcome 1: £ strengthens to £1 = $1·65. $1,500,000 is bought for £909,091. The option is not exercised.
Outcome 2: £ weakens to £1 = $1·35. £1,000,000 would buy only $1,350,000. The option to sell £1,000,000 for $1,500,000 is exercised.

Exercise 5.3

Question
It is 6 January and the following information is available:

£1 = US$1·8295–1·8305
£1 = DM2·9750–2·9800
US$1 = DM1·6265–1·6275

LIFFE sterling currency futures are as shown in Table 5.8.
IMM Deutschmark futures are as shown in Table 5.9.
Philadelphia Stock Exchange DM/US$ options are as shown in Table 5.10.
Philadelphia Stock Exchange £/US$ options are as shown in Table 5.11.

A British paper mill imports wood which is priced in US dollars and exports paper priced in Deutschmarks. Its import payments for the coming year are expected to be $10 million whilst its export receipts are anticipated to be DM15 million. These cash flows are expected to be evenly spread over the year. Four-fifths of the cash flows are expected with confidence, the other 20% are less certain.

(a) Suggest a strategy for hedging the company's currency risks in the event of poor liquidity beyond the next two delivery/expiry dates and assuming that

Table 5.10

	Calls		Puts	
Strike price	January	February	January	February
0.60	2.310	3.721	0.820	2.224
0.61	1.509	3.003	1.029	2.520
0.62	1.011	2.504	1.525	3.031
0.63	0.810	2.218	2.320	3.750
0.64	0.631	1.979	3.161	4.495

Table 5.11

	Calls		Puts	
Strike price	January	February	January	February
1.70	17.35	17.35	0.30	0.30
1.75	12.35	12.35	0.30	0.70
1.80	3.40	7.10	1.05	1.35
1.85	1.75	2.50	2.20	3.90

the company wishes to minimise risk and take no view on currency movements.

(b) How might this strategy be changed if the company becomes willing to bear some risk in order to reduce hedging costs and adopts the view that the US dollar is more likely to fall than to rise against the Deutschmark?

Answer

(a) The DM12 million confidently anticipated receipts can be hedged with DM/$ futures. The appropriate number of contracts would be 96. Because of the even spread over time of the cash flows the company treasurer might prefer to use equal numbers of futures for the March, June, September and December maturity dates. However, since liquidity is poor beyond the nearest two maturity dates, it would be more appropriate to sell 24 March contracts and 72 June contracts. Later exposures are thus being covered by means of June contracts and the hedger is vulnerable to distant changes in the exchange rate that are not paralleled by movements in the June futures price. (A sophisticated hedger might deal with this problem by buying March–June DM/$ futures straddles, buying 72 March contracts and selling 72 June contracts: 24 for the September maturity and 48 for the December maturity. With the straddles the net outcome would be to buy 48 March contracts and sell 144 June contracts.)

Selling 24 March contracts locks in the sale of DM3 million for $1,850,400. The 72 June contracts lock in the sale of DM9 million for $5,605,200. Thus $7,455,600 are covered out of the $8 million confidently expected to be required. There is thus a shortfall of $544,400 which can be covered with £/$ futures. To cover this shortfall 3 March £/$ currency futures contracts might be sold, along with 9 June £/$ currency futures contracts.

The 20% of the exposure that is uncertain would be covered by means of options. The absence of liquidity beyond the next two expiry dates suggests the need constantly to roll forward the option holding (N.B. delta hedging would not be appropriate since that is suitable only for confidently expected cash flows).

The DM3 million could be covered by buying 48 February DM/$ 0·61 puts. This covers about $1,843,318 of the $2 million exposure. The remaining exposure of $156,682 could be covered with £/$ options. Seven February £/US$ 1·80 puts might be bought (on the basis of each contract relating to £12,500).

(b) If the company treasurer took the view that the US dollar was more likely to fall than rise against the DM and he is more willing to accept some risk, the extent of cover might be reduced. The numbers of futures contracts might be smaller than suggested above, or the uncertain part of the exposure might be left unhedged.

Out-of-the-money puts, e.g. 0·60, could be used instead of at-the-money options. Less would be lost (by way of premiums) in the event of a rise in the DM against the dollar.

Hedging and trading: the profiles

It is useful to visualise a hedger as seeking to make gains from options in order to offset cash market losses. When the option is looked upon in isolation, the profit/loss profile is the opposite to that which emerges if the option and the cash position being hedged are combined.

Consider the case of a call option. Since the hedger faces a cash market loss in the event of a price rise, the options gain merely serves to offset this loss. A fall in price brings a cash market gain which is not offset by an options loss (other than the premium paid).

From Figure 5.7 it can be seen that the call option is a more suitable hedging tool than futures and forwards for a UK exporter to the United States who anticipates a fall in sterling against the US dollar, who wants to profit from the anticipated appreciation of the US dollar receivables, but who seeks downside protection in case his expectations prove to be wrong.

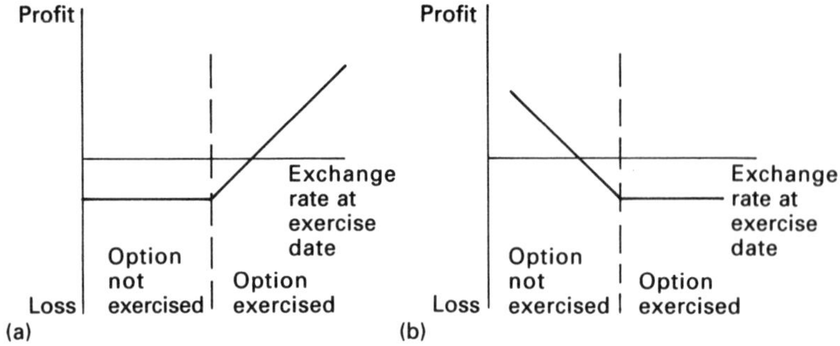

Figure 5.7 (a) A call option in isolation; (b) a call option in combination with a hedged cash position

Vertical spreads

Vertical spreads involve the simultaneous buying and selling of options on the same underlying instrument for the same expiry month but with different exercise prices. Figure 5.8 illustrates a bull call spread.

Spot exchange rate £1=$1·22.
A $1·25 call is bought at a premium of 2 cents/£.
A $1·30 call is sold at a premium of 0·5 cents/£.

The vertical distance between the at-expiry and prior-to-expiry profiles represents the net time value. The net time value is the time value of the purchased option minus the time value of the written option. The net time value is positive when the purchased (i.e. long) option is at the money, but

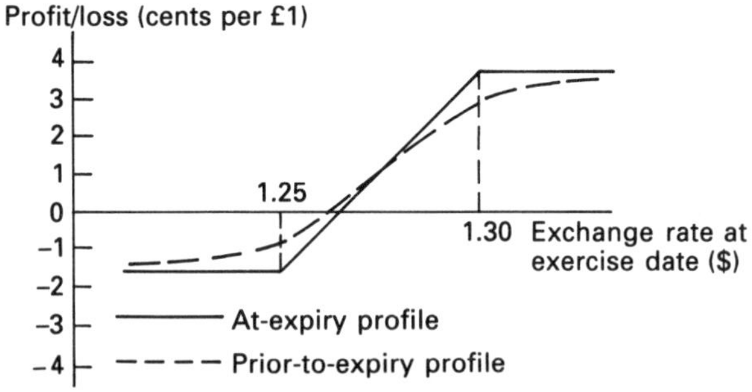

Figure 5.8 Bull call spread

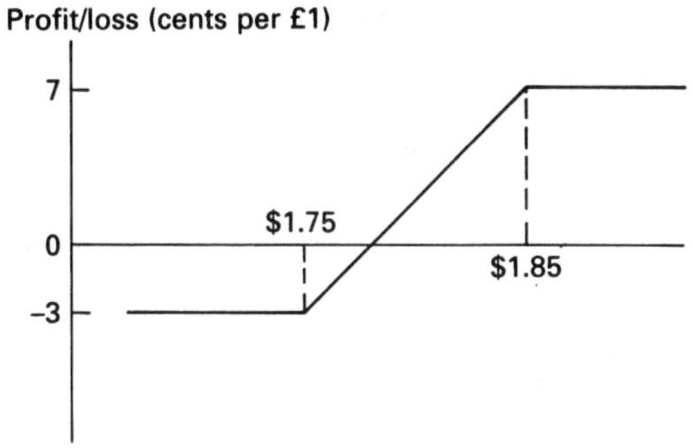

Figure 5.9 Bull spread

negative when the written (i.e. short) option is at the money (since the premium of an option is at its maximum when the option is at the money).

Such a spread might appeal to a hedger who seeks insurance against a rise in the spot price of sterling above $1·25 whilst feeling that a strengthening of sterling beyond £1=$1·30 is unlikely. This latter view leads to the writing of the $1·30 call so that beyond $1·30 (intrinsic value) gains from the $1·25 call would be offset by losses on the $1·30 call, but with the benefit that the premium paid is reduced by 0·5 cents per £1.

Example 5.2

Figure 5.9 illustrates a bull spread.
A $1·75 call is bought for 4 cents/£.
A $1·85 call is sold for 1 cent/£.
The net premium = 3 cents/£.
Below $1·75 neither option is exercised: the loss is the net premium of 3 cents/£.
Maximum profit occurs above $1·85:

Profit from exercising $1·75 option
Minus loss from exercise of $1·85 option
Minus initial net premium
Equals 7 cents/£

(Above $1·85 the additional profits from the long $1·75 call are offset by losses from the short $1·85 call.)

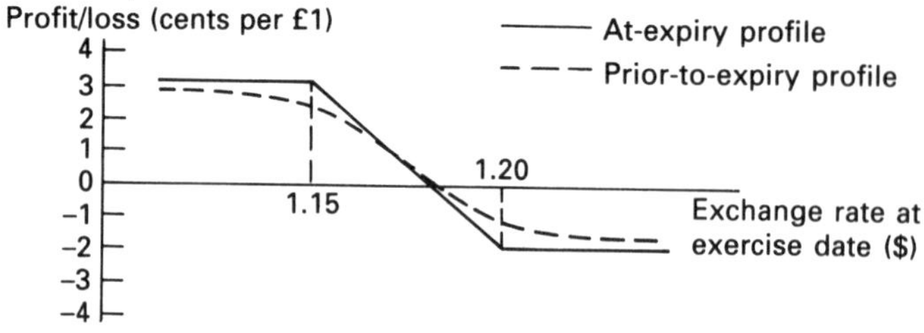

Figure 5.10 Bear put spread

Figure 5.10 illustrates a bear put spread.

Spot exchange rate £1=$1·22.
A $1·20 put is bought at a premium of 2·5 cents/£.
A $1·15 put is sold at a premium of 0·6 cents/£.

Considering the intrinsic value (at-expiry) profile, at spot prices above $1·20 neither option would be exercised and the transactor makes a net loss equal to the balance of the premiums, 2·5−0·6=1·9 cents. As the value of sterling falls below $1·20, there is a potential gain from selling sterling at the exercise price of $1·20 and buying it more cheaply. This potential gain increases until it reaches 5 cents per £1 when the exchange rate is £1=$1·15. The net gain at $1·15, taking account of the net premium, is 5·0−1·9=3·1 cents. If the price of sterling falls below $1·15, the $1·15 put will be exercised, obliging the transactor to buy at $1·15 whilst selling at a lower price. Thus as the price of sterling falls below $1·15, the additional gains from exercising the $1·20 put are cancelled by the losses on the $1·15 put, leaving the net profit at a constant 3·1 cents per £1.

A hedger wanting to insure against the possibility that sterling will depreciate beyond £1=$1·20 but holding the view that the depreciation could not go beyond £1=$1·15 would buy such a put spread. He reduces the net premium payable from 2·5 to 1·9 cents per £1 at the cost of forgoing protection from depreciation beyond $1·15.

Example 5.3

Figure 5.11 illustrates a bear spread.
A $1·75 put is bought for 5 cents/£.
A $1·65 put is sold for 1 cent/£.

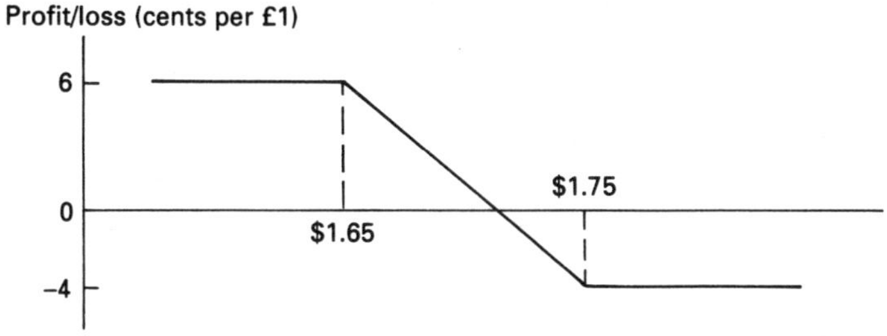

Figure 5.11 Bear spread

The net premium is 4 cents/£.
Above \$1·75 neither option is exercised: the loss is the net premium of 4 cents/£.
Below \$1·65 both options are exercised:

Profit from \$1·75 option
Minus loss from \$1·65 option
Minus net premium paid
Equals net profit of 6 cents/£

(Below \$1·65 the additional profits from the long \$1·75 put are offset by losses from the short \$1·65 put.)

In addition to the bull call spreads and bear put spreads there are bull put spreads and bear call spreads. Writing a put option with a high exercise price (and high premium) and buying a put option with a low exercise price (and consequent low premium) creates a bull put spread. A bear call spread involves selling a call option with a low exercise price (and high premium) and buying a call option with a high exercise price (and low premium). In the event of the price of sterling falling below the lower exercise price, neither option would be exercised and the difference between the premiums would accrue as profit.

Traded options versus OTC options

An 'over-the-counter' (OTC) option is typically provided by a bank and is tailor-made to meet the requirements of the customer. The customer can stipulate the amount of currency (or other financial instrument), the strike (exercise) price, the expiry date and whether the option is of the American or European type. American-type options can be exercised on any business day up to the expiry date, whereas European-type options can be exercised on the expiry date only.

Traded options, which are options bought and sold on an exchange, are standardised. There is limited choice as to amount of the underlying instrument, strike price and expiry date. The customer must also accept an American-type option. For example, the sterling currency option traded on LIFFE must be traded in blocks of £25,000, the exercise prices available are at 5 cent intervals (e.g. $1·30, $1·35, $1·40 per £1) and there are just five expiry dates available at one time. Standardisation is necessary to ensure adequate liquidity in traded options markets.

Hedging without exercising options

A hedger may choose to sell the options that he holds rather than exercise them. This is particularly likely in the case of traded options. The procedure is illustrated by the following hypothetical example.

Suppose that the spot exchange rate is £1 = $1·25 and a UK exporter anticipates receipt of dollars in two months. He buys sterling call options with an exercise price of $1·25 at the cost of a premium of 2 cents per £1. On the date of receiving the dollars, he finds that sterling has strengthened to £1 = $1·30. He could exercise the options and pay $1·25 per £1. Taking into account the 2 cents per £1 option premium, he would be paying a total price of $1·27 per £1 for sterling. Alternatively, he could sell the options. The increase in the price of sterling from $1·25 to $1·30 would raise the market value of $1·25 call options. The premiums might rise, for example, from 2 cents to 5·5 cents per £1. The hedger could sell his options at a profit of 3·5 cents per £1 and then buy sterling at the new spot price of $1·30. Taking account of the profit on the options, the price effectively paid for sterling is $1·30 – $0·035 = $1·265 per £1.

For traded options it is to be expected that hedgers would sell rather than exercise them. This is because time value is very unlikely to be negative. Table 5.12 shows a hypothetical set of values that illustrates this point. It is assumed that the chosen strike price is $1·25 per £1 and that a premium of 2 cents per £1 has previously been paid.

So long as an option is sold prior to the expiry date, some time value is likely to remain. In Table 5.12 the time value of 2 cents per £1 which made up the 2 cents premium for the $1·25 at-the-money call option has eroded as the time left to expiry has been reduced. The time value for a $1·25 at-the-money call option is now 1 cent per £1. The time value further declines as the option moves into the money, but intrinsic value increases cent for

Table 5.12

Spot price ($)	Premium ($) Intrinsic value	Time value	Effective price if option sold ($)	Effective price if option exercised ($)
1.250	0.000	0.010	1.260	1.270
1.260	0.010	0.009	1.261	1.270
1.270	0.020	0.008	1.262	1.270
1.280	0.030	0.007	1.263	1.270
1.300	0.050	0.005	1.265	1.270
1.350	0.100	0.002	1.268	1.270
1.400	0.150	0.001	1.269	1.270

cent. If the option is sold for the new premium and sterling is bought at the existing spot price, the effective price paid for sterling is given by the following:

$$\text{Spot price} + \text{Original premium} - \text{New premium} = \text{Effective price}$$

The original premium is $0·02 and the new premium is equal to the sum of the intrinsic and time values. For example,

$$\$1{\cdot}28 + \$0{\cdot}02 - \$0{\cdot}037 = \$1{\cdot}263$$

It can be seen from Table 5.12 that so long as some time value remains there is an advantage in selling the option and buying sterling at the spot rate rather than exercising the option. The difference between the two alternative effective prices of sterling is equal to the time value. Exercising an option realises only the intrinsic value; selling the option realises both the intrinsic and the time values.

Delta hedging an OTC option

The delta of an option is the ratio of the change in the price of that option to the change in the price of the underlying instrument. Knowledge of option deltas allows hedgers to cover exposures in a manner that can precisely cover day-to-day variations in the price of the underlying instrument.

A fixed hedge aims to match the value of the exposure with the amount covered by the option: for example, covering a holding of 5,000 UK shares with five options. Fixed hedges are most appropriate to cases in which the risk being hedged occurs on the expiry date of the option: for example, when an anticipated sale of shares is due to occur on the expiry date of the options. Fixed hedges are less suitable for covering prior-to-expiry risk. Profits from changes in intrinsic value can be offset by losses from variations in time value so that prior-to-expiry, and hence day-to-day, hedging requires the number of options used to be factored up. This is achieved by delta hedging.

Delta hedging (also known as ratio hedging) involves the number of option contracts being factored up by the reciprocal of the option delta. So, for example, if 5,000 shares are to be hedged with options whose delta is 0·5, the appropriate number of option contracts would be ten. Likewise an option delta of 0·625 would entail the use of 5 × (1/0·625) = 8 contracts.

The use of delta hedging can be illustrated by the case of a bank that wishes to cover an over-the-counter option that it has written for a client. In addition to traded options, which are standardised (as to size, expiry date and available exercise prices), there are over-the-counter options written by banks. An over-the-counter option is tailor-made to a customer's specific requirements in terms of size, expiry date and exercise price. The writing of over-the-counter options subjects banks to risks that can be offset by delta hedging with traded options.

Since the delta of an option is the ratio of the change in its premium to the change in the price of the underlying financial instrument, it follows that if, for example, the dollar price of sterling rose by 1 cent and as a result the premium on a sterling call option increased by 0·4 cents, the delta of the option would be 0·4. Correspondingly, the number of option contracts required for full cover would be 2·5 times that required for a hedge that anticipates that delivery will take place (i.e. a fixed hedge).

The fair price of an option is the premium that would be expected in the light of the magnitudes of the variables that determine its value: for example, the spot price, the exercise price, the time to expiry and the expected volatility of the price of the underlying instrument. Fair prices are calculated by means of mathematical models, typically based on either the Black–Scholes (see Appendix II) or the Cox–Rubinstein equations.

A bank writing over-the-counter options might wish to avoid losses arising from increases in premiums. If option premiums rise subsequent to a bank writing an option for an agreed premium, that bank could be in what is effectively a loss-making position. If the fair price of the option written exceeds the premium agreed, the balance of probabilities is that the option will be exercised at a net loss to the bank. This loss-making position might alternatively be explained in terms of the bank needing to pay more, for an option that exactly offsets the one that it has written, than it received for the option that it has written.

Suppose, for example, that a bank has written an over-the-counter sterling call option for the purchase of £1 million. The spot exchange rate and exercise price are both \$1·23, so the option is at the money. The bank charges a premium of 3 cents per £1 but calculates that the fair price would have been 2·9 cents per £1. The bank is in the position of having made a net gain of 0·1 cents per £1: that is, \$1,000. The bank wishes to protect this profit from the possibility of the fair price rising. It does this by buying traded options. It looks for traded options with characteristics as close as possible to those of the over-the-counter option: that is, options similar in respect of expiry date and exercise price. If the fair price of the written option were to rise, so too would the premiums on traded options and hence there would be a profit on the traded options to compensate for the loss on the over-the-counter option. However, a perfect offset could occur only in the event of the traded options being identical in the relevant attributes to the over-the-counter option.

The differences between the over-the-counter option written by the bank and the traded options used to hedge risks arising from the over-the-counter option would tend to cause the deltas to differ. For example, the delta of the over-the-counter option (as calculated from mathematical models using the same variables as the models used to estimate fair prices) might be 0·54 whereas the delta of the relevant traded options is 0·60. The fact that the traded options premiums show greater sensitivity to exchange rate movements than the over-the-counter option fair price means that correspondingly fewer traded options are required for the hedge.

If the hedger were to choose options traded on LIFFE he would find that they are traded in units of £25,000, each unit being known as a contract. Hedging a £1 million over-the-counter option might appear to require forty traded option contracts. However, the higher delta of the traded options means that fewer than forty are required. The requisite number is found with the use of the ratio of the deltas.

$$\frac{\text{Size of over-the-counter option}}{\text{Size of each option contract}} \times \frac{\text{Delta of over-the-counter option}}{\text{Delta of traded options}} = \text{Required number of contracts}$$

In the current example the numbers are

$$\frac{£1{,}000{,}000}{£25{,}000} \times \frac{0{\cdot}54}{0{\cdot}60} = 36$$

The fact that the responsiveness of the fair price of the over-the-counter option to exchange rate movements is only 90 per cent of the responsiveness of the traded options means that the optimal number of traded options contracts is thirty-six. Use of a greater number of contracts would probably involve gains or losses on the traded options being greater than those on the over-the-counter option, so that hedging could be expected to be imperfect.

A delta hedge needs to be continuously monitored. Deltas change in response to variations in exchange rates, expectations of volatility and time remaining to expiry. The ratio of the deltas could change as a result, so that the number of contracts may need to be altered. Hence there is a need for monitoring and, when necessary, rebalancing the hedge.

Transacting in options under a margin system

The procedures whereby money passes hands between people who deal in traded options on LIFFE is based on the margin system. It is useful to begin with an introduction to the margin arrangements.

Any transactor in LIFFE options, whether buyer or seller, is required to put up an initial margin. This is a sum of money deposited with the International Commodities Clearing House (ICCH) and is ultimately returnable to the transactor. The initial margin is equal to the initial margin on the corresponding LIFFE futures contract multiplied by the delta of the option. So if the initial margin on a LIFFE sterling currency futures contract were $1,000 and the delta of a particular option were 0·64, then the required initial margin would be $640. The delta is recalculated daily and hence the initial margin is subject to daily variation.

As option premiums vary from day to day, gains and losses are incurred as a result. The daily calculation of profits and losses is known as marking to market. After each business day, those incurring losses must realise them by paying variation margin; correspondingly, profit-making option positions are rewarded in the form of variation margin. The purpose of initial margin is the provision of a source of funds from which variation margin can be drawn in the event of an option holder or writer being unable to meet the variation margin requirements. Such a transactor could be compelled to terminate his options position so as to avoid losses that cannot be met. It is through the medium of variation margin that hedgers normally obtain their compensation for exchange rate movements. Option holders typically do not expect options to result directly in the exchange of currencies. The buying and selling of currencies will usually take place on the foreign exchange spot market. Although a holder of an option may choose to exercise the option, such a procedure is unlikely since the time value component of the option premium would thereby be lost, whereas the time value would be realised if the option were instead closed out by means of a sale. In the event of an option being exercised, the premium is payable when the option is exercised, and is the premium at the time of exercising rather than the premium on the date of buying the option (the variation margin received compensates for the difference between the two premiums).

Consider a hypothetical example. Someone buys a sterling call option with an exercise price of $1·25 per £1 at a premium of 2 cents per £1 when the spot price of sterling is $1·25 per £1. On the date of selling the option, the spot price of sterling is $1·30 and the option premium is 6 cents. The seller of the option realises a net gain of 4 cents per £1. He will have received this by means of variation margin payments over time as the option premium rose. He will not actually have paid the 2 cents per £1 premium upon buying the option nor have received the 6 cents per £1 upon selling, but the 4 cents per £1 received in variation margin is equivalent to buying the option at 2 cents and selling at 6 cents per £1. The effective price of sterling is $1·26 ($1·30 spot price minus 4 cents compensation). This is better than the $1·27 guaranteed by the purchase of the option ($1·25 exercise price plus 2 cents premium) since the transactor has been able to sell remaining time value at 1 cent per £1 (time value = premium minus intrinsic value, 1 cent = 6 cents minus 5 cents, the intrinsic value of 5 cents being the excess of the spot price over the exercise price).

The person to whom the option is sold obtains an option with an exercise price of $1·25 when the spot price of sterling is $1·30. Although the option premium stands at 6 cents per £1, this new buyer of the option does not make any payment at the time of buying the option. Suppose that the new buyer holds the option until its expiry date, at which time the spot price of sterling stands at $1·35. At the expiry date there is no time value, but the intrinsic value of the option is $1·35 − $1·25 = 10 cents. While the new buyer was holding the option the premium rose from 6 cents to 10 cents per £1 and correspondingly he will have received 4 cents per £1 in variation margin. He closes out the option and buys sterling at the spot price of $1·35 having received 4 cents compensation, so that his effective exchange rate is £1 = $1·31. The final outcome is equivalent to having paid 6 cents per £1 premium for a call option with an exercise price of $1·25. His effective price for sterling is equal to his guaranteed maximum price of $1·31.

If the initial seller of the option did not close out his position until expiry, then during this process he will have paid a total of 8 cents per £1 in variation margin. This is equivalent to honouring a $1·25 call option when the spot price of sterling is $1·35 after receiving 2 cents per £1 by way of a premium payment.

Avoiding time value loss

The tendency for time value decay to be slow at first but to accelerate as the expiry date is approached has implications for hedging. A hedger who buys an option and subsequently sells it prior to its expiry date faces a decline in time value arising from the passage of time. This loss of time value is minimised if options with distant expiry dates are used, since time value decays slowly when the expiry date is distant. The hedger would be avoiding the rapid loss of time value that is experienced close to the expiry date.

A consequence of this strategy is that the premium is likely to contain considerable time value and this causes substantial exposure to the risk of time value loss arising from movements in the price of the underlying instrument or in expected volatility. Time value peaks when an option is at the money and declines as it becomes in the money, with the decline continuing as it moves deeper in the money. A hedger requiring a gain from an option becoming in the money (or deeper in the money) would be faced with a loss of time value that partially offsets the gain from rising intrinsic value. Also the high time value increases the option holder's time value loss in the event of the option becoming out of the money (or moving deeper out of the money) or in the event of a decline in market expectations of volatility. One way to reduce the amount of time value purchased, and hence to reduce exposure to factors that influence time value, is to buy in-the-money or out-of-the-money options rather than at-the-money options.

Two types of zero cost option

Zero cost options provide hedgers with protection against adverse movements in prices, allow profits from favourable movements, but involve no expenditure on premiums. However, such zero cost options do have their disadvantages when compared with ordinary options, as will be demonstrated in the cases of two categories of zero cost option.

The first category is often referred to as the cylinder option. This involves buying and writing options on the same quantity at different exercise prices. The second category involves buying and writing options on different quantities but at the same exercise price.

To illustrate these strategies the example of a UK exporter with US dollar receivables will be considered. The principles involved are, of course, readily extendable to hedging needs arising from other instruments and involving other types of option: stock, gilt, stock index, etc.

CYLINDER OPTIONS

The hedger would buy a sterling call option so as to guarantee a maximum purchase price of sterling. Simultaneously, a put option would be written committing the hedger to a minimum buying price. The two exercise prices would fall either side of the spot (and forward) price of sterling and be approximately equidistant from it. In other words, the two options would be out of the money to about the same extent. This is necessary for the put premium received to offset the call premium paid. The (at-expiry) profit/loss profile of such a cylinder is illustrated by Figure 5.12.

When the profit/loss profile of Figure 5.12 is combined with the short position in sterling (long position in US dollars) which is being hedged, the result is the profile illustrated by Figure 5.13. As can be seen from the lower section of Figure 5.13, the absence of a net premium is obtained at the cost of incomplete protection from a rise in the price of sterling and a restricted opportunity to benefit from a fall in the price. The hedger is not protected from a rise in the price of sterling between the spot price and the maximum buying price. At the same time there is no scope for gaining from a fall in the price of sterling below the minimum buying price.

Figure 5.13 provides the at-expiry profit/loss profiles. A hedger who sells rather than exercises options, as would typically be the case when traded options are used, would be more concerned with the prior-to-

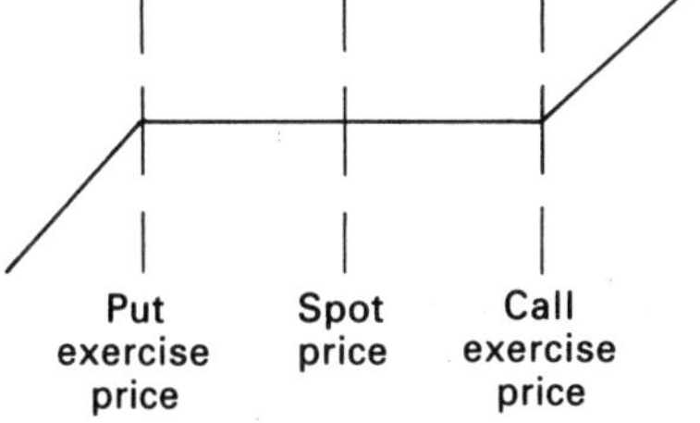

Figure 5.12 Profit/loss profile of a cylinder option at expiry

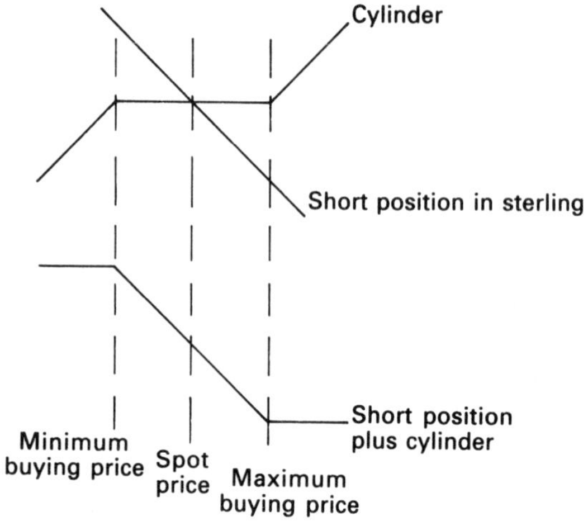

Figure 5.13 Profile of a cylinder option in combination with a short position in sterling at expiry

expiry profiles. These are illustrated in Figure 5.14. The broken line curves in Figure 5.14 depict the prior-to-expiry profit/loss profiles. These are the profiles that appertain when options are sold rather than exercised. They incorporate the time value that is received when an option is sold, but not when it is exercised.

The prior-to-expiry profit/loss profiles are likely to be the relevant ones for users of traded options. They moderate the impact of price movements. More protection is offered against a rise in the price of sterling, whilst less profit is obtained from a fall in the price (it is useful to bear in mind that the profits and losses would have been measured along the vertical axis, had it been drawn).

Example 5.4

Figure 5.15 shows an example of a cylinder option.

The hedger remains vulnerable to movements within the \$1·70 to \$1·80 range.

Any deviation of the exchange rate from the \$1·70 to \$1·80 range is offset by profits/losses on options.

The option premiums tend to offset each other – possibly involving zero net cost.

The protection against a decline beyond \$1·70 is obtained at the cost of losing the benefit of a price rise beyond \$1·80.

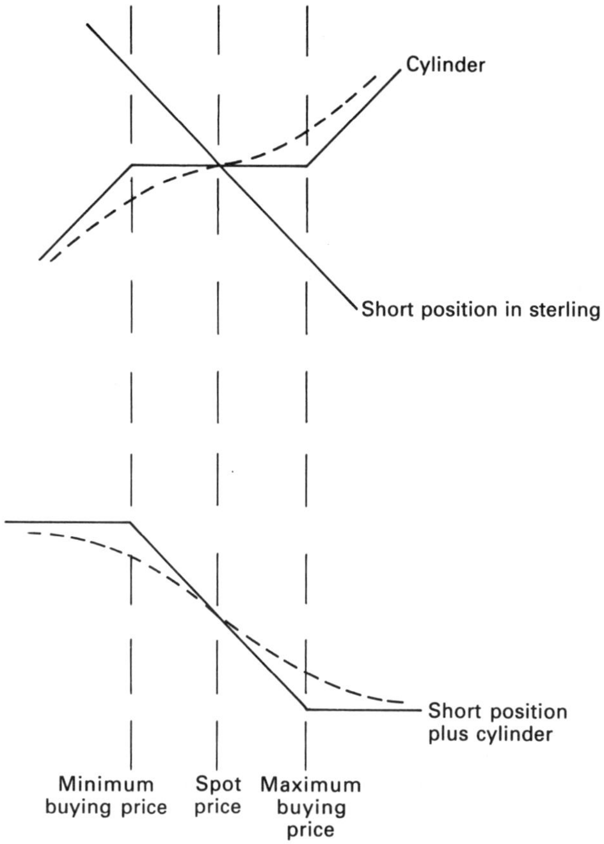

Figure 5.14 Profile of a cylinder option in combination with a short position in sterling prior to expiry

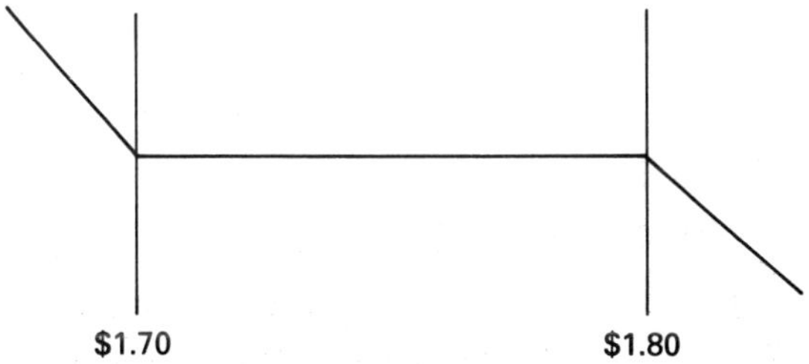

Figure 5.15

Table 5.13

Strike price	Calls	Puts
195	6.80 (0.84)	1.65 (−0.16)
200	2.79 (0.50)	2.69 (−0.50)
205	1.75 (0.15)	6.60 (−0.85)

Exercise 5.4

Question

The June S & P 500 stock index futures price stands at 200.
June S & P 500 stock index futures options prices (deltas in brackets) are as shown in Table 5.13.
Design a strategy for a hedger who seeks some protection from a fall in the market whilst preserving the ability to enjoy some gain from a rise.

Answer

The hedger might, for example, buy June 195 puts and sell an equal number of June 205 calls. The cylinders thereby created meet the stipulated requirements.

SINGLE EXERCISE PRICE ZERO COST OPTIONS

An example of this type of zero cost option involves the purchase of out-of-the-money call options and the writing of a smaller number of in-the-money put options. (Use of at-the-money calls and puts of equal number would be merely a synthetic long forward. Buying in-the-money calls financed by writing a larger number of out-of-the-money puts would entail the risk of unlimited loss from rises in the price of sterling above the strike price if the puts match the underlying instrument, and unlimited loss from falls in the price of sterling if the calls match the underlying instrument: in other words, synthetic short option positions would be created.) This combination would result in a kinked profit/loss profile of the form illustrated by Figure 5.16.

This is equivalent to a combination of synthetic long forwards and call options. In other words, the profit/loss profile of Figure 5.16 can be broken down into the two components of Figure 5.17. (Since part of the exposure is covered by the synthetic and part by the option component, it follows that the total coverage in a fixed hedge corresponds to the aggregate size of the calls. The size of the exposure is matched by the call options.)

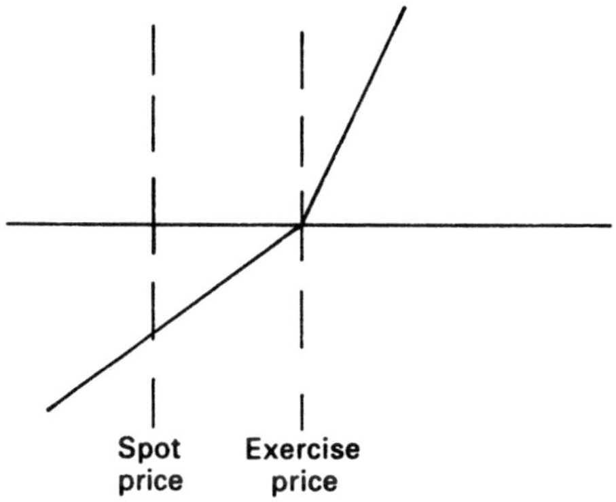

Figure 5.16 Profit/loss profile of a single exercise price zero cost option

When single exercise price zero cost options are broken down in the way illustrated by Figure 5.17, the relative merits and demerits of this strategy become apparent. Inevitably, zero cost options have some disadvantages in comparison with simple options. Diagram (a) in Figure 5.17 shows that part of the exposure is covered by a synthetic forward that provides a relatively unfavourable guaranteed price. Meanwhile the remainder of the exposure is only partially covered: there is no cover for a movement of the price of sterling between the spot price and the exercise price. So although this strategy provides significant advantages – a high degree of protection from upward price movements, some scope for benefiting from a price fall (within the call option component of Figure 5.17) and no net premium to be paid – it also has its drawbacks. Neither type of zero cost option succeeds in providing something for nothing.

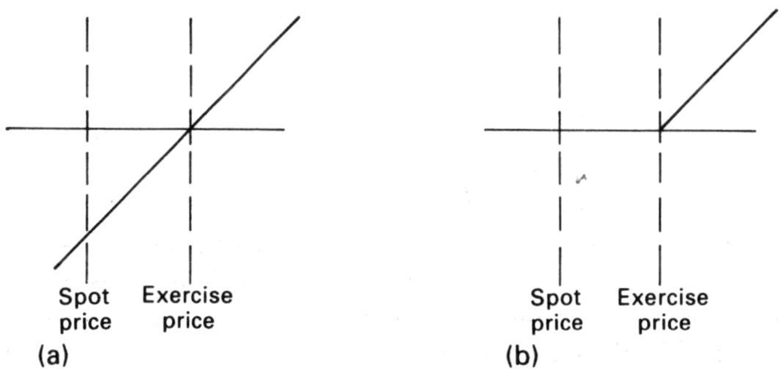

Figure 5.17 The components of the single exercise price zero cost option: (a) synthetic forward; (b) call option

Table 5.14

	Calls			Puts		
	October	January	April	October	January	April
200	28	37	43	4	9	13
220	15	25	30	11	17	20
240	7	16	22	23	28	32

Residual exposure

It has been suggested above that the short position being hedged should be matched in size by the call options. This would produce a synthetic put giving a negative delta and profit potential from price falls. If the view taken is that the price of the underlying instrument is more likely to rise, matching its size to the put options might be appropriate since that would produce a net call option position with a positive delta. The elimination of all market exposure – that is, the achievement of delta neutrality – could be attained by a position in which the coverage of the calls exceeds the size of the underlying instrument, whilst the coverage of the puts is less than the size of the underlying instrument. This delta-neutral position would constitute a long straddle.

A long straddle would provide an exposure to changes in market expectations of volatility that would provide profits in the event of a rise in expected volatility. A hedger who takes the view that market expectations of volatility will fall might prefer a short straddle. If the single exercise price zero cost option takes the form of buying in-the-money calls and financing them by writing a larger number of out-of-the-money puts, the potential profiles from combining the options with the underlying short position would be those of a short call, a short put or a short straddle. Such short positions would tend to provide profits in the event of market expectations of volatility declining.

Exercise 5.5

Question

It is 12 August, the price of GEC shares is 221p and the option prices are as shown in Table 5.14.

Suppose that a portfolio manager is confident that the price of GEC shares will rise, to the extent of discounting any possibility of downside risk, but is uncertain as to the timing and extent of that rise. Suggest a strategy that avoids initial premium outlay whilst allowing substantial profits in the event of a considerable price rise.

Answer

A possible strategy is that of buying calls and selling puts which involves the number of puts sold exceeding the number of calls bought so that at 221 there is a net premium receipt. For example:

Buy 1 April 220 call at 30.
Write 2 April 220 puts at 20.
Net premium receipt $20+20-30=10$.
(A bid–offer spread of 2p would change the calculation to $18+18-30=6$.)

The most distant options (i.e. April) are required because of the uncertainty about the timing of the rise.

6

Trading with options

Basic principles

Whereas hedging seeks to make profits from options in order to offset losses on an underlying exposure, trading seeks to make profits from options for their own sake.

Trading with options is based on views as to whether the existing price of an option series is likely to change. A trader believing that the price of an option series will rise might buy, whilst an option that is seen as prone to a price fall may be written. The foregoing observation begs the question as to how a trader can ascertain whether an option series is over- or underpriced. The trader must have an understanding of the determinants of option prices, or employ computer software that is based on an appropriate model of option pricing. A detailed assessment of the determinants of option prices will be attempted later in this chapter. For the moment it is sufficient to know that the intrinsic value of an option provides a lower boundary to its theoretical price. In principle, the minimum price that an option can have is its intrinsic value.

As an option series moves into the money, and becomes deeper in the money, its intrinsic value will rise and with it the value of the option. So trading strategies might be based on option series moving into the money, or becoming deeper in the money. These strategies parallel hedging strategies.

Trading strategies based on increases in intrinsic value are concerned with the direction and extent of movements in the price of the underlying instrument. The simplest trading strategies are those involving the purchase or sale of a single option series. A trader expecting a rise in the price of the underlying instrument might buy a call or write a put (see Figure 6.1). The choice between the long call and short put, along with choices relating to strike prices and expiry dates, would be influenced by

Figure 6.1 (a) Long call; (b) short put

factors such as the extent of the expected movement, the confidence with which the expectation is held and the level of risk that the trader is prepared to tolerate.

If the extent of the expected movement in the price of the underlying instrument is considerable, out-of-the-money long calls would be appropriate since the relatively low premiums would allow large percentage profits. If the expected movement is more modest, out-of-the-money options may not be appropriate since the amount of intrinsic value generated by the movement in the price of the underlying instrument would be curtailed to the extent that the option is out of the money. If the expected rise in the price of the underlying instrument is considerable, a long call would be more appropriate than a short put with the same strike price. A more modest expectation might suggest the use of a short put. A long call would be more appropriate if the trader lacked strong confidence in his expectation or was particularly risk averse, since the short put entails the potential for very large losses in the event of a fall in the price of the underlying instrument.

The degree of confidence and the level of risk aversion would also influence the strike price chosen. A trader with little tolerance of risk might opt for the payment of a small premium in order to limit the sum of money risked, and would therefore choose an out-of-the-money call option. If a trader with limited confidence in his forecast, or who is very risk averse, were to write a put option, then an out-of-the-money option would be appropriate. The price of the underlying instrument would have further to move before it provided the writer with losses.

A trader anticipating a fall in the price of the underlying instrument might buy a put or write a call (see Figure 6.2). The considerations bearing

Figure 6.2 (a) Long put; (b) short call

Figure 6.3 (a) Bull spread; (b) bear spread

upon the relevant choices parallel those mentioned in relation to the bullish trader.

Forecasts as to the direction and extent of movements in the price of the underlying instrument could alternatively suggest the use of bull or bear spreads (Figure 6.3). A bull spread can be created with either calls or puts. For example, a long call at the lower strike price and a short call at the higher strike price would produce a bull spread. As the price of the underlying instrument rises from the lower strike price, there is an increasing intrinsic value of the long call. However, as the price of the underlying instrument rises beyond the higher strike price, the additional profit from the long call is cancelled by losses on the short call. So beyond the higher strike price there is no net change in the profit/loss situation. This is illustrated by a horizontal line.

If the price of the underlying instrument were to remain below the lower strike price neither option would be exercised. The profit/loss would equal the net premium receipt/payment. Since the long call would have the higher premium there would be a net premium payment, so there would be a loss below the lower strike price. The maximum profit would be received in the event of the price of the underlying instrument exceeding the higher strike price. That profit would equal the difference between the strike prices minus the net premium payment.

The bull spread could alternatively be constructed by writing a put at the higher strike price and buying a put at the lower strike price. As the price of the underlying instrument falls further below the strike price of the short put, the loss resulting from exercise increases. However, beyond the lower strike price the loss would be offset by profits from the long put. So below the lower strike price there is a horizontal line depicting an unchanging profit/loss position.

If the price of the underlying instrument were to remain above the higher strike price neither option would be exercised. In that event the profit/loss would equal the net premium received/paid. The short put would have the higher premium and hence there would be a net premium

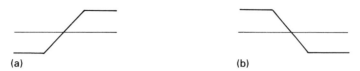

receipt. This is the maximum profit available from the spread. The maximum loss is equal to the difference between the strike prices minus the net premium receipt. This maximum loss would arise from a price of the underlying instrument below the lower strike price.

A trader would use a bull spread if he expected a rise in the price of the underlying instrument but felt that such a rise would not be substantial. If he thought it unlikely that the price of the underlying instrument would rise beyond the higher strike price, he would, for example, write a call at the higher strike price so as partially to offset the premium paid for the call with the lower strike price. The reduced net premium that results would involve a lower level of risk for the trader, so this strategy might be preferred by a very risk-averse trader or one who had limited confidence in his forecast.

Bear spreads can also be constructed with either calls or puts. A short call at the lower exercise price, together with a long call at the higher exercise price, would produce the spread. So would a long put at the higher exercise price, together with a short put at the lower exercise price. A bear spread might be adopted by a trader wishing to take a position on a fall in the price of the underlying instrument, but feeling either that the fall will be limited in extent or that the risk and uncertainty are such that the profit potential can be restricted in order to reduce the net premium payment.

It was pointed out at the beginning of this chapter that trading with options is based on views as to whether the existing price of an option will change. One determinant of the price of an option is the price of the underlying instrument. If this price is perceived to be incorrect, and hence likely to change, a corresponding variation in the price of the option could be anticipated. The trading strategies described thus far are based on such expectations of movements in the price of the underlying instrument. A complete guide to options trading needs to pay attention to the other determinants of option prices.

Exercise 6.1

Question

The June S & P stock index futures price stands at 200.

June S & P 500 stock index futures options prices (deltas in brackets) are as shown in Table 6.1.

Suggest a low-risk strategy for a trader with a mildly bearish view of the market. What is the maximum profit (if any), maximum loss (if any) and break-even point?

Table 6.1

Strike price	Calls	Puts
195	6.80 (0.84)	1.65 (−0.16)
200	2.79 (0.50)	2.69 (−0.50)
205	1.75 (0.15)	6.60 (−0.85)

Answer
A possibility would be a bear put spread.

Buy a June 200 put for 2·69.
Write a June 195 put for 1·65.

Maximum profit is

$$[5-(2{\cdot}69-1{\cdot}65)]\times \$500=\$1{,}980$$

Maximum loss is

$$(2{\cdot}69-1{\cdot}65)\times \$500=\$520$$

(which would be realised if neither option were exercised).
Break-even point is

$$200-(2{\cdot}69-1{\cdot}65)=198{\cdot}96$$

The determinants of option premiums

The most popular way of calculating the 'fair price' of an option is by means of the Black–Scholes model. This equates the price (premium) with the expected profit from a naked option. 'Expected' profit is used in the sense of possible profit outcomes weighted by their probabilities of occurrence.

Figure 6.4 illustrates this with respect to options on the FTSE 100 stock index. The curve in the upper part of Figure 6.4 is known as a normal distribution curve and indicates the probabilities of the various possible outcomes. The profile ABC in the lower part shows the profit possibilities from buying a call option (ignoring the premium at this stage).

Suppose that the area under the normal distribution curve between 1600 and 1610, as a proportion of the total area under the curve, is 0·19. This means that there is a 19 per cent chance that the index will fall between 1600 and 1610. If the area under the curve between 1610 and 1620 is 0·15 of the total area there is a 15 per cent probability of the index being between 1610 and 1620. The statistical expectation of the profit from the call option

Table 6.2

Range of index values	Range of profit possibilities	Probability of occurrence	Contribution to expectation of profit
1600–10	0–10	0.19	5 × 0.19 = 0.95
1610–20	10–20	0.15	15 × 0.15 = 2.25
1620–30	20–30	0.09	25 × 0.09 = 2.25
1630–40	30–40	0.05	35 × 0.05 = 1.75
1640–50	40–50	0.01	45 × 0.01 = 0.45
1650–60	50–60	0.01	55 × 0.01 = 0.55
		——	Expected ——
		0.50	profit = 8.20

is given by the sum of the possible profits when each possible profit is weighted by its probability of occurrence. The calculation of this expected profit is illustrated by Table 6.2 in which, for the sake of simplification, the possible profits are represented by the mid-points of the respective ranges.

Table 6.2 involves some simplifications that would be avoided in the actual calculation of expected profit. In particular, the mid-point of a range is not the best measure of the average possible outcome within the range. Nevertheless the table serves to illustrate the principles behind the calculation of the price (premium) of an option using the Black–Scholes model. In the example shown, the premium, expressed in index points, is 8·20. At £10 per index point this would correspond to a money price of £82 per contract.

The various factors that affect the premium can be viewed in relation to

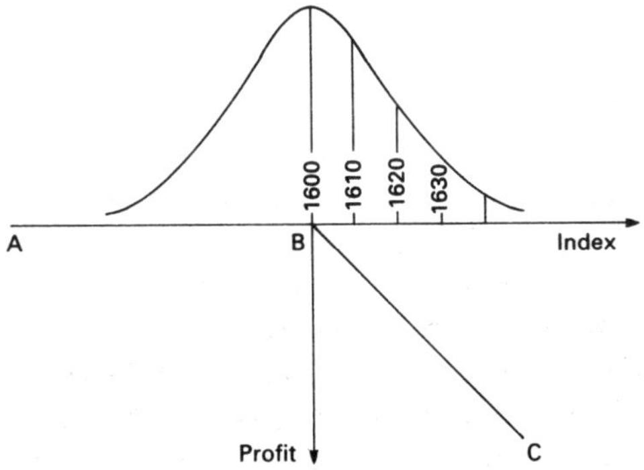

Figure 6.4 Probability distribution of possible future index levels (with exercise price equal to spot price)

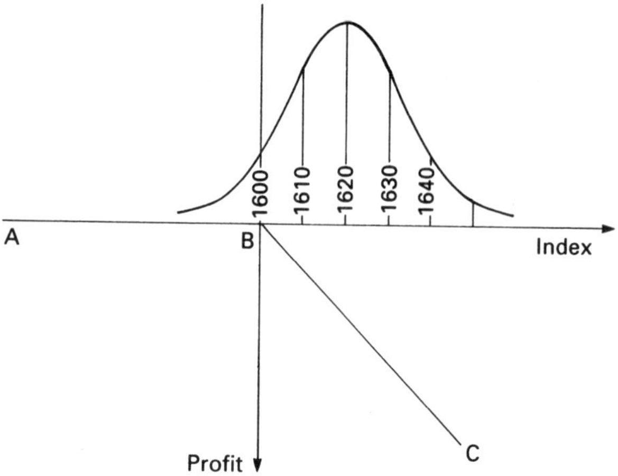

Figure 6.5 Probability distribution of possible future index levels (where exercise price and spot price differ)

Figure 6.4. A particularly important determinant is the relationship between the exercise price (index) and the index at the time that the option is purchased. Figure 6.4 assumes that the exercise price is equal to the spot price, each being 1600 index points. If the spot price were to differ from the exercise price this difference would have an impact on the premium. Figure 6.5 illustrates a case in which the spot price is 1620 whilst the exercise price is 1600. In this case the type of calculation illustrated by Table 6.2 would produce an expected profit greater than 8·20 index points.

The option illustrated by Figure 6.5 is in the money. The illustrated option would yield a 20 index point profit if exercised because the guaranteed buying price, at 1600 index points, is 20 index points below the current market price. This intrinsic value must be reflected in the price of the option and sets a lower boundary to the premium. The potential for immediate profit has to be paid for.

Time value is at its greatest when the option is at the money and declines as the option moves towards being either in the money or out of the money. This could be demonstrated by numerous replications of Table 6.2 based on variations on Figures 6.4 and 6.5 with different positions of the normal distribution curve. This behaviour of time value can be explained intuitively.

An out-of-the-money option has to reach the at-the-money position before movements of the index can start generating profitable opportunities for exercise. Thus an option buyer would regard an out-of-the-money option as less valuable than an at-the-money option since some leeway has to be made up before it reaches the threshold of profitability, whereas an at-the-money option is already at this threshold. Consequently, the option buyer is prepared to pay less for an out-of-the-money option. Conversely, the option writer would accept a lower premium because of his reduced chance of loss. (This line of reasoning also underlines the role of the market forces of demand and supply in the establishment of option prices. Black–Scholes calculations merely serve as guidelines to buyers and writers.)

The time value of an in-the-money-option would be lower than if that option were at the money because of the possibility of erosion of the intrinsic value. In the case of a call option, a rise in the index would increase the intrinsic value of options that were either in the money or at the money prior to the rise in the index. However, a fall in the index would reduce the intrinsic value of an in-the-money option, whereas an at-the-money option has no intrinsic value to be eroded. This potential for loss of intrinsic value is reflected in a lower time value.

Another determinant of the size of premiums is the expected volatility of the index. A high volatility would mean that the normal distribution of Figures 6.4 and 6.5 would spread out and flatten, indicating an increased chance of extreme values of the index. A calculation similar to that of Table 6.2 but with a normal distribution curve exhibiting a greater variance would produce a higher expected profit. Thus premiums rise as expected volatility increases since the probability of high profits is enhanced.

The term 'volatility' could be seen as referring to the standard deviation of the distribution of possible spot prices at the end of a particular period of time. This standard deviation depends upon the length of time involved. It is obvious that this standard deviation will increase as the period lengthens (graphically depicted by the normal distribution curve becoming wider and flatter) since the likelihood of substantial movements from the original price becomes greater. What is less obvious is the precise relationship between the standard deviation and time.

The standard deviation is proportional to the square root of the period of time involved. So the volatility over t days is equal to the square root of t times the daily volatility. The non-proportional relationship between volatility and time arises from the possibility that some price movements may reverse previous ones rather than adding to the degree of divergence.

This relationship between volatility and the square root of time explains

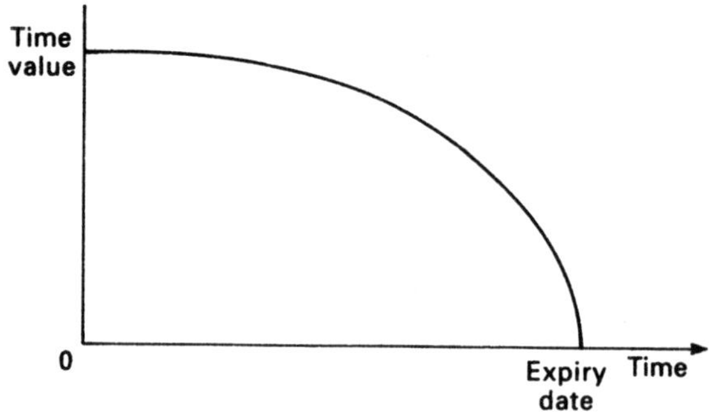

Figure 6.6 Time value decay

the observed pattern of time value decay. Time value decays at an accelerating rate as the expiry date is approached. In fact, time value is proportional to the square root of the amount of time remaining before expiry. This pattern of time value decay, slow when expiry is distant but becoming rapid close to expiry, is illustrated by Figure 6.6.

From what has just been said it is clear that time to expiry also influences the option price. Longer periods to expiry are associated with higher option premiums. A long period to expiry provides more opportunity for the index to move sufficiently above a call option exercise price (or below a put option exercise price) to generate a net profit. The enhanced likelihood of profitable exercise would tend to raise the price that a buyer is prepared to pay and that a writer would need to receive. (The point could alternatively be expressed in terms of a longer period leading to a greater variance of the normal distribution curve.)

Interest rates also have an influence on option premiums. The influence of interest rates can be understood by seeing options as a means of changing the timing of transactions in the underlying instrument. An investor can buy call options with the intention of taking delivery of the corresponding shares when the option expires, and in the meantime can receive interest on the money that will be used. The attractiveness of this procedure relative to buying the shares immediately is improved by a rise in interest rates payable on the money held. It follows that when interest rates are high the demand for call options will be somewhat greater, and option prices will be boosted by this additional demand.

Put options can be used to postpone the sale of shares. Instead of selling shares immediately, the investor might buy put options with the intention of selling in the future. Pending the sale of the shares, the investor would forgo interest on the money that would have been received from an immediate sale. Using puts in this way becomes less attractive as the interest receipts forgone rise. So investors are less likely to buy puts for this purpose when interest rates are high. High interest rates are therefore associated with a somewhat lower demand for put options and hence lower put option premiums.

In the case of stock options the prospect of an ex-dividend date can have an impact on the premium of an option. When a stock goes ex-dividend its price falls by an amount approximately equal to the anticipated dividend. So an ex-dividend date can be seen as providing a price fall that is anticipated. The price fall will cause a reduction in the premiums of call options and an increase in those of put options. The option premiums would normally discount the anticipated fall in the share price well before the ex-dividend date.

If the expected dividend is very large, it may even effectively circumscribe the life of a call option. An anticipated substantial fall in the share price might, especially in a stable market, be regarded by investors as effectively terminating the life of that option (reflected by a collapse in time value). Conversely, the life of a put option might be seen as effectively beginning on the ex-dividend date.

The Black–Scholes equation has a number of variations, partly depending on the nature of the underlying instrument. A general form is shown by the following equation:

$$\text{Option price} = PN(d_1) - Se^{-rt}N(d_2)$$

$$d_1 = \frac{\text{In}\left(\frac{P}{S}\right) + \left(r + \frac{v^2}{2}\right)t}{v\sqrt{t}}$$

$$d_2 = d_1 - v\sqrt{t}$$

$$v = \sqrt{\frac{\sum_{i=1}^{n}\left(P_i - P\right)^2}{n-1}}$$

and where P = price of the underlying instrument
S = strike price
t = time remaining before expiry
r = risk-free interest rate

v = volatility
In = natural logarithm
$N()$ = cumulative normal density function
e = exponential

This equation takes no account of dividends, but it can be amended to do so. A more significant deficiency is its failure to take account of early (i.e. prior-to-expiry) exercise possibilities. For this reason it is really suitable for European-style options only (those that can be exercised only at expiry). Other models are more appropriate to American-style options: for example, the binomial models known as Cox–Rubinstein models. A more detailed mathematical analysis of the Black–Scholes option pricing model is given in Appendix II.

Hedging short option positions by replication

Replication refers to the artificial creation of a long option position that mirrors the option that has been written. An alternative way of looking at option pricing is to look at the cost to an option writer of hedging that option by means of replicating it. Replication may take place in either a cash market or a derivatives market. Obviously replication using derivatives ties up less cash. In the case of replicating stock index options, the appropriate derivative would be stock index futures.

Hedging by means of replication would be based on the option delta. If it can be assumed that on a day-to-day basis movements in FTSE 100 stock index futures prices match changes in the FTSE 100 index, then written FTSE 100 traded options can be hedged by holding futures in an amount calculated as follows:

$$\frac{£10}{£25} \times \text{number of options contracts} \times \text{delta of option}$$

The term £10/£25 arises from the relative sizes of FTSE 100 options (£10 per index point) and FTSE 100 futures (£25 per index point) contracts. The number of contracts required must be adjusted in the light of the delta since the price movement of the option is delta times the index movement, and hence the price movement of the option is matched by a number of futures contracts that is factored down by the delta. In this way, profits/losses on the written option will be matched by losses/profits on futures contracts. In other words, there will effectively be a long option position to match the short option position. Short calls would be hedged by means of long futures, whilst short puts would be replicated with short futures. The cost of hedging by means of such replication may determine the premiums required by option writers.

The cost to the writer of an option of hedging that option by replication arises from the relationship between the option delta and the price of the underlying instrument. Long option positions are gamma positive, which means that the delta rises as the price of the underlying instrument increases (−1 to 0 in the case of puts, 0 to 1 in the case of calls). This implies that a movement in the price of the underlying instrument, by changing the option delta, renders the quantity of the instrument used for hedging the option inappropriate. A rise in the price of the underlying instrument means that more of the hedging instrument must be purchased; a fall in the price of the underlying instrument means that some of the hedging instrument needs to be sold.

So as the price of the underlying instrument rises, the hedger of the option needs to buy cash market or futures market instruments in order to maintain the hedge; a fall in the price of the underlying instrument, on the other hand, requires the sale of those cash or futures market instruments. The hedger of the option thus finds that replication involves buying the instrument used for replication when its price is relatively high and selling it when its price is relatively low (a situation accentuated by the bid–offer spread). This is the cost to the option writer, who uses replication of a long option position in order to cover the short option position.

The time value of an option will be such as to compensate for this cost. This cost increases with volatility and time to expiry. In consequence, the time value of the option bears a positive relationship to expected volatility and time to expiry.

Hedging short option positions by means of replication introduces a source of market instability. A rise in the stock index raises the deltas of call options. The number of futures contracts required for replication rises and the increased demand for futures contracts tends to raise their prices. The rise in the prices of futures contracts can initiate program trading orientated towards buying spot and selling via futures contracts. The spot purchases in the stock markets cause further upward movements in the stock index and hence raise option deltas further. So an upward movement in stock prices can become self-reinforcing. The converse process operates to exaggerate a fall in stock prices.

The instrument used for the replication of stock options would be the underlying stock. In the case of currency options it might be the currency itself, or futures based on that currency. Short-term interest rate options might be replicated by short-term interest rate futures or by forward rate agreements (FRAs – a form of OTC short-term interest rate futures). In all these cases, hedging by replication can be a source of market instability.

Time value and options trading

The discussion of options trading earlier in this chapter was based on changes in intrinsic value with no attention being paid to time value. However, time value is not only something that might be the basis of trading in itself; it is also something that should be borne in mind when a trade is primarily concerned with movements in intrinsic value.

Consider a trade that involves the purchase of a single call option series. An at-the-money call could provide the holder with a loss even in the event of a rise in the price of the underlying instrument. If the rise in the price of the underlying instrument is modest and takes a long time to come about, the profit from the increase in intrinsic value could be more than offset by a fall in time value. This is more likely in the case of an option that is close to expiry since such an option would be subject to the rapid time value decay that occurs close to the expiry date. This case illustrates the point that it is not only the direction and extent of the movement in the price of the underlying instrument, but also the speed of the movement that a trader must consider when contemplating a trade.

The point is even more apparent in the case of an out-of-the-money call. Such a call might fail to become in the money as a result of a rise in the price of the underlying instrument. In such a case any chance of a profit depends upon the price rise of the underlying instrument occurring quickly, and well before expiry. The profit would depend upon the increase in time value resulting from the price rise of the underlying instrument outweighing the loss of time value caused by the passage of time.

Some trading strategies are based entirely on anticipated movements in time value. These strategies include calendar spreads, alternatively known as horizontal spreads. (The various expiry months are depicted horizontally in the financial press and so strategies using the same strike price but differing expiry dates are referred to as horizontal spreads. Strategies using the same expiry date but differing strike prices are referred to as vertical spreads, the various strike prices appearing vertically in the financial press. If the options used differ with respect to both expiry date and strike price, the strategy is called a diagonal spread.)

A calendar spread seeks to profit from the acceleration in time value decay as the expiry date approaches. A trader using a calendar spread would take a short position in an option series with a nearby expiry month and a long position in a series with a distant expiry (the two series would be identical in every respect other than the expiry month). The short option position can be seen as a liability, whereas the long option is an asset. The time value of the option with the nearby maturity date would decay more rapidly than that of the option with the distant maturity date. The value of the liability declines more quickly than the value of the asset. If the other determinants of time value remain unchanged, the passage of time will yield a profit for the trader.

The rate of decline of an option premium per unit of time elapsing is known as the theta of the option. The (absolute value of the) theta of an option increases as expiry is approached. Thetas are greatest for at-the-money options.

In order to benefit most from the rapid time value decay of the near-dated option, the option should be allowed to run to the expiry date (it would be advisable to use out-of-the-money options for the near date so as to reduce the risk of early exercise: in other words, the risk that the option holder will exercise the option before the expiry date). The profit from the calendar spread is then equal to the time value of the far-dated option (on the expiry date of the near-dated option) minus the net premium cost of initially establishing the calendar spread. The time value of the far-dated option will be at its maximum when that option is at the money, and will decline as the price of the underlying instrument deviates from the exercise price. The profit/loss profile of the calendar spread thus takes the form indicated in Figure 6.7.

An increase in expected volatility would also raise the time value of the

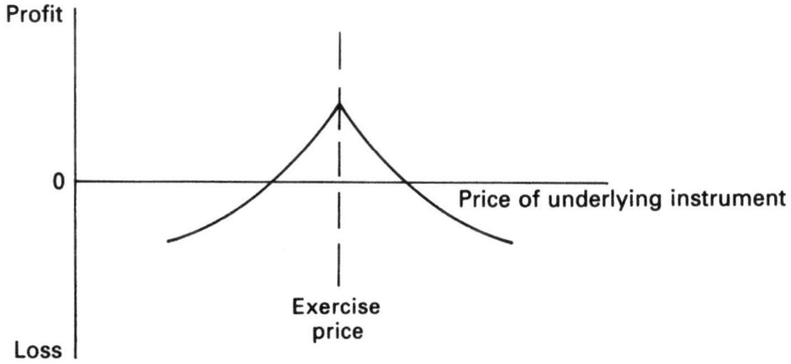

Figure 6.7 Profit/loss profile of a calendar spread

Table 6.3

Strike price	Premium	Implied volatility	Delta
330	44	6.800	0.7
360	28	7.000	0.5
390	18	8.900	0.3

far-dated option. For this reason a calendar spread might be particularly attractive to a trader who believes that the market is underestimating future volatility.

Another trading strategy based on time value is often referred to as valuation trading. This involves identifying relatively over- and underpriced options and trading them in delta-neutral combinations.

Coming to a view as to whether an option is over-, under- or correctly priced requires attention to the volatility implied by the option premium. Just as the theoretical option premium (alternatively known as the fair price) can be ascertained from knowledge of the determinants of option prices, including volatility, so too can the value of one determinant be ascertained from knowledge of the option premium and the other determinants. So it is possible to calculate, using models such as Black–Scholes or Cox–Rubinstein, the volatility implied by an option premium. This is a major way of ascertaining market expectations of volatility, which is the only determinant of option prices that is not directly observable.

An overpriced option series is one whose premium implies a higher than average level of volatility; the converse applies for an underpriced option. If the underlying instrument and the expiry date are the same, the implied volatility should be the same. If implied volatilities differ, there may be an opportunity for valuation trading.

Suppose that a trader encounters the premiums for call options on the shares of Shoddigoods plc shown in Table 6.3, and using an options pricing model derives the implied volatilities and deltas indicated. (The options share a common expiry month.) The 330p calls are relatively underpriced whilst the 390p calls are relatively overpriced. The valuation trader might write 390p calls whilst buying 330p calls. In order to achieve delta neutrality, and hence immunity from movements in the price of the underlying instrument, the numbers of options contracts should be in the ratio of the deltas. Writing seven 390p calls for every three 330p calls bought would achieve this delta neutrality.

Table 6.4

Strike price	Premium	Fair price	% deviation of premium from fair price	Delta
330	44	46	−4.3	0.7
360	28	30	−6.7	0.5
390	18	15	+20.0	0.3

This oversimplifies the decision facing the trader. The trader really seeks to trade the option series whose over- or underpricing is greatest in percentage terms. These may not coincide with those with the most extreme implied volatilities. The series with the most extreme implied volatilities would exhibit the greatest percentage deviations of time value, but if intrinsic value is present then this may not be reflected in the relative percentage deviations of premiums. If an option series has considerable intrinsic value, a high percentage deviation of time value may correspond to a relatively low percentage deviation of the premium.

Table 6.3 therefore needs to be adjusted. Firstly, a column of theoretical (fair) prices needs to be added (see Table 6.4). In order to ascertain these fair prices, the trader needs a single measure of volatility to apply to each of the option series. This measure of volatility could be derived from the implied volatilities depicted in Table 6.3. Secondly, a column showing percentage deviations of actual premiums from fair prices is needed. It is this column that would guide the trader's actions. He would buy those with the greatest percentage undervaluation and sell those showing the highest percentage overvaluation. Although the 330p calls have the lowest implied volatility, the percentage undervaluation is greatest in the case of the 360p calls. The valuation trader would buy 360p calls and sell 390p calls. The ratio of five 390p calls to every three 360p calls would achieve delta neutrality.

Another class of trading strategies based on time value arises from the relationship between time value and market expectations of volatility.

Volatility trading

Volatility trading can be looked upon as taking positions on changes in market expectations of price volatility. The main strategies for trading volatility are straddles, strangles and butterflies.

STRADDLES

A long straddle is the simultaneous purchase of a call and a put on the same stock, at the same exercise (strike) price and for the same expiry month (see Figure 6.8). A short straddle is the simultaneous sale of two such options (see Figure 6.9). A trader buying a straddle is taking the view that volatility will be high in the future, whereas the seller of a straddle takes the view that volatility will be low.

Suppose that shares in Shoddigoods plc are 99p and that on 1 December January 100p call options are 2p whilst January 100p put options are 3p. A long straddle could be constructed by simultaneously buying a January 100p call and a January 100p put so as to produce the profit/loss profile illustrated by Figure 6.10. The holder of the long straddle depicted in the figure would make net profits if the stock price moved outside the range 95p–105p. The maximum loss would be the sum of the premiums paid, 5p. This loss would be incurred if the stock price moved to, and stayed at, 100p.

A short straddle could be produced by means of writing a January 100p call and simultaneously writing a January 100p put. The resulting profit/loss profile is illustrated by Figure 6.11. The seller of the short straddle shown in the figure will make a profit if the stock price remains within the range 95p–105p. The maximum profit of 5p, equal to the sum of the premiums received, would be made in the event of the stock price moving to and stabilising at 100p.

Thus the holder of a long straddle hopes for high volatility, whereas the holder of a short straddle desires low volatility. It is more likely, however, that they take positions on changes in market expectations of price volatility rather than on price volatility itself. This requires consideration of profit/loss profiles which take account of time value.

Figure 6.12 incorporates time value into the profit/loss profile of the long straddle illustrated by Figure 6.10. The intrinsic value of an option is

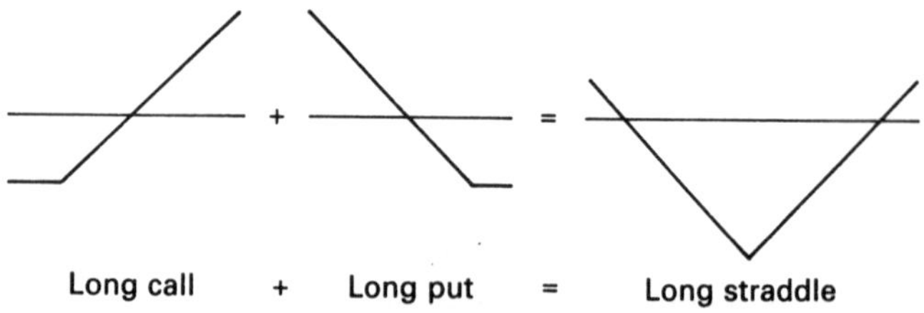

Figure 6.8 Long straddle

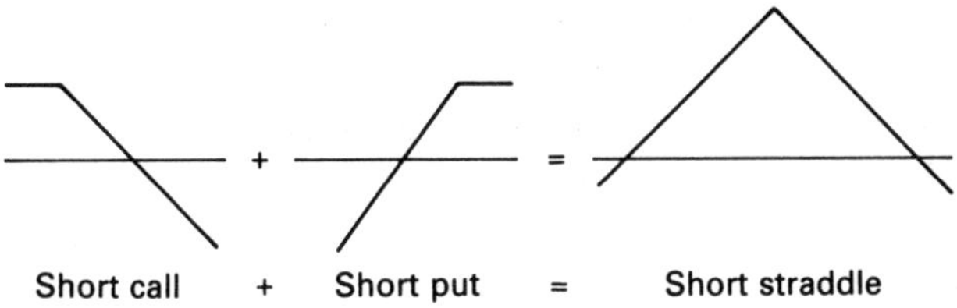

Figure 6.9 Short straddle

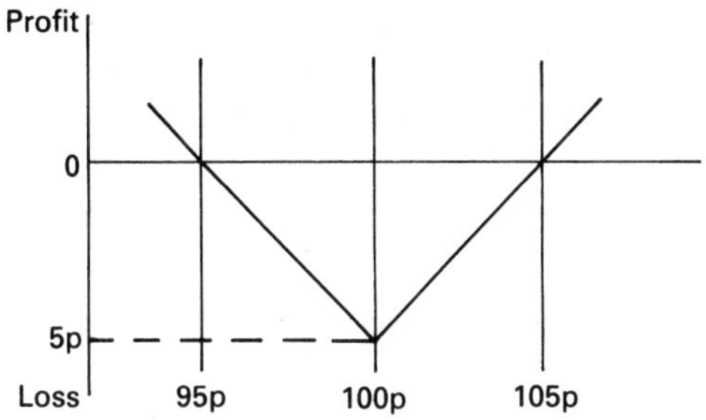

Figure 6.10 Long straddle

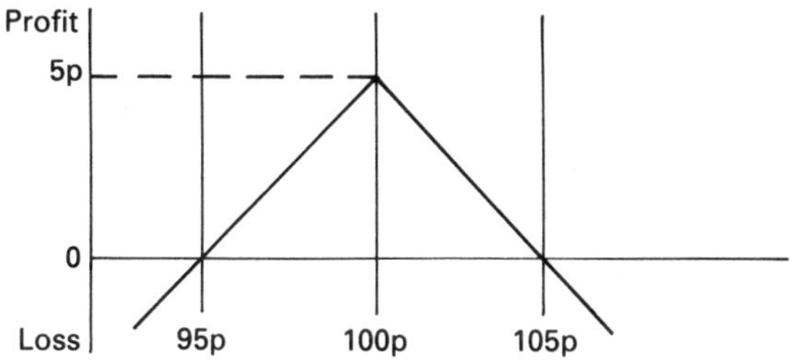

Figure 6.11 Short straddle

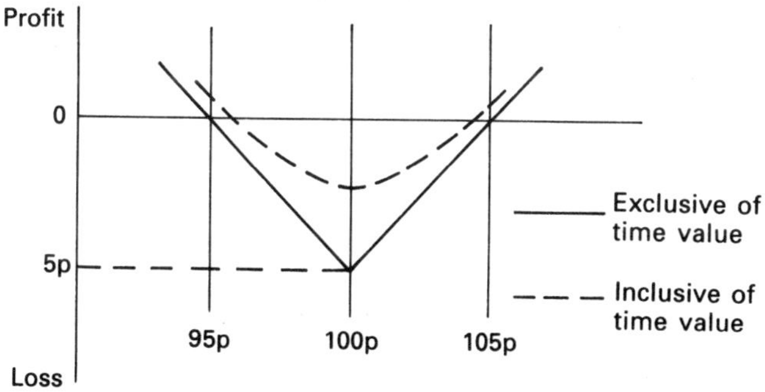

Figure 6.12 Long straddle profile including time value

the profit (without deduction of premium) to be obtained from immediate exercise of the option. The profit/loss profiles of Figures 6.8 to 6.11 reflect intrinsic value. Option premiums consist of time value as well as intrinsic value. Time value can be looked upon as a payment for the possibility that the intrinsic value might increase prior to the expiry date. When an option is sold, rather than exercised, time value is received in addition to the intrinsic value. Figures 6.8 to 6.11 are based on exercising options, while Figure 6.12 is based on selling them.

The broken line of Figure 6.12 represents the price received upon sale of the options minus the price originally paid for the options: that is, the new sum of the premiums minus the original sum of the premiums. The vertical distance between the two profiles represents the time value.

One of the factors that determine time value is the market expectation of volatility. If it is expected that the price of the stock will be highly volatile in the period up to the expiry date of the option, the time value will be relatively high, reflecting the strong possibility of a substantial increase in intrinsic value.

A trader who takes the view that the market's expectation of future volatility will increase might buy options so as to profit from the increase in their prices resulting from enhanced time value. However, buying options individually provides an exposure to direction of price movement as well as to expected volatility. The trader may not wish to take a view as to which way the stock price will move. He would then seek a position that is unaffected by stock price change as such, but which can yield profits from a rise in expected volatility. This objective might be satisfied by a long straddle that is delta neutral.

The delta of an option is the ratio of the change in the price of the option to the change in the underlying stock price. Call options have positive deltas whilst put options have negative deltas. Call and put option deltas thus tend to offset each other. This offset can produce a situation in which the option premiums, when considered together, show little net response to movements in the underlying stock price.

A straddle therefore allows the trader to take a position on changes in expectations of volatility whilst providing little exposure to movements of the stock price. Straddles would typically be established so that both options are as close as possible to being at the money. At-the-money call options have deltas of about 0·5 and at-the-money put options have deltas around −0·5. So if both options are at the money the net delta is close to zero. The net delta of the options is represented by the gradient of the broken line in Figure 6.12.

Table 6.5

Strike price	Calls	Puts
195	6.80 (0.84)	1.65 (−0.16)
200	2.79 (0.50)	2.69 (−0.50)
205	1.75 (0.15)	6.60 (−0.85)

The gradient is equal to, or close to, zero when the stock price is equal to the exercise price of 100p. When the gradient of the profit/loss profile is equal to zero the position is said to be delta neutral. The position illustrated by Figure 6.12, however, is gamma positive. The gamma is a measure of the responsiveness of the delta to stock price movements (see Appendix III). The profile in Figure 6.12 moves from being delta negative, to being delta neutral, to being delta positive as the stock price rises. It is thus termed gamma positive. If the stock price is volatile, this is beneficial to the holder of the options since a rise in the stock price above 100p establishes a delta-positive position, which produces profits from a rising stock price, whilst a fall in the stock price to below 100p causes the position to become delta negative and thus prone to benefit from falls in the stock price.

Exercise 6.2

Question

The June S & P 500 stock index futures price stands at 200.

June S & P 500 stock index futures options prices (deltas in brackets) are as shown in Table 6.5.

Describe a strategy using options *and* futures that will result in a profit from a movement of the futures price, irrespective of direction, in the event of market expectations of volatility remaining constant. What might cause a loss to be incurred?

Answer

Buy 2 June 200 calls:	$\text{Delta} = 2 \times 0{\cdot}5$
Sell 1 June futures contract:	$\text{Delta} = -1$
	$\text{Net delta} = 0$

A fall in the futures price would cause the options delta to decline. The net delta of the position thus becomes negative and the trader benefits from the price fall.

A rise in the futures price would cause the options delta to rise. The net delta of the position thus becomes positive and the trader profits from the price rise.

In other words, the position is gamma positive.

Losses could be incurred if market expectations of volatility were to decline and thereby reduce option prices. Also if time were to pass and the futures price remained stable there would be a decline in options prices which would render the overall position loss making.

STRANGLES

Strangles differ from straddles in that the two options have different exercise prices. A strangle would typically be constructed using an out-of-the-money call and an out-of-the-money put (see Figures 6.13 and 6.14). (It could be constructed with an in-the-money call and an in-the-money put, or with one option being in the money and the other out of the money. However, in the case of short strangles it must be borne in mind that strategies involving in-the-money options run a relatively high risk of early exercise: that is, the short option position could be closed out by an option holder choosing to exercise.) The buyer of a strangle takes the view that volatility is going to be high, whilst the seller of a strangle is taking a position on low volatility.

If shares in Shoddigoods plc are 99p, a long strangle on 1 December might be produced by buying a January 90p put option and a January 110p call option. If the premium of each option is 1p, the profit/loss profile of Figure 6.15 would be the result. The holder of the strangle depicted by Figure 6.15 would make a profit if the stock price moved outside the range

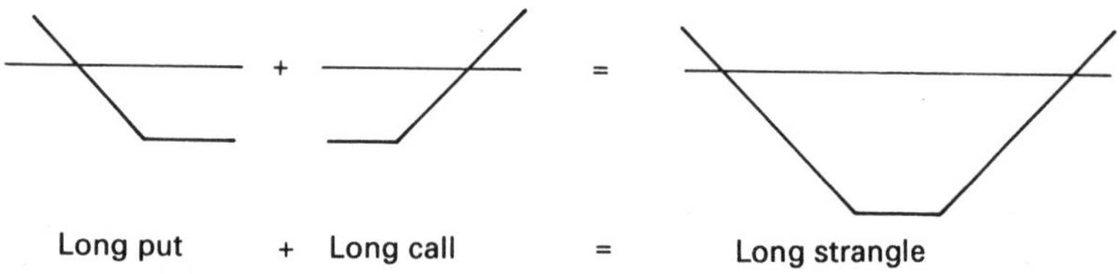

Figure 6.13 Long strangle

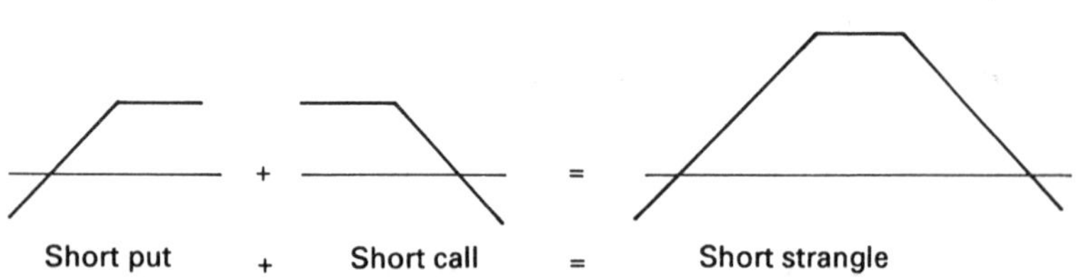

Figure 6.14 Short strangle

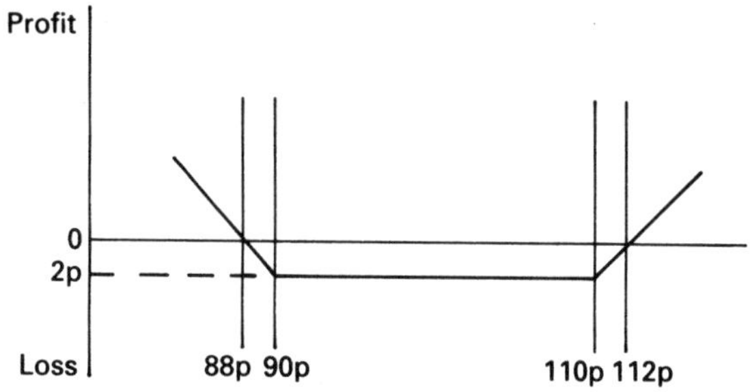

Figure 6.15 Long strangle

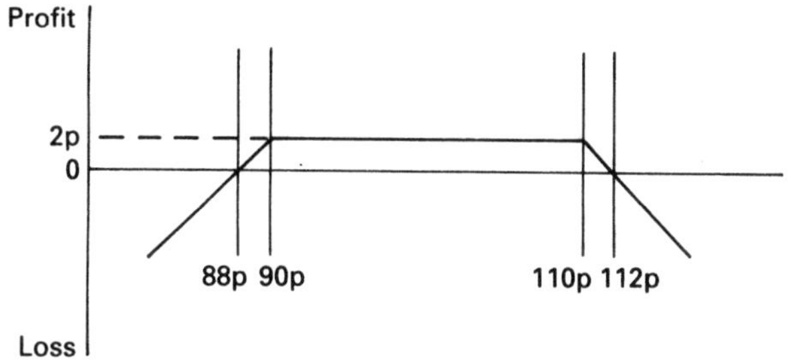

Figure 6.16 Short strangle

88p–112p. The maximum loss of 2p, the sum of the premiums paid, would be incurred in the event of the stock price remaining in the range 90p–110p. A short strangle, created by writing a January 90p put and a January 110p call, is illustrated by Figure 6.16, which is a mirror image of Figure 6.15.

Although the long and short strangles are suitable for taking positions on changes in volatility, they are more likely to be used for taking positions on changes in market expectations of volatility, with the combining of calls and puts being for the purpose of achieving delta neutrality. Figure 6.17 illustrates the profit/loss profile of the short strangle, inclusive of time value, for two different market expectations of volatility.

The volatility trader with a short strangle hopes for a reduction in market expectations of volatility so that the time value of both options falls and moves the profit/loss profile closer to the intrinsic value (i.e. straight-line) profile. Such a change would tend to move the position into profit so long as the share price does not simultaneously undergo a substantial rise or fall.

The writer of option contracts can be regarded as having incurred

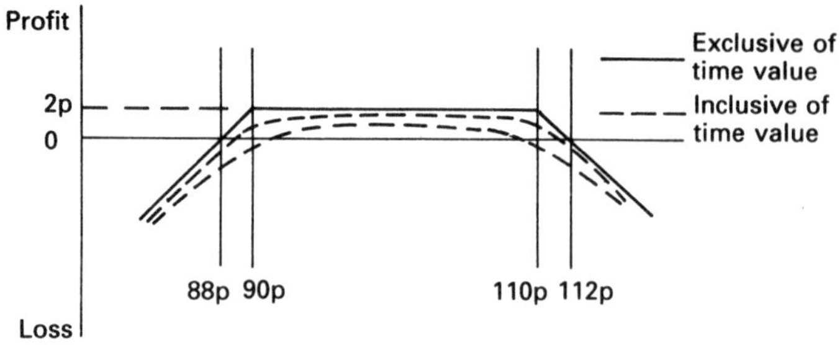

Figure 6.17 Short strangle profile including time value

liabilities in exchange for premium receipts. The prices of options represent the extent of the liabilities. The intrinsic value is the sum immediately lost in the event of the buyer of the option exercising it; the time value reflects the possibility that this potential loss might increase prior to expiry. A lower volatility suggests a diminished likelihood of intrinsic value rising (or coming into being) so if the market expectation of volatility falls, so will the time value paid and received when options change hands. The option writer will enjoy a decline in his liabilities and hence an improvement in his profit/loss position. This will show up as a movement of the profit/loss profile (broken line) towards the profit/loss profile that excludes time value (unbroken line) since the vertical distance between these two profiles represents time value.

The buyer of a strangle hopes for an increase in market expectations of share price volatility, which will cause time value to rise and the profit/loss profile to move away from the profile that excludes time value, as illustrated by Figure 6.18.

Both Figures 6.17 and 6.18 serve to demonstrate the interrelationship of the two dimensions of volatility trading. Both strategies seek to profit from

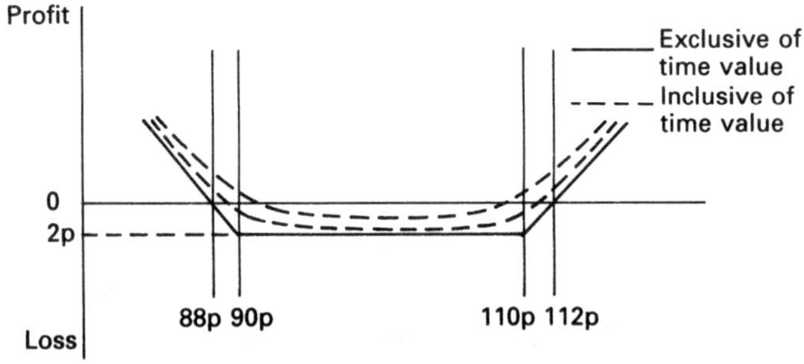

Figure 6.18 Long strangle profile including time value

the changes in time value that ensue from variations in the market expectations of future volatility. At the same time, the profit potential is dependent upon the actual volatility of the share price as represented by the extent of movement of the share price from its original value. In the case of the short strangle (Figure 6.17) the share price should remain within a range, whereas in the case of the long strangle (Figure 6.18) profits are enhanced by substantial deviations of the share price from its original level.

BUTTERFLIES

Long and short butterflies are illustrated by Figures 6.19 and 6.20 respectively. Butterfly spreads can be constructed in a number of ways. A long butterfly can be formed in the following ways:

1. Buy an in-the-money call, write two at-the-money calls and buy an out-of-the-money call. In the context of Figure 6.19 this means buying a 90p call, writing two 100p calls and buying a 110p call.

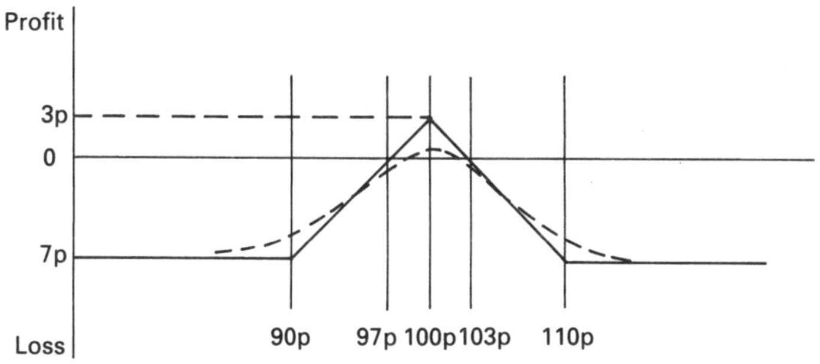

Figure 6.19 Long butterfly

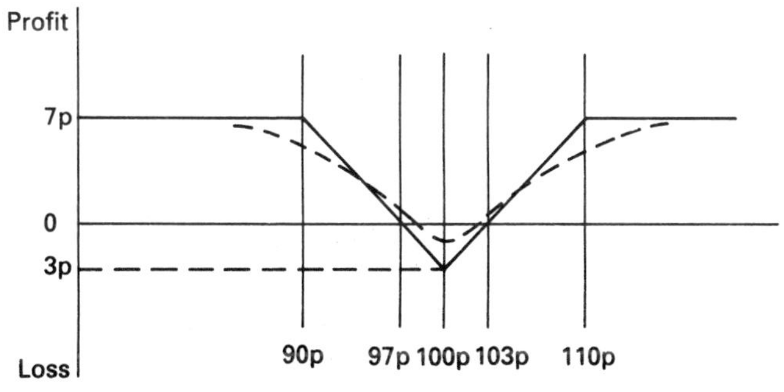

Figure 6.20 Short butterfly

2. Buy an in-the-money put, write two at-the-money puts and buy an out-of-the-money put. In the context of Figure 6.19 this means buying a 110p put, writing two 100p puts and buying a 90p put.
3. Buy an out-of-the-money put, write an at-the-money put, write an at-the-money call and buy an out-of-the-money call. In the context of Figure 6.19 this means buying a 90p put, writing a 100p put, writing a 100p call and buying a 110p call.

A short butterfly can be constructed in the following ways:

1. Write an in-the-money call, buy two at-the-money calls and write one out-of-the-money call. With reference to Figure 6.20 this means writing a 90p call, buying two 100p calls and writing a 110p call.
2. Write an in-the-money put, buy two at-the-money puts and write an out-of-the-money put. In relation to Figure 6.20 this means writing a 110p put, buying two 100p puts and writing a 90p put.
3. Write an out-of-the-money put, buy an at-the-money put, buy an at-the-money call and write an out-of-the-money call. In the context of Figure 6.20 this would involve writing a 90p put, buying a 100p put, buying a 100p call and writing a 110p call.

Although all these butterflies ideally involve at-the-money options, it is unlikely in practice that any options will be precisely at the money. In reality, traders would use those options that are closest to being at the money.

The reason for using options close to being at the money as the middle options in butterfly spreads is the achievement of a delta that is as close as possible to zero. This reflects the concern with trading on changes in time value that arise from variations in market expectations of volatility, rather than with trading on a direction of change in price. Delta neutrality also provides a position for the short butterfly that allows gains from share price movements in either direction, and a position for the long butterfly that renders share price stability desirable since losses would accrue from share price movements in either direction.

Exercise 6.3

Question

The June long gilt futures price is 119-29.

Long gilt futures options prices (deltas in brackets) are as shown in Table 6.6 Design a strategy that would allow a trader to gain from a narrow price range in the long gilt futures market whilst limiting the maximum possible loss. Indicate the maximum profit, maximum loss(es) and break-even point(s).

Table 6.6

	Calls		Puts	
	June	September	June	September
116	4-49 (0.83)	5-35 (0.79)	0-55 (−0.17)	1-51 (−0.21)
118	3-18 (0.65)	4-20 (0.61)	1-24 (−0.35)	2-36 (−0.39)
120	2-18 (0.45)	3-18 (0.46)	2-24 (−0.55)	3-34 (−0.54)
122	1-22 (0.23)	2-27 (0.28)	3-28 (−0.77)	4-43 (−0.72)
124	0-52 (0.09)	1-48 (0.13)	4-58 (−0.91)	6-00 (−0.87)

Answer

The trader might buy a butterfly spread. For example, selling a June 120 call for 2-18 and a June 120 put for 2-24 whilst buying a June 118 put for 1-24 and a June 122 call for 1-22 would achieve the objective.

The maximum profit is option receipts minus option payments:

$$(2\text{-}18 + 2\text{-}24) - (1\text{-}24 + 1\text{-}22) = 1\text{-}60$$

(This would be achieved at a futures price of 120, at which price none of the options could be profitably exercised.)

The maximum loss is 2 minus maximum profit:

$$2 - (1\text{-}60) = 0\text{-}04$$

The break-even points occur at 120 + / − 1-60, i.e. 118-04 and 121-60.

COMPARISON OF VOLATILITY TRADING STRATEGIES

Figures 6.21 and 6.22 provide comparisons of profit/loss profiles for straddles, strangles and butterflies. Figure 6.21 shows the profiles exclusive of time value (the profiles that would exist on the expiry date of the options). Figure 6.22 illustrates the profiles inclusive of time value.

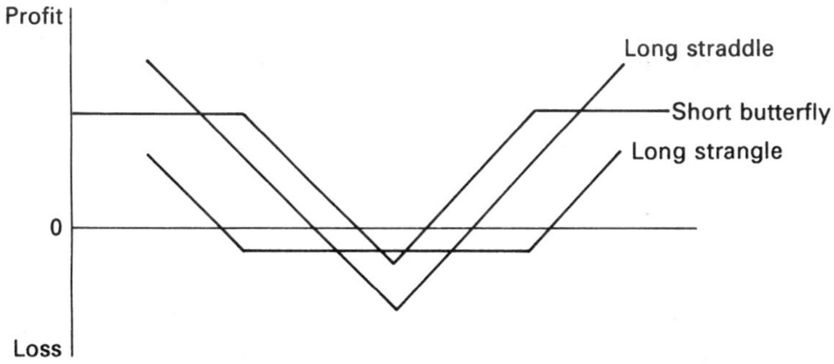

Figure 6.21 Volatility trading strategies exclusive of time value

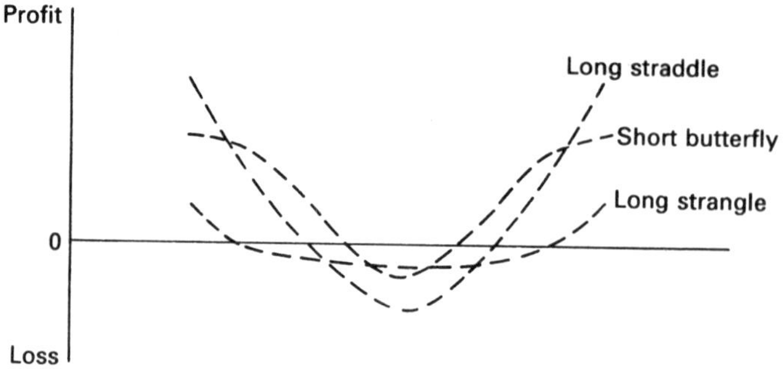

Figure 6.22 Volatility trading strategies inclusive of time value

Straddles tend to provide the highest potential profits, but also the greatest potential losses. Strangles involve a low maximum loss but a greater likelihood of it occurring. Butterflies have small potential losses but at the cost of limited profit possibilities. The volatility trading strategies thus conform to the general rule that higher potential profits are obtained at the cost of higher risk – a rule applicable to all options strategies, indeed all investments.

RATIO SPREADS

Ratio spreads can be looked upon as hybrid volatility trading strategies in that they mirror one of the basic strategies on the up side and another on the down side. Figure 6.23 illustrates the four generic possibilities.

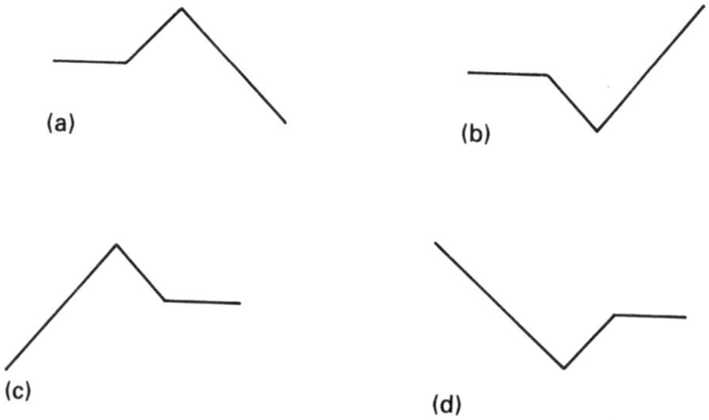

Figure 6.23 Ratio spreads: (a) call ratio spread; (b) call ratio backspread; (c) put ratio spread; (d) put ratio backspread

Call ratio spreads can be seen as involving a butterfly on the down side and a straddle on the up side. This position is created by buying calls with the lower strike price whilst writing a greater number of calls at the higher strike price. This strategy might be used by a trader who anticipates stability of the price of the underlying instrument around the higher strike price but is anxious about a possible price fall, against which he seeks protection.

The call ratio backspread can also be seen as a butterfly on the down side and a straddle on the up side. This strategy is established by writing calls at the lower strike price and buying a greater number of calls at the higher strike price. This position might be established by a bullish trader who seeks profits from movement in either direction. He feels that an upward movement is the most likely but suspects that a downward movement is possible.

The put ratio spread can be looked upon as a straddle on the down side together with a butterfly on the up side. It could be established by buying puts with the higher strike price and selling a greater number of puts at the lower strike price. Maximum profit is achieved if the price of the underlying instrument stabilises at the lower strike price. The position affords protection against a rise in the price of the underlying instrument (perhaps even providing a modest profit for prices above the higher strike price).

The put ratio backspread can also be viewed as a straddle on the down side combined with a butterfly on the up side. It could be established by means of writing puts with the higher strike price and buying a larger number of puts with the lower strike price. This position is a bearish one that is based on an anticipation of high volatility that is most likely to be manifested on the down side.

Hitherto the options trading strategies have been based on holding options either singly or in combination with each other. Trading strategies might alternatively involve options in combination with other derivatives such as futures, or with the underlying instrument.

Exercise 6.4

Question

The prices of £/$ options on the Philadelphia Stock Exchange are as shown in Table 6.7.

The spot price of sterling is $1·6000.

Suppose that a trader takes the view that the market has underestimated the future

Table 6.7

	Calls		Puts	
	April	May	April	May
1.55	4.55	5.05	0.70	1.40
1.60	1.40	2.15	2.35	3.60
1.65	0.50	0.90	6.20	7.30

volatility of the £/$ rate and that sterling is much more likely to fall than rise. Suggest a trading strategy that involves net premium receipts. What is the maximum loss from the strategy and what is the profit at expiry if the value of sterling is 10 cents higher than the spot rate when the strategy is established?

Answer
The trader might adopt a put ratio backspread. For example, he could write one May 1·65 put and buy two May 1·60 puts. (The distant expiry date options are chosen since they have the higher time value and hence greater exposure to changes in market expectations of volatility.)

The maximum loss occurs at $1·60 at expiry. The net premium received would be 0·10 cents × 12,500 = $12·50 (7·30 − 3·60 − 3·60 = 0·10). The loss from the short put (ignoring the premium) at 1·60 is

$0·05 × 12,500 = $625

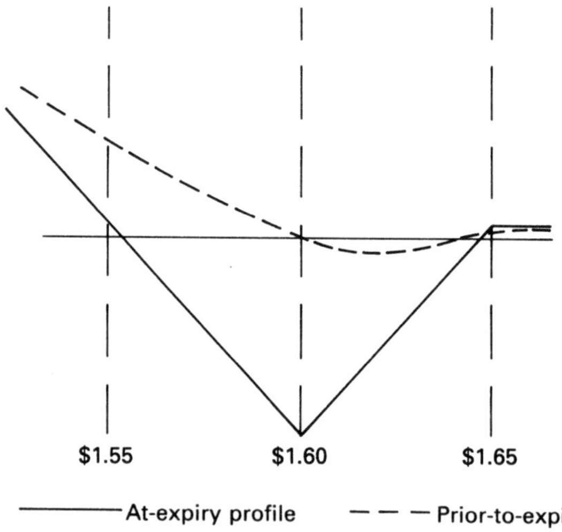

Figure 6.24 At-expiry and prior-to-expiry (immediately after establishing the position) profiles of the put ratio backspread

Therefore the net loss at \$1·60 is

$$\$625-\$12{\cdot}50=\$612{\cdot}50$$

The profit at expiry would be equal to the net premium, i.e. \$12·50, when the price of sterling is \$1·70. Neither option would be exercised, so the profit would equal the net premium receipt (see Figure 6.24).

At the moment that the options position is established there must be zero net profit/loss at the spot price of sterling (if the price and expected volatility of the underlying instrument and time to expiry have not changed, neither profit nor loss could have developed). A rise in market expectations of volatility would raise the prior-to-expiry profile (in the region of \$1·60). A decline in the price of sterling would generate a profit.

7

Arbitrage with options

Arbitrage is the process of making riskless profits from buying an instrument and simultaneously selling a similar instrument. It involves taking advantage of price anomalies such as unjustified price differences. Arbitrage with options is often pursued through the medium of creating synthetic positions.

Synthetics

A synthetic long position can be created by buying a call option and writing a put option. A synthetic short position is constructed by buying a put option and writing a call. Figure 7.1 illustrates a synthetic long position in Nogood plc stock.

The simultaneous purchase of a call option and writing of a put, both at the exercise price of 140p, creates a synthetic purchase at 140p. At prices above 140p it is worthwhile to exercise the option to buy stock at 140p, whereas below 140p the buyer of the put option could profitably exercise the option to sell at 140p. Thus above 140p the holder of the synthetic chooses to buy at 140p, whilst below 140p he is obliged to buy at 140p: either way he buys at 140p.

The line depicting the profit/loss profile of the synthetic is obtained by summing the profits or losses on the two options at each price. The assumption that the premiums for the two options are the same, at 2p, implies that the profit/loss profile of the synthetic crosses the horizontal at 140p. At 140p, the exercise price of the two options, the premium received and the premium paid are equal so that there is neither a net gain nor a net loss. This means that the synthetic is equivalent to a purchase of stock at 140p. If the option premiums had differed, the profit/loss profile of the synthetic would have intersected the horizontal at a different price, so that the synthetic would have been equivalent to a purchase at a price other

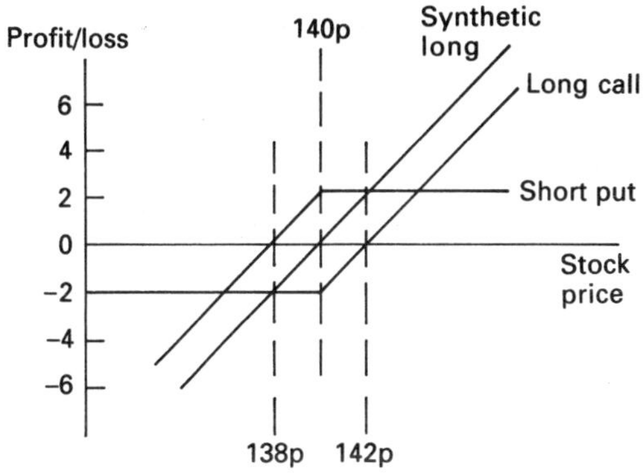

Figure 7.1 Creation of a synthetic long position

than 140p. Suppose that, in Figure 7.1, the call option premium were 3p. Then the synthetic price would be 141p, represented by the exercise price of 140p plus the net premium payment of 1p.

Figure 7.1 involves at-expiry profiles. The derivation of the synthetic futures position is, however, essentially the same when prior-to-expiry profiles are used. When a long call is combined with a short put with the same exercise price, the sum of the deltas will be approximately 1 (a long put plus a short call with the same exercise price would exhibit a combined delta of about −1). So, in Figure 7.1, any deviation of the stock price from 140p would result in a change in the net value of the options that approximately matches the price change of the stock. In other words, there is a synthetic at about 140p prior to expiry as well as at expiry.

SYNTHETIC FTSE 100 POSITIONS

By combining FTSE 100 stock index options (traded on the London Traded Options Market) it is possible to produce synthetic positions in a stock index. For example, simultaneously establishing long call and short put positions at the same exercise price effectively generates a long position.

If the FTSE index turns out to be less than the exercise price, the short put obliges the transactor to buy at the exercise price (the exercise price in this context refers to an FTSE index). This 'purchase' would take the form of a compensation payment to the option buyer to make up the difference between sales receipts at actual market prices and those that would have been received if the FTSE index had turned out to be at the exercise price. If

Table 7.1 Chicago Mercantile Exchange futures prices

	Sterling currency	Deutschmark currency
June	1.8405	0.6056

Table 7.2 Philadelphia Stock Exchange £/US$ options

Strike price	Calls (June)	Puts (June)
1.825	5.20	3.45
1.850	3.95	4.70

the FTSE index turns out to be higher than the exercise price, the transactor will 'purchase' at the exercise price (he would receive compensation for having to buy at the higher prices ruling in the market). So whatever the FTSE index turns out to be, the transactor effectively buys at the stock prices that correspond to the index implied by the synthetic. Likewise a short call and long put at the same exercise price produce a synthetic short position.

Exercise 7.1

Question
It is 15 March and the information given in Tables 7.1–7.3 is available. Compare the DM/£ exchange rates implied by the currency futures with those implicit in the options prices.

Answer
Rate implied by futures:

$$(\text{DM}/\pounds) = (\text{DM}/\$) \times (\$/\pounds) = (1{\cdot}8405/0{\cdot}6056) = 3{\cdot}0391$$

Rates implied by options:

Synthetic (DM/\$)	0·60 + 0·0002 = 0·6002		
	0·61 − 0·0093 = 0·6007		
Synthetic (£/\$)	1·825 + 0·0175 = 1·8425		
	1·850 − 0·0075 = 1·8425		
Cross-rates (DM/£)			(1·8425)
		(0·6002)	3·0698
		(0·6007)	3·0673

The rates implied are 3·0698 and 3·0673.

Table 7.3 Philadelphia Stock Exchange DM/US$ options

Strike price	Calls (June)	Puts (June)
0.60	1.20	1.18
0.61	0.77	1.70

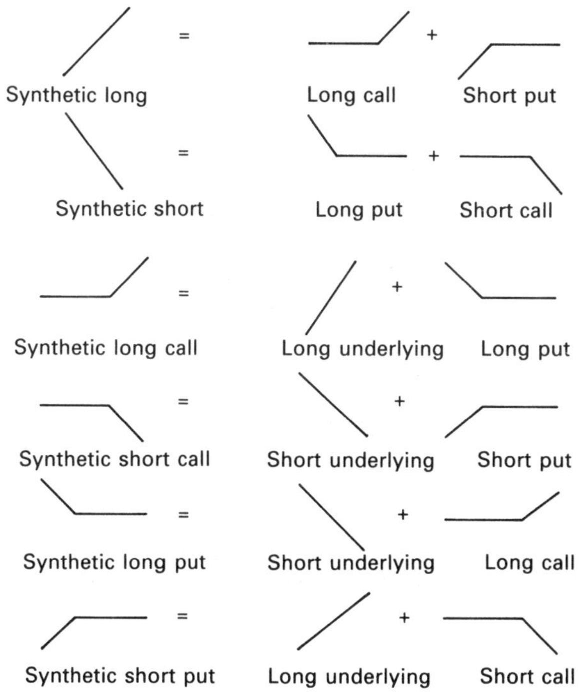

Figure 7.2 Synthetics and their components

Figure 7.2 shows the feasible synthetics together with their components. The profit/loss profile of each instrument is illustrated.

Reversals, conversions and options boxes

A reversal involves the construction of a synthetic long position and the simultaneous holding of a short position in the underlying instrument (which may take the form of a short futures position). The difference

Table 7.4

Strike price	Calls	Puts
92.75	0.40	0.07
93.00	0.19	0.18
93.25	0.10	0.28
93.50	0.04	0.46

between the synthetic price obtained and the market price is locked in for the duration of the reversal, since profits/losses on the underlying instrument would be matched by losses/profits on the synthetic. This is a technique for locking in a profit on one or more of the component instruments (since an overall profit must arise from the mispricing of one or more of the components), and it provides an alternative to closing out. By closing out a position the profit (or loss) is realised immediately, whereas a reversal delays the realisation of the profit without putting it in jeopardy.

Exercise 7.2

Question
The December eurodollar futures price is 93·08, whilst December eurodollar futures options prices are as shown in Table 7.4.
What is the best arbitrage opportunity?

Answer
The best arbitrage opportunity arises from buying a 93 call, selling a 93 put and selling a futures contract. The buying price of the synthetic is

$$93{\cdot}00 + 0{\cdot}19 - 0{\cdot}18 = 93{\cdot}01$$

whilst the selling price of the futures contract is 93·08.

A conversion involves the creation of a synthetic short position together with holding a simultaneous long position. Again it is a technique for postponing the realisation of a profit whilst guaranteeing the size of the profit to be realised. An options box consists of a synthetic long together with a synthetic short and serves the same function as conversions and reversals.

Since it is possible to close out a synthetic position (by means of closing sales and purchases) at any time between the present and the expiry date,

Table 7.5

Number	Share	Price	Beta
1,000	Barclays	416	0.85
1,000	Whitbread 'A'	292	0.90
1,000	Marks and Spencer	170	0.75
1,000	Thorn EMI	666	0.95
1,000	Grand Metropolitan	451	0.80
1,000	Commercial Union	339	0.88

Table 7.6

	Calls	Puts
1800	74	20
1850	39	36
1900	23	72

the synthetic price created can be regarded either as a synthetic spot price or as a synthetic futures price. Likewise synthetics can be arbitraged against either spot or futures instruments.

Exercise 7.3

Question
It is 27 October. An investor holds the portfolio shown in Table 7.5.
The FTSE 100 index stands at 1850.
November FTSE 100 option prices include those given in Table 7.6.

(a) Do the options provide opportunities for profitable arbitrage?
(b) Suggest two strategies for reducing the risk on the portfolio whilst avoiding initial premium outlay.
(c) On 11 November the FTSE 100 index stands at 1780. For both strategies suggest (with appropriate calculations and explanations) a plausible net profit/loss outcome from the options on the assumption that none of the options was exercised prior to 11 November.

Answer
(a) The implied FTSE 100 indices are 1854, 1853 and 1851 from the 1800, 1850 and 1900 options respectively. An options box involving 1800 and 1900 options should yield an arbitrage profit. Buying an 1800 put and writing an 1800 call produces a synthetic short at 1854. Buying a 1900 call and writing a 1900 put produces a synthetic long at 1851. However, this arbitrage opportunity will not be available if bid–offer spreads are not sufficiently fine.

(b) The market exposure provided by the portfolio is calculated thus:

$$\begin{aligned}&\pounds4{,}160 \times 0{\cdot}85\\&+\pounds2{,}920 \times 0{\cdot}90\\&+\pounds1{,}700 \times 0{\cdot}75\\&+\pounds6{,}660 \times 0{\cdot}95\\&+\pounds4{,}510 \times 0{\cdot}80\\&+\pounds3{,}390 \times 0{\cdot}88 = \pounds20{,}357{\cdot}2\end{aligned}$$

One strategy would be to buy an 1800 put for 20 and finance it by writing an 1800 call at 74: that is, a synthetic short FTSE 100 futures position is created. (The 1800 strike price options give a slightly better selling price than the 1850 options.)

Another strategy would be to use a cylinder. An 1800 put could be bought and a 1900 call written.

(c) The synthetic short would involve a put with an intrinsic value of 20. Time value might plausibly be 20 for the put and 22 for the call. So the long put would be worth £400 and the short call £220, providing a net value of £180 for a position that originally involved a receipt of £540. So there is an overall profit of £720.

The cylinder would involve an in-the-money long put which has intrinsic value of 20. Its time value might be 20. The deep out-of-the-money call would have little time value, possibly 4. The long put would thus have a price of 40 and the short call a price of 4. The position cost −3 to establish (there was a net receipt of 3). The net profit is thus (40−4+3) × £10 = £390.

Put/call parity

Put/call parity suggests that the put and the call should have the same time value when they are identical with respect to the underlying instrument, the strike price and the expiry date. If this equality of time values does not hold, there may be arbitrage profits available from the use of reversals or conversions.

However, when the anticipated rate of return on an asset differs from the financing cost of holding that asset, the 'no arbitrage' condition is not equality of the time values: in other words, put/call parity (in the above form) would not be expected to exist. The time values would differ to the same extent as the return on the asset differs from the financing cost.

Suppose, for example, that put/call parity held for a particular stock but that the financing cost was at 10 per cent p.a. whilst the expected dividend yield was 5 per cent p.a. The existence of put/call parity implies that the price of the stock is equal to the price at which a synthetic futures position can be created (the price generated by the synthetic being the strike price plus the intrinsic value of the call or minus the intrinsic value of the put). In other words, an investor could guarantee a future buying price equal to the present price. It would be possible for that investor to take a long synthetic position, deposit the funds at 10 per cent p.a. and then acquire the shares through the synthetic. The shares would be acquired at the same price but in the interim the 10 per cent p.a. on the deposited money would exceed the 5 per cent p.a. dividends forgone. In such a situation the 'no arbitrage' condition would involve the call option time value exceeding the put option time value to the extent required to raise the synthetic futures price above the spot price just enough to match the excess of the financing cost (return on deposits) over the expected dividend yield. (Note that when buying by means of synthetics it is advisable to avoid short option positions that are in the money since such options run a significant risk of early exercise: that is, exercise before the expiry date.)

An alternative form of put/call parity takes this into account by discounting the exercise price in order to convert it into a present value. The synthetic purchase or sale is treated as occurring on the expiry date of the options and the price is discounted to the present in order to render it comparable with the spot price. Put/call parity in this form uses the difference between the spot price and the discounted exercise price in place of the intrinsic value. In equation form it can be expressed as follows:

$$C-P=S-\frac{K}{(1+rt)}$$

(the continuously compounding formulation would be $C-P=S-\frac{K}{(1+r)^t}$ or $C-P=S-Ke^{-rt}$) where

C = call price
P = put price
S = spot price
K = strike price
r = interest rate (annualised)
t = number of days to expiry date divided by 365
e = natural logarithm

This is an alternative put/call parity formulation to the previous one: $C-P=S-K$.

$C-P=S-K$ states that the excess of the call price over the put price is equal to the extent that the call option is in the money, and hence that the time values are equal. $C-P=S-[K/(1+rt)]$ implies that the excess of the call price over the put price is greater than the intrinsic value of the call option and hence that the time value of the call exceeds that of the put.

It is to be noted that the formulation above discounts with the interest rate rather than with the excess of the interest rate over the expected dividend yield. If dividends are expected during the relevant time period, the difference between the interest rate and the expected dividend yield would be the appropriate rate of discount.

The put/call parity relationship is used in Appendix II to analyse further the Black–Scholes option pricing model.

Making riskless profits from mispriced options

Perhaps the first response to the observation that an option is mispriced is to buy if it is cheap and write if it is expensive. Such positions, however, leave the trader exposed to adverse market movements. The profit potential is accompanied by risk; indeed, it is likely that a small profit potential is accompanied by substantial risk. In such a situation it would make sense to seek to profit from the mispriced option by means of a delta-neutral strategy: in other words, a strategy which involves no net exposure to movements in the price of the underlying financial instrument. What follows is based on LIFFE long gilt futures options, but most of the principles involved are readily adaptable to other types of option.

Suppose it is 24 May and the prices of September long gilt futures options are as shown in Table 7.7 (deltas in brackets). The September long gilt futures price is 95-15.

An analyst concludes that the 96 calls are underpriced. A valuation trading strategy would involve buying 96 calls whilst adopting an offsetting position elsewhere so as to achieve zero net market exposure. The offsetting position might involve writing other calls, buying puts or taking a short position in the underlying futures contracts.

This strategy would require ratios based on option deltas. For example, three 92 puts could be bought in order to offset each 96 call (the delta of $3 \times -0{\cdot}15$ offsets the delta of $0{\cdot}45$). Alternatively, nine futures contracts could be sold to offset every twenty 96 calls bought (the delta of $9 \times -1{\cdot}00$ offsets the delta of $20 \times 0{\cdot}45$).

Such valuation trading strategies require constant rebalancing as deltas change and it is likely that there is not a complete offset. The need for constant monitoring accompanied by the buying/selling required to minimise net exposure can be expensive, and the fact that complete neutrality would be rarely obtained leaves the position open to risk.

Table 7.7

Strike price	Calls	Puts
90	5-38 (0.96)	0-08 (−0.04)
92	3-50 (0.85)	0-20 (−0.15)
94	2-13 (0.65)	0-47 (−0.35)
96	0-49 (0.45)	1-35 (−0.55)
98	0-26 (0.25)	2-60 (−0.75)
100	0-09 (0.08)	4-43 (−0.92)
102	0-06 (0.02)	6-40 (−0.98)

An alternative strategy would be an arbitrage using reversals. (There is some confusion between conversions and reversals. For present purposes I shall consider a synthetic long position combined with a short futures position to be a reversal – and a short synthetic with a long futures to be a conversion.) This would avoid the need for monitoring and rebalancing whilst achieving complete delta neutrality (i.e. no net exposure to movements in the price of the underlying futures contract).

A synthetic long futures can be created by buying a call and writing a put. In order to profit from the underpriced 96 call, the trader would buy a 96 call, write a 96 put and sell a futures contract. The effective buying price would be

$$96 + 0\text{-}49 - 1\text{-}35 = 95\text{-}14$$

when expressed in 1/64ths. Although long gilt futures options are priced in 1/64ths, the long gilt futures are priced in 1/32nds. So the above price is equivalent to a long gilt futures price of 95-7.

The synthetic thus generates a buying price of 95-7 when the price of the futures contract is 95-15. So it is possible to buy at 95-7 and simultaneously sell at 95-15. An arbitrage profit of 8/32nds is generated, which amounts to £125 (8 × £15·625) for each combination of one long call, one short put and one short futures. Whilst holding the reversal the arbitrageur has no net exposure to movements in the price of the futures contract. In other words, the net delta is zero:

$$0{\cdot}45 - (-0{\cdot}55) - 1{\cdot}00 = 0$$

An alternative strategy involves three-month sterling interest rate futures. Suppose that the June long gilt futures price is 95-26 and the interest yield implied by the June long gilt futures price is 10·37 per cent p.a. (the coupon divided by the product of the futures price and the price factor of the cheapest-to-deliver gilt), whilst the June three-month sterling futures price is 91·06.

By taking a short position in June long gilt futures and simultaneously constructing a synthetic long futures position for September, a three-month borrowing rate can be synthesised. The June futures price is 95-26 and the synthetic September futures price is 95-7, whilst the interest yield implied by the June long gilt futures price is 10·37 per cent p.a. This implies a three-month borrowing rate of 7·87 per cent p.a. (subtracting the rate of depreciation implied by the June price of 95-26 and the September price of 95-7 from the interest yield of 10·37 per cent p.a.). June three-month sterling futures imply an interest rate of 8·94 per cent p.a.

The ability to lock in a borrowing rate of 7·87 per cent p.a. along with a lending rate of 8·94 per cent p.a. could be used to generate a low-risk profit. This might be achieved by selling twenty-one June long gilt futures, synthesising a long position in twenty-one September futures and buying two three-month sterling interest rate futures. (Twenty-one June long gilt futures at a price of 95-26 gives an exposure of £1,006,031; twenty-one synthetic long gilt futures at a price of 95-7 gives an exposure of £999,797; so there is an average gilt futures exposure of £1,002,914 against a three-month sterling exposure of £1,000,000).

This latter type of strategy would be particularly attractive if the June long gilt futures price were higher than expected and the June three-month sterling interest rate futures price appeared to be low.

Exercise 7.4

Question

Given the option prices for 9% Nov/2018 T-bonds shown in Table 7.8:
Accrued interest by 23 February is 1·06.
Accrued interest by 23 May is 3·21.
How could forward interest rates be locked in using synthetics and what might those rates be?

Answer

A synthetic long position using February 114 options would involve

Buy 1 call at $\frac{5}{8}$.
Sell 1 put at $2\frac{7}{16}$.

The effective purchase price of a synthetic long position for the end of February is

$$114+\tfrac{5}{8}-2\tfrac{7}{16}+1{\cdot}06=113{\cdot}2475$$

Table 7.8

	Call	Put
February 114	$\frac{1}{2}$–$\frac{5}{8}$	$2\frac{7}{16}$–$\frac{9}{16}$
May 112	$1\frac{1}{2}$–$\frac{5}{8}$	$1\frac{5}{8}$–$\frac{7}{8}$

A synthetic short position using May 112 options would involve

Buy 1 put at $1\frac{7}{8}$.
Sell 1 call at $1\frac{1}{2}$.

The effective sale price of the synthetic short position for the end of May is

$$112-1\tfrac{7}{8}+1\tfrac{1}{2}+3{\cdot}21=114{\cdot}835$$
$$113{\cdot}2475(1+i)=114{\cdot}835$$
$$1+i=1{\cdot}014$$

Annualised lending rate is 5·73% p.a. (using continuous compounding).
A synthetic short position using February 114 options would involve

Buy 1 put at $2\frac{9}{16}$.
Sell 1 call at $\frac{1}{2}$.

The effective sale price of a synthetic short position for the end of February is

$$114-2\tfrac{9}{16}+\tfrac{1}{2}+1{\cdot}06=112{\cdot}9975$$

A synthetic long position using May 112 options would involve

Buy 1 call at $1\frac{5}{8}$.
Sell 1 put at $1\frac{5}{8}$.

The effective purchase price of a synthetic long position for the end of May is

$$112+1\tfrac{5}{8}-1\tfrac{5}{8}+3{\cdot}21=115{\cdot}21$$
$$112{\cdot}9975(1+i)=115{\cdot}21$$
$$1+i=1{\cdot}0196$$

Annualised borrowing rate is 8·065% p.a. (using continuous compounding).

8

Derivatives in portfolio management

Previous chapters have considered ways in which derivatives can be used by portfolio managers. These include buying stock, gilt or stock index puts in order to protect the value of a portfolio, buying calls in order to obtain protection against price rises prior to purchase, using short or long stock index or bond futures for the same purposes, and so forth. This chapter will describe some uses of derivatives not hitherto considered.

Covered writing

Covered writing refers to selling call options corresponding to assets held or selling put options when the liquidity for the purchase of the underlying instrument is held. So covered writing involves the portfolio manager being prepared for the eventuality of being exercised against.

It may be the case that a portfolio manager has in mind a share price at which he would be prepared to buy and another at which he would be prepared to sell. For example, he might be prepared to buy more shares in XYZ plc if the share price falls to 180p and sell some of his existing holding if the price reaches 220p. In such a situation it would make sense for the fund manager to write 180p puts and write 220p calls. Writing these options would provide premium receipts whilst bringing about the desired transactions in the event of the share price passing 180p or 220p.

Covered writing would also be a strategy that arises from a view that the market will be stable for a period of time.

Using call options in a stable market

If a fund manager expects the market to be stable (and if he considers that other market participants have, on average, underestimated the stability), writing call options that are covered by his portfolio is a rational strategy. The premiums received from such covered writing augment the returns on the portfolio.

The analysis can be expressed in terms of options on individual stocks covered by holdings of those stocks (for delivery if the option writer is assigned) or in terms of stock index options covered by a portfolio of stocks (which can be partially liquidated in order to provide any requisite cash settlement). The analysis will be based on the FTSE 100 stock index options.

Suppose it is 15 April and a fund manager has a balanced portfolio of UK equities with a value of £1,000,000 and a beta of approximately 1. (A beta of 1 suggests that each 1 per cent move in the market as a whole would cause a 1 per cent change in the value of the portfolio.) Suppose further that the FTSE 100 index stands at 1787 and the FTSE 100 call options for April expiry with a strike price of 1800 are priced at 20. The fund manager can write up to fifty-five option contracts whilst being fully covered: £1,000,000/£17,870 = 55·96. Note that the denominator is £10 multiplied by the current index rather than £10 multiplied by the strike price. (If the options were exercised, the effective value of the portfolio would be £1,000,000 × (1800/1787) = £1,007,275, which when divided by £18,000 gives 55·96, the number previously obtained. The need to divide by the current index multiplied by £10 rather than by the strike price multiplied by £10 can be seen more readily by reference to the case of equity options. Ten thousand Jaguar shares would be covered by ten option contracts. So if the share price were 270p and the strike price 300p, the appropriate number of contracts is £27,000/£2,700 rather than £27,000/£3,000.)

Writing fifty-five contracts would yield 55 × £200 = £11,000 (ignoring the bid–offer spread and other transactions costs). This yield is in addition to the dividend yield from the shares held. The drawback is that, if the market rises by more than thirteen points over the two weeks remaining to expiry, the fund manager will forgo any market rise beyond those thirteen points, so this strategy would be attractive only if no strong market rise in the short term is expected.

RATES OF RETURN

The yield can be expressed as a rate of return. For convenience, dividend yields and transactions costs will be ignored.

Initial value of portfolio	£1,000,000
Less option premiums received	– £ 11,000
Net cash investment	£ 989,000

The potential rate of return can be expressed as 'return if unchanged' or as 'return if exercised'. The 'return if unchanged' is the rate of return in the event of the FTSE 100 index remaining at 1787, in which event the 1800 calls would not be exercised:

Unchanged value of portfolio	£1,000,000
Less net cash investment	−£ 989,000
Profit	£ 11,000

Rate of return = £11,000/£989,000 or 1·11 per cent, which is approximately 30 per cent on an annualised basis. It is to be noted that the appropriate denominator is the net cash investment and not the value of the portfolio.

When ascertaining the 'return if exercised' it is necessary to take into account the profit on the portfolio arising from the market movement:

Portfolio value upon exercise	£1,007,275	(£1,000,000 × 1800/1787)
Less net cash investment	£ 989,000	
Profit	£ 18,275	

Rate of return = £18,275/£989,000 or 1·85 per cent, which is approximately 55 per cent on an annualised basis. It is to be noted that in the case of FTSE 100 options 'portfolio value upon exercise' refers to the new value of the original portfolio minus the cash settlement made upon assignment.

Of course incorporating the bid–offer spread and the other transactions costs would slightly reduce the rates of return. Recognition of the bid–offer spread would reduce the option premiums received and option sale commissions raise the net cash investment.

Exercise 8.1

Question

It is 15 March.

FTSE option prices on the London Traded Options Market are as shown in Table 8.1.

The FTSE 100 index is 1839.

A portfolio manager has a balanced fund worth £1,000,000, with a beta equal to the beta of the FTSE 100 index. Describe a strategy that could be pursued in order to increase returns in a stable market environment. Ignoring transactions costs and dividend receipts, calculate the rate of return achieved if on the option expiry date the FTSE 100 index is (a) 1750, (b) 1839 and (c) 1950.

Table 8.1

	Calls			Puts		
Strike price	March	April	May	March	April	May
1800	64	88	110	23	47	65
1850	35	60	83	45	73	88
1900	16	38	60	77	103	115

Answer

Write April 1850 call options. The number of contracts required for near-complete cover is fifty-four (£1,000,000/£18,390=54·38).

Value of stock	£1,000,000
Less option premiums received	−£ 32,400
Net cash investment	£ 967,600

In cases (a) and (b) the option would be unexercised

(a)	Value of stock	£ 951,604	$\left(\frac{1750}{1839} \times £1{,}000{,}000\right)$
	Less net cash investment	−£ 967,600	
	Net profit/loss	−£ 15,996	

Rate of return $\frac{-£\ 15{,}996}{£\ 967{,}600} \times 100 = -1{\cdot}65\%$ (−13·2% on an annualised basis)

(b)	Value of stock	£1,000,000	
	Less net cash investment	−£ 967,600	
	Net profit/loss	£ 32,400	

Rate of return $\frac{-£\ 32{,}400}{£\ 967{,}600} \times 100 = 3{\cdot}35\%$ (−26·79% on an annualised basis)

In case (c) the option would be exercised

(c)	Value of stock	£1,005,982	$\left(\frac{1850}{1839} \times £1{,}000{,}000\right)$
	Less net cash investment	−£ 967,600	
	Net profit/loss	£ 38,382	

Rate of return $\frac{-£\ 38{,}382}{£\ 967{,}600} \times 100 = 3{\cdot}97\%$ (−31·76% on an annualised basis)

(In case (c) the rate of return would be a little higher than indicated since 0·38/54·38 = 0·7% of the portfolio would not be matched by options and would therefore benefit from the full rise in the index to 1950.)

DOWNSIDE PROTECTION

The option premiums received can be looked upon as providing some protection against a fall in the value of the portfolio. In the above case, a decline in the value of the original portfolio to £989,000 after writing the options would leave the fund manager in his original position of holding assets to the value of £1 million (£989,000 plus the option premiums received of £11,000). The written options might thus be regarded as providing 1·1 per cent downside protection.

Thus covered call writes provide additional yield, which can be interpreted as downside protection, at the cost of forgoing some (or all) of the upside potential. Obviously different option series provide different configurations of additional yield (downside protection) and upside potential.

Exercise 8.2

Question

It is 12 August, the price of GEC shares is 221p and the option prices are as shown in Table 8.2.

A portfolio manager holds 100,000 shares. Suggest (a) a high-risk/high-reward, (b) a low-risk/low-reward covered write strategy. Calculate the percentage return from the covered write on a 'return if exercised' and a 'return if unchanged' basis for each of the two strategies. Also calculate the percentage downside protection. (Assume that no dividends are due before expiry and that the commission on option sales is £10 per contract whilst stock sale commission is 1% of the total.)

Answer

(a) Writing 240 calls would be a suitable strategy (producing a synthetic short put).

(b) Writing 200 calls would be a suitable strategy (producing a synthetic short put).

(When ascertaining which strategy is high-risk/high-reward and which is low-risk/low-reward, the relevant profiles are those of the options combined with the underlying instrument: in other words, the synthetic short puts.)

Distant-dated options might be more appropriate for (a) and near-dated options

Table 8.2

	Calls			Puts		
	October	January	April	October	January	April
200	29	37	48	4	9	13
220	16	25	36	11	17	20
240	8	15	26	23	28	32

for (b). On the assumption that the sale of 100 options does not affect the premium and that October options are chosen, the percentage returns could be calculated thus:

		£
(a)	Stock cost (100,000 shares at 221p)	221,000
	Less option premiums received	– 8,000
	Plus option sale commissions	1,000
	Net cash investment	214,000

	£
'Return if exercised'	
Stock sale proceeds (100,000 at 240p)	240,000
Less net cash investment	–214,000
Less stock sale commissions	– 2,400
Net profit if exercised	23,600

$$\text{Return if exercised } (\%) = \frac{£23,600}{£214,000} \times 100 = 11{\cdot}0\%$$

	£
'Return if unchanged'	
Unchanged stock value	221,000
Less net cash investment	214,000
Profit if unchanged	7,000

$$\text{Return if unchanged } (\%) = \frac{£7,000}{£214,000} \times 100 = 3{\cdot}3\%$$

		£
(b)	Stock cost (100,000 at 221p)	221,000
	Less option premiums received	– 29,000
	Plus option sale commissions	1,000
	Net cash investment	193,000

	£
'Return if exercised'	
Stock sale proceeds (100,000 at 200p)	200,000
Less net cash investment	−193,000
Less stock sale commissions	− 2,000
Net profit if exercised	5,000

$$\text{Return if exercised (\%)} = \frac{£5,000}{£193,000} \times 100 = 2{\cdot}6\%$$

'Return if unchanged'

If the price remained at 221p the options would be exercised and therefore the 'return if unchanged' would be equal to the 'return if exercised'.

The percentage downside protection is calculated thus:

(a) $$\text{Break-even price} = \frac{\text{Net cash investment}}{\text{Number of shares}} = \frac{£214,000}{100,000} = 214\text{p}$$

Initial stock price	221
Less break-even price	−214
Points of protection	7

As a % of original stock price 7/221 × 100 = 3·2%

(b) $$\text{Break-even price} = \frac{\text{Net cash investment}}{\text{Number of shares}} = \frac{£193,000}{100,000} = 193\text{p}$$

Initial stock price	221
Less break-even price	−193
Points of protection	28

As a % of original stock price 28/221 × 100 = 12·7%

(Note that the points of downside protection equal the option premium minus the option sale commission, i.e. the net receipts from the sale of the options.)

HIGHER REWARDS WITH LOWER RISKS

Whether the premium receipts are interpreted as additional yield or downside protection, the strategy of covered call writing can improve the risk/reward trade-off. The statistical variance of the possible profit/loss outcome is reduced by the curtailment of upside potential, and since statistical variance is regarded as a measure of risk it follows that risk is reduced. Meanwhile the premium receipts are increasing the returns on the portfolio. So higher rewards are accompanied by lower risks (although a reduction of 'risk' that entails curtailment of the up side but not of the down side must be regarded as a dubious benefit).

Interpretation of the premium receipts as downside protection rather than as additional yield seems to imply that the covered call write dampens both upside and downside movements, thus reducing risk whilst leaving expected returns unchanged (although it might be argued that expected returns, in the sense of statistical expectation, are changed since the nature of the upside curtailment differs from that of the downside protection).

CONVERTING A COVERED CALL WRITE INTO A SHORT STRADDLE

A covered call write effectively produces a synthetic short put (see Figure 8.1). By writing further call options a short straddle can be constructed (see Figure 8.2). It is to be noted that this short straddle is not constructed in the usual way by writing calls and puts. It is constructed by writing calls in conjunction with a portfolio of shares.

Since twice as many calls are being written, compared with the covered call write previously discussed, the addition to the yield is twice as much. However, losses can now be incurred as a result of movements of the stock index in either direction. The fund manager must be sure that the index will remain close to the strike price of the options.

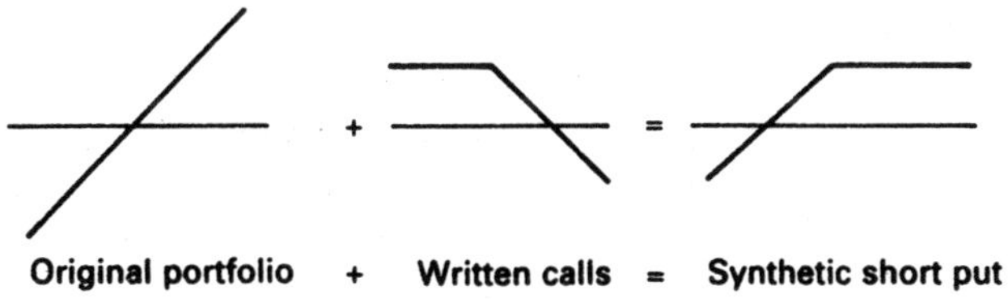

Figure 8.1 Synthetic short put from a covered call write

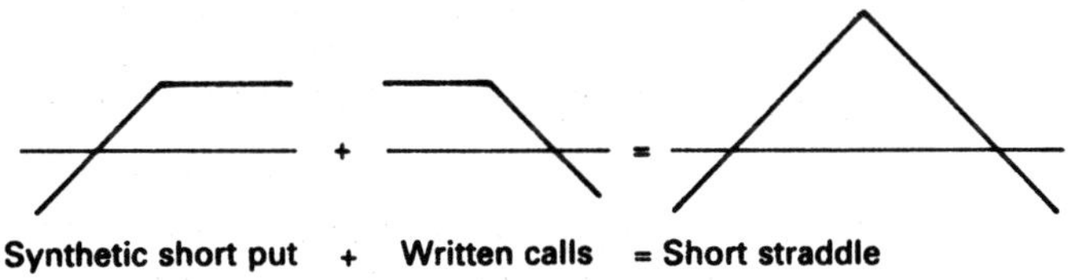

Figure 8.2 Converting a covered call write into a short straddle

Table 8.3

	Calls			Puts		
	August	September	October	August	September	October
2200	107	140	165	10	28	42
2250	72	105	132	25	45	60
2300	40	77	103	47	68	83
2350	20	55	78	75	95	105
2400	10	37	57	122	128	135

Exercise 8.3

Question

It is 12 August and the FTSE 100 index stands at 2286·1.
The prices of the FTSE 100 options are as shown in Table 8.3.
A fund manager with a balanced equity portfolio of £10 million does not initially want to take a position that is not covered by current assets but wants to use options to increase returns on the existing portfolio. However, he feels that he could subsequently decide to relax his fully covered requirement in order to take a position based on an expectation of low volatility. Suggest a strategy.

Answer

The fund manager could decide to write calls. Since the position could subsequently be adjusted to a volatility trade, at-the-money calls would seem appropriate. The 2300 calls are the nearest to being at the money. Each 2300 call corresponds to £23,000 of stock on exercise.

$$\frac{£10{,}000{,}000}{£22{,}861} = 437{\cdot}4 \text{ (£22,861 = FTSE 100 index} \times \text{£10)}$$

The fund manager can write up to 437 call options whilst remaining fully covered by current assets. (If the index rose to 2300, the value of the portfolio would move to £10,000,000 × (2300/2286·1) = £10,060,802. This is the maximum value of the portfolio since beyond 2300 the calls would be exercised: £10,060,802/£23,000 = 437·4.)

Taking a position that would profit from low volatility might be achieved by writing further 2300 call options. For example, writing a further 437 call options creates a synthetic short straddle.

VALUATION TRADING

The fund manager could be indulging in a form of valuation trading. He writes the call options because he considers them to be overpriced. It would seem to be irrational for him to sell underpriced options. Individual estimates of fair prices depend upon individual estimates of market volatility. The current price of an option reflects the market's expectation of volatility. An individual market participant will consider the option to be overpriced if he considers that volatility will be less than the market expects. Hence the statement in parentheses in the sentence on page 148, 'and if he considers that other market participants have, on average, underestimated the stability'.

Using bond futures to reduce portfolio volatility

One definition of volatility, known as perturbation, uses the impact of a specific interest rate change (e.g. 1 per cent) on the price of the bond. Another definition of volatility, namely duration, is the relationship between the percentage (proportionate) change in the value of the bond and the percentage (proportionate) change in $(1+r)$ that caused it, where r is the redemption yield. Although the percentage change in $(1+r)$ is closely related to the change in the percentage rate of interest, the two are not identical.

A fund manager may feel that in order to render volatilities of different bonds comparable (in particular the volatilities of the hedged bond and the cheapest-to-deliver bond) volatility needs to be expressed in terms of perturbation. However, he may find that the available data relate to duration. The first task is then one of converting duration into a measure that is closer to perturbation. The following expression achieves this:

$$(\text{Duration} \times \text{Clean price})/(1+\text{Redemption yield})$$

Division by (1 + Redemption yield) changes the formulation

$$\frac{\text{Proportionate change in price}}{\text{Proportionate change in } (1+r)} \text{ into } \frac{\text{Proportionate change in price}}{\text{Absolute change in } (1+r)}$$

Multiplication by the clean price converts proportionate changes in price into absolute changes in price. These adjustments convert duration into

$$\frac{\text{Change in price}}{\text{Change in } (1+\text{Redemption yield})}$$

which is equivalent to

$$\frac{\text{Change in price}}{\text{Change in redemption yield}}$$

Table 8.4

Clean price	Duration	Price factor	Redemption yield
111-04	7.248	1.0363064	11.1

This expression differs from perturbation only in using the change in redemption yield rather than the change in the rate of interest as denominator. Changes in redemption yields and changes in interest rates tend to be closely related to each other.

The risk of a portfolio is greatly affected by the volatility of the individual assets which belong to that portfolio. Volatility is a corollary of market exposure: an increase in volatility is a consequence of greater exposure and vice versa. Reducing exposure with futures entails diminution of volatility. To illustrate the use of futures to reduce volatility the example of a bond holding will be used.

Suppose it is 10 January and a fund manager holds £10 million nominal of Treasury 11¾% 03/07. The clean price is 104-16, the duration 7·122 and the redemption yield 10·9. The volatility of this gilt holding is deemed to be too great and the fund manager decides to use futures in order to halve the volatility. Suppose further that the cheapest to deliver into the March long gilt futures contract is the Treasury 12½% 03/05 which has the characteristics shown in Table 8.4.

The volatility of the holding of Treasury 11¾% 03/07 can be expressed as follows:

$$\text{Nominal value (in millions)} \times \text{Duration} \times \text{Clean price} \times \frac{1}{(1+r)} \times \frac{1}{100}$$

$$\text{i.e.} \quad \frac{10 \times 7{\cdot}122 \times 104{\cdot}5}{100 \times 1{\cdot}109} = 67{\cdot}110$$

Halving the volatility would require the elimination of about 33·555. An amount of volatility approximately equal to this can be eliminated by taking a short position in long gilt futures.

The volatility per £1 million nominal of cheapest to deliver (Treasury 12½% 03/05) is as follows:

$$\frac{7{\cdot}248 \times 111{\cdot}125}{100 \times 1{\cdot}111} = 7{\cdot}25$$

The number of futures contracts required to cover £1 million nominal of the cheapest to deliver is as follows:

$$(1{,}000{,}000/50{,}000) \times 1{\cdot}0363064 = 20{\cdot}726$$

It follows that the number of futures contracts that need to be sold in order to eliminate 33·555 from the volatility is as follows:

$$(33{\cdot}555/7{\cdot}25) \times 20{\cdot}726 = 95{\cdot}926$$

So the volatility of the gilt holding would be approximately halved by the sale of 96 March long gilt futures contracts.

The fund manager does not, unfortunately, reduce the volatility of his portfolio at zero cost. The greater the extent to which volatility is eliminated, the closer the portfolio yield moves towards that on completely risk-free assets (which for present purposes might be regarded as the interest rate on three-month deposits).

This situation arises from the cash-and-carry arbitrage that determines gilt futures prices. If the running yield on the cheapest to deliver exceeds the interest to be paid on money used to finance the holding of the gilts, the basis will be such as to provide a loss from the short futures position (relative to the long gilt position) so as to cancel out the excess of the running yield over the financing cost. Arbitrage will ensure that the futures price lies below the cash price so that convergence would provide a loss from the combined cash and futures position sufficient to bring the net return into line with short-term money rates. Consequently, to the extent that a portfolio is matched with a short position in gilt futures, the futures would tend to bring the return on the portfolio into line with short-term money market rates.

Exercise 8.4

Question

It is 1 February and a gilt portfolio holder wishes to extend the average maturity of the portfolio whilst avoiding increasing the volatility of the portfolio.

The information shown in Table 8.5 is available.

Accrued interest on Treasury 11¾% 03/07 is 3-02. Accrued interest on Exchequer 15% 97 is 4-29.

The cheapest to deliver into the March long gilt futures contract is the Treasury 9½% 03/05 which has the characteristics shown in Table 8.6.

He sells £10 million nominal of Exchequer 15% 97 and uses the proceeds to buy Treasury 11¾% 03/07. How can expected volatility be maintained at the original level? (For the purposes of this exercise assume that there is no significant difference between the redemption yields of the gilts.)

Table 8.5

Gilt	Clean price	Duration
Treasury $11\frac{3}{4}$% 03/07	104-16	7.122
Exchequer 15% 97	130-08	5.542

Table 8.6

Clean price	Duration	Price factor
111-04	7.248	1.0363064

Answer

The proceeds are £10 million $\times \frac{135\text{-}05}{100}$ = £13·516 million.

Therefore £13·516 million is used to buy £13·516/(107-18/100), that is £12·565 million nominal of Treasury $11\frac{3}{4}$% 03/07.

Volatility sold is 10 × 5·542 × [(130-08)/100] = 72·185.

Volatility bought is 12·565 × 7·122 × [(104-16)/100] = 93·515.

Volatility to be eliminated is 93·515 − 72·185 = 21·330.

Volatility bought/sold per £1 million nominal of CTD is 7·248 × [(111-04)/100] = 8·054.

Number of long gilt futures contracts required to match £1 million nominal of CTD is

$$\frac{1{,}000{,}000}{50{,}000} \times 1{\cdot}0363064 = 20{\cdot}73$$

Volatility to be eliminated is 21·330.

Number of long gilt futures contracts to be sold is

$$\frac{21{\cdot}330}{8{\cdot}054} \times 20{\cdot}73 = 54{\cdot}9 \text{ contracts}$$

which is approximated by fifty-five contracts.

Long puts, short calls and short synthetics can all be used to reduce the market exposure of a portfolio of stock. Either stock or stock index options could be used. Such a hedging strategy is, however, not without its cost. The greater the extent to which the portfolio is covered, the closer its expected return will approach that on risk-free investments (short-term money market funds).

This can be seen most clearly by reference to a complete form of cover.

A synthetic short position in a particular stock could totally hedge a holding of the respective stock. This position would constitute a conversion. The return on a conversion arises from the excess of the synthetic price over the spot price of the stock and the dividend receipts from the stockholding. Arbitrage should ensure that together these equal the financing cost of holding the stock. This financing cost reflects short-term money market interest rates. So the return on the conversion – that is, a stockholding that is totally hedged by a synthetic short – approximates to short-term money market interest rates.

Using cylinders to reduce portfolio risk

The risk of a portfolio is frequently expressed in terms of the variance of the distribution of possible outcomes. This is illustrated by Figure 8.3 which shows a fund manager's subjective evaluation of the probability of various possible values of a portfolio of stocks three months from the present.

The mean of the possible values weighted by their probabilities (in other words, the statistical expectation) is £10 million. This value of £10 million reflects a rate of return over the current value of the portfolio (which might, for example, be £9,900,000). However, an apparent cost of this expected profit is considerable uncertainty as to the outcome, with the range of possibilities including values less than £9,900,000.

The portfolio manager could reduce the extent of possible variation at negligible (if any) cost by means of an options cylinder. This involves buying FTSE 100 put options in order to impose a minimum prospective value on the portfolio and financing this purchase by writing (i.e. selling) call options at a higher strike price.

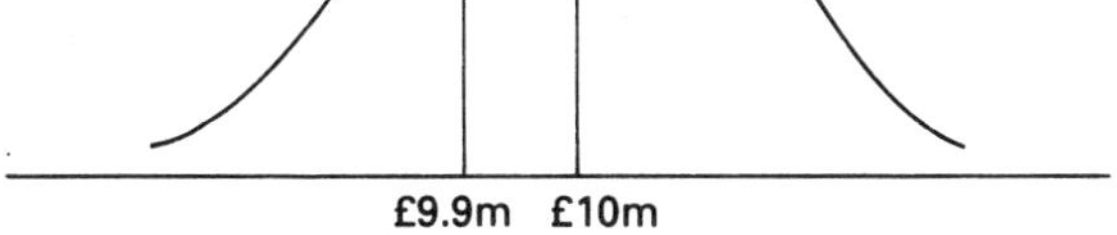

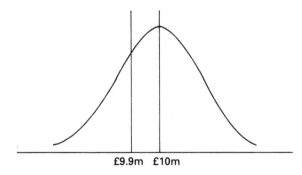

Figure 8.3 Probability distribution of possible future values of a portfolio

Suppose it is mid-October and the portfolio manager is considering the prospective value of the fund in mid-January. Suppose further that the current FTSE 100 index stands at 1980 and that January 1950 put options can be bought for 80 whilst January 2050 call options can be sold for 77. This implies a premium cost of £30 [(80-77) × £10] per pair of options. (These option premiums imply that the forward level of the FTSE 100 is about 2000.)

A 1950 put option gives the fund manager the right to sell a notional quantity of stock for £19,500. That notional quantity would sell for £19,800 at the current FTSE 100 index value of 1980. A 2050 call option that has been written obliges the fund manager to sell that same quantity of stock at £20,500 to the buyer of the option should that buyer choose to exercise the option. The fund manager would choose to exercise a 1950 put option if the index fell below 1950 and would be exercised against by the holder of the 2050 call option if the index rose above 2050. So the cylinder constrains the fund manager to an index range of 1950 to 2050. In so doing it reduces the statistical variance of the value of the portfolio and hence reduces the risk faced by the fund manager.

The question arises as to the appropriate number of option contracts. Since a 1950 option relates to £19,500, it is tempting to assume that the appropriate number of options would be 9,750,000 divided by 19,500, which equals 500. This £9,750,000 would be the value of the portfolio at an index value of 1950 if the portfolio beta equalled the FTSE 100 beta. However, the portfolio beta might differ from the FTSE 100 beta. If the portfolio had the higher beta, the number of option contracts would need to be ratioed up in proportion to the ratio of the betas, whilst ratioing down would be appropriate if the portfolio had the lower beta.

Exercising FTSE 100 options does not involve stock being delivered. Effectively the fund manager would be locked into a range of values (£9,750,000 to £10,250,000 if the beta of the portfolio is the same as the beta of the FTSE 100 index) by being compensated with a positive cash flow in the event of a decline beyond the bottom of the range and suffering by way of a monetary loss in the event of the value rising above the top of the range.

Making profits from relative share price movements

The case to be considered is one in which an investor believes that the stock prices of a particular sector are due to perform more favourably than is generally expected by the market. However, the investor's view is that

Table 8.7

20,000	Marks and Spencer at 174p	(0.81)
15,000	Sainsbury at 217p	(0.80)
10,000	Storehouse at 257p	(0.91)
10,000	Kingfisher at 292p	(0.83)
15,000	Boots at 208p	(0.88)
20,000	Dixons at 180p	(0.90)
30,000	Sears at 121p	(1.00)
25,000	Tesco at 147p	(0.81)

those shares will perform well *relative* to the market, and not necessarily in absolute terms. In other words, he expects the stock prices either to move up by more than the extent predicted by the general market rise and the stock betas, or to fall by less than the amount implied by the general market decline adjusted by the betas of the stocks.

AVOIDING GENERAL MARKET EXPOSURE

The investor may choose to take his position in the stocks concerned by means of a stockholding or by means of options. The stockholding approach will be considered first.

Suppose that the investor believes that the stocks of retail firms are undervalued relative to the rest of the market but wishes to avoid the exposure to overall market movements that such stocks provide. He could proceed by buying stocks in retail groups whilst hedging the general market exposure with futures or options. Perhaps his stock purchases might be as shown in Table 8.7 (the stock betas are in parentheses).

In order to ascertain the appropriate number of futures or options contracts to hedge this stockholding, the investor must calculate the market exposure. This involves multiplying the value of each stockholding by the corresponding beta:

$$
\begin{aligned}
20{,}000 \times £1{\cdot}74 \times 0{\cdot}81 &= £28{,}188{\cdot}0\\
15{,}000 \times £2{\cdot}17 \times 0{\cdot}80 &= £26{,}040{\cdot}0\\
10{,}000 \times £2{\cdot}57 \times 0{\cdot}91 &= £23{,}387{\cdot}0\\
10{,}000 \times £2{\cdot}92 \times 0{\cdot}83 &= £24{,}236{\cdot}0\\
15{,}000 \times £2{\cdot}08 \times 0{\cdot}88 &= £27{,}456{\cdot}0\\
20{,}000 \times £1{\cdot}80 \times 0{\cdot}90 &= £32{,}400{\cdot}0\\
30{,}000 \times £1{\cdot}21 \times 1{\cdot}00 &= £36{,}300{\cdot}0\\
25{,}000 \times £1{\cdot}47 \times 0{\cdot}81 &= £29{,}767{\cdot}5\\
\hline
& £227{,}774{\cdot}5
\end{aligned}
$$

The nearest maturity date FTSE futures contract is priced at 1820·0 which implies £45,500 per contract (1820·0 × £25). Dividing £227,774·5 by £45,500 gives 5·006. Thus the stockholding can be hedged by selling five FTSE futures contracts (the investor might intentionally construct a portfolio whose market exposure matches that of a discrete number of futures contracts).

As an alternative to selling futures the investor might construct a synthetic short position using FTSE options. A synthetic short position can be created by buying put options and writing an equal number of call options at the same exercise price (see Figure 8.4). At prices below the exercise price a holder of put options will find it profitable to exercise the options to sell at the exercise price and will therefore do so. At prices above the exercise price holders of call options will profit from exercising the options to buy at the exercise price and will do so, compelling the writers to sell at the exercise price. So the holder of the combination illustrated by Figure 8.4 will sell at the exercise price whatever the price turns out to be. In effect the holder of the combination has a short position.

The investor, instead of selling FTSE futures, might construct synthetic shorts with a strike price of 1800. The bid price of the call options might be 40 whilst the offer price of the put options is 30. So writing a call and buying a put yields a net profit of 10. The effective selling price guaranteed by the synthetic is therefore 1800 + 10 = 1810. The net profit from the premiums must be added to the receipts guaranteed by the exercise price.

Each combination of long put option and short call option corresponds to stock worth £18,100 (1810 × £10). If complete cover against general market movements is required, the investor does not want a situation in which the requisite number of synthetics is not discrete. The establishment of the type of strategy being considered would, however, involve simultaneous calculation of the number of shares and the number of the options. The investor would establish a stockholding that (very nearly) corresponds to a discrete number of option contracts. If the investor intended to use futures for the hedging then the portfolio described above

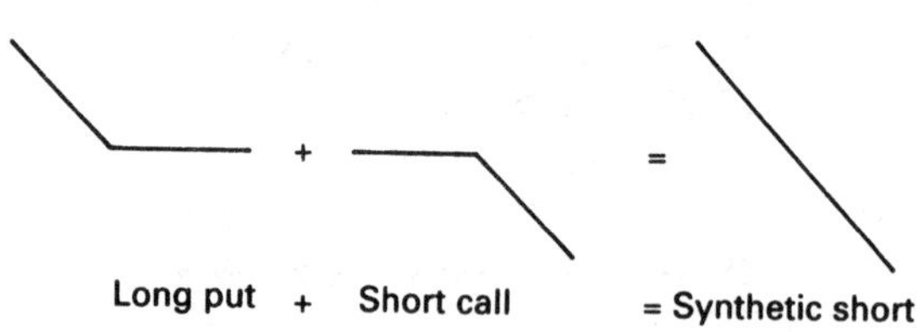

Figure 8.4 Creation of a synthetic short

does (very nearly) correspond to a discrete number of instruments (five futures contracts).

USING OPTIONS IN THE PLACE OF STOCKS

An investor looking to profit from rises in certain stock prices relative to the market as a whole whilst avoiding exposure to general market movements could use options on the stocks rather than shares in the stocks. The gearing offered by options can substantially reduce the initial monetary outlays, and options allow positions to be taken on price *falls* relative to the market as a whole.

A synthetic long position on a stock can be constructed by means of buying a call option and simultaneously writing a put option. This is illustrated by Figure 8.5. (Synthetic short positions can be constructed along the lines illustrated by Figure 8.4.)

The premium paid for the call option is offset by the premium received from writing the put option, so that any net money outlay is very small. The stock price guaranteed by the synthetic, when account is taken of the exercise price and the net premium receipt/payment, approximates to the market price of the stock. For example, the price of Marks and Spencer shares might be 174p and the premium on the nearest maturity 180p calls 6p whilst the premium on the corresponding 180p puts is 10p. There is a net receipt of 4p from the options which, when subtracted from the 180p exercise price, produces an effective buying price of 176p – which is close to the actual stock price.

The portfolio of stocks in retail groups can thus be simulated with synthetics. For example, instead of buying 20,000 Marks and Spencer shares at a price of 174p, the investor can buy twenty 180p call options at 6p and write twenty 180p put options at 10p, which simulates the purchase of 20,000 shares at an effective price of 176p. (In the case of the Marks and Spencer simulation there was a net monetary receipt. Other simulations might involve net payments, but overall the creation of the simulated

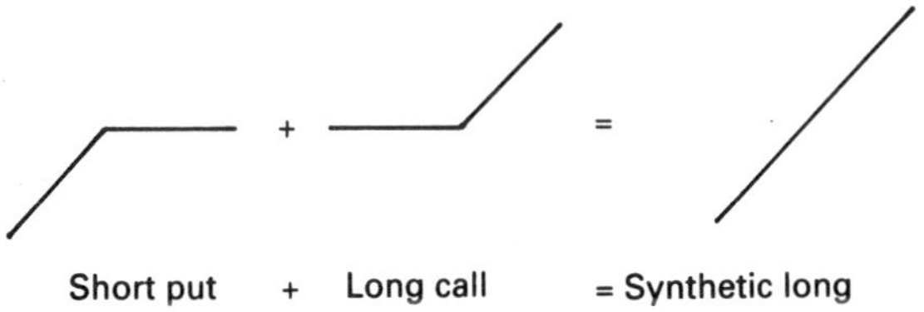

Figure 8.5 Creation of a synthetic long

Table 8.8

	Calls			Puts		
Strike price	March	April	May	March	April	May
1800	64	88	110	23	47	65
1850	35	60	83	45	73	88
1900	16	38	60	77	103	115

Table 8.9

	Calls		Puts	
Strike price	April	July	April	July
140	33 (0.95)	37 (0.91)	1 (−0.05)	5 (−0.09)
160	16 (0.75)	21 (0.67)	3 (−0.25)	12 (−0.33)
180	5 (0.34)	10 (0.41)	13 (−0.66)	21 (−0.59)

portfolio would involve very small net money flows. The simulated portfolio thus ties up far less liquidity than an actual portfolio; indeed it may even involve net receipts.)

The simulated portfolio can then be hedged with stock index futures or stock index options in the same way as the actual portfolio (the same betas would be used). So an investor can profit from relative stock price movements whilst avoiding general market exposure without buying any shares – and with a comparatively small initial cash outlay.

Exercise 8.5

Question

It is 15 March and LIFFE FTSE 100 futures prices are

March 1837·0
June 1856·0

FTSE option prices on the London Traded Options Market are as shown in Table 8.8.

The FTSE 100 index is 1839.

On 15 March British Airways shares have a price of 172p and a beta of 1·12. British Airways option prices (deltas in brackets) are as shown in Table 8.9.

How can a trader take a position on a fall in British Airways relative to the market as a whole in the following two situations whilst avoiding exposure to overall market movements?

(a) Adequate FTSE futures liquidity, inadequate FTSE options liquidity (calls and puts).
(b) Inadequate FTSE futures liquidity, adequate FTSE options liquidity (calls and puts), unknown FTSE option deltas.

Answer

(a) Buy BA puts, e.g. one July 160 put. Equivalent market exposure is

£1,720 × −0·33 × 1·12 = £635·71 (£1,720 is based on the current stock price)

The market exposure could be neutralised by buying June FTSE futures. One contract would give an equivalent market exposure of

$$£25 \times 1856{\cdot}0 = £46{,}400$$

This would neutralise the market exposure from £46,400/£635·71 = 72·99 option contracts. So the trader would buy seventy-three July 160 puts and cover the general market exposure by buying a June FTSE futures contract.
(b) In this case the general market exposure from the British Airways puts could be covered by a synthetic long FTSE position.
Buying a May 1850 FTSE call option and selling a May 1850 FTSE put option would produce a synthetic purchase for

$$1850 + 83 - 88 = 1845$$

This provides a market exposure of £18,450 which would neutralise the market exposure from (£18,450/£635·71) = 29·02 July 160 British Airways puts. So twenty-nine BA puts might be bought along with the synthetic long FTSE.
Alternatively, synthetic short BA stock might be used (avoiding writing in-the-money contracts).

The forgoing strategies have sought to derive *absolute* profits from relative price movements. An investor's objective, however, might be to obtain *relative* profits from relative price movements. The following strategies would satisfy this latter objective.

RENDERING THE PORTFOLIO BETA EQUAL TO ONE

If an investor wishes to perform well relative to the market, he can use futures or options to equate the beta of his portfolio to unity. His portfolio would then (apart from the hoped-for relative rise in the prices of the stocks of retail groups) move in line with the market as a whole.

Suppose the investor establishes the stockholding shown in Table 8.10 (the stock betas are in brackets). The market exposure provided by this portfolio is calculated as follows:

Table 8.10

50,000	Marks and Spencer at 174p	(0.81)
40,000	Sainsbury at 217p	(0.83)
25,000	Storehouse at 257p	(0.91)
25,000	Kingfisher at 292p	(0.84)
40,000	Boots at 208p	(0.88)
50,000	Dixons at 180p	(0.94)
75,000	Sears at 121p	(0.92)
75,000	Tesco at 147p	(0.82)

$$
\begin{aligned}
50{,}000 \times £1{\cdot}74 \times 0{\cdot}81 &= £70{,}470{\cdot}0\\
40{,}000 \times £2{\cdot}17 \times 0{\cdot}83 &= £72{,}044{\cdot}0\\
25{,}000 \times £2{\cdot}57 \times 0{\cdot}91 &= £58{,}467{\cdot}5\\
25{,}000 \times £2{\cdot}92 \times 0{\cdot}84 &= £61{,}320{\cdot}0\\
40{,}000 \times £2{\cdot}08 \times 0{\cdot}88 &= £73{,}216{\cdot}0\\
50{,}000 \times £1{\cdot}80 \times 0{\cdot}94 &= £84{,}600{\cdot}0\\
75{,}000 \times £1{\cdot}21 \times 0{\cdot}92 &= £83{,}490{\cdot}0\\
75{,}000 \times £1{\cdot}47 \times 0.82 &= £90{,}405{\cdot}0\\
\hline
& £594{,}012{\cdot}5
\end{aligned}
$$

The market value of the portfolio is equal to £685,250. This implies that the beta of the portfolio is

$$594{,}012{\cdot}5/685{,}250 = 0{\cdot}867$$

and that the additional exposure required to render the portfolio beta equal to 1 is

$$£685{,}250 - £594{,}012{\cdot}5 = £91{,}237{\cdot}5$$

If the price of the nearest maturity FTSE futures contract is 1820 (equivalent to $1820 \times £25 = £45{,}500$ of stock), the additional exposure would be provided by buying two FTSE futures contracts.

Alternatively, the beta of the portfolio could be raised by means of constructing synthetic FTSE positions. If the FTSE option prices are those previously cited, each combination of long call and short put (synthetic long forward) would correspond to stock worth £18,100 (the net premium payment of 10 is added to the exercise price of 1800 and the result is multiplied by £10). The exposure deficiency of £91,237·5 could be covered by 5·04 (£91,237·5/£18,100) synthetic FTSE forwards. So the investor's objective could be fulfilled by five long synthetic FTSE forwards.

Table 8.11

Quantity	Share	Price	Beta
20,000	British Airways	109	1.15
30,000	British Gas	80	0.90
5,000	ICI	1,403	0.95
10,000	Jaguar	630	1.25
10,000	Blue Circle	709	0.98

The portfolio of stocks could be replaced by a portfolio of synthetics. Instead of 50,000 Marks and Spencer shares at 174p, the investor could buy fifty 180p call options at 6p and write fifty 180p put options at 10p (all options having the same maturity date), thus guaranteeing the purchase of 50,000 shares at an effective price of 176p. The other shares could be replaced by options in the same way. The cash outlay would be far less when using options than when using shares.

Options allow for the construction of short positions. This enables an investor to take a position on a decline in the prices of stocks of particular companies, or groups of companies, relative to the market as a whole. For example, by buying puts and writing calls an investor could construct a portfolio of short synthetics on the stocks of the retail companies mentioned previously.

A portfolio of synthetics would have a beta which is calculated in the same way as the beta of a portfolio of stocks. The beta of the portfolio of synthetics could then be rendered equal to unity using futures or options in the same way as the beta of the portfolio of stocks. By this means an investor can take a position on a rise or fall in the prices of a group of stocks relative to the market as a whole whilst keeping the value of the portfolio in line with the market as a whole (except for the hoped-for relative movement).

Exercise 8.6

Question

It is 3 March. An investment manager holds the portfolio shown in Table 8.11. The FTSE 100 index stands at 1983·1 and the FTSE 100 futures prices are

March	June
2001·0	2038·5

Jaguar option prices (with deltas in brackets) are as shown in Table 8.12. Suggest a strategy that the portfolio manager might follow if he expects (and

Table 8.12

	Calls			Puts		
	March	June	September	March	June	September
550	83 (0.95)	100 (0.9)	115 (0.85)	1 (−0.05)	10 (−0.1)	12 (−0.15)
600	38 (0.9)	65 (0.82)	80 (0.75)	7 (−0.1)	25 (−0.18)	30 (−0.25)
650	14 (0.40)	40 (0.43)	53 (0.46)	35 (−0.6)	47 (−0.57)	55 (−0.54)

Table 8.13

	Price	Value (£)	Beta
20,000 British Airways	109	21,800	1.15
30,000 British Gas	80	24,000	0.90
5,000 ICI	1,403	70,150	0.95
10,000 Jaguar	630	63,000	1.25
10,000 Blue Circle	709	70,900	0.98
		249,850	

wishes to gain from) a rise in Jaguar stock relative to the market as a whole whilst keeping movements in the value of the portfolio in line with the FTSE 100 index (except for the effect of Jaguar's hoped-for relative rise on the value of the portfolio). Assume that the portfolio manager wishes to take no view as to movements in the market as a whole. He does not want to change the stock make-up of the portfolio but does have excess funds available.

Answer
(See Table 8.13.)

$$\begin{aligned} & 21{,}800 \times 1{\cdot}15 \\ + \; & 24{,}000 \times 0{\cdot}90 \\ + \; & 70{,}150 \times 0{\cdot}95 \\ + \; & 63{,}000 \times 1{\cdot}25 \\ + \; & 70{,}900 \times 0{\cdot}98 \\ = \; & 261{,}544{\cdot}5 \end{aligned}$$

The weighted average beta is

$$\frac{261{,}544{\cdot}5}{249{,}850} = 1{\cdot}05$$

A short position in FTSE futures could bring the weighted average beta closer to 1. The value of a June FTSE futures contract is $2038{\cdot}5 \times £25 = £50{,}962{\cdot}50$. Assuming that the delta of a futures contract is 1·00 the number of contracts that need to be sold in order to equate the weighted average beta to 1 is

$$\frac{261{,}544{\cdot}5 - 249{,}850}{50{,}962{\cdot}50} = 0{\cdot}229$$

Therefore 0·771 of the futures contract would be surplus in the sense of eliminating too much market exposure. There is a need for Jaguar call options in order to compensate for this 0·771. If a discrete number of Jaguar call options fail to match the 0·771, an alternative would be to sell two FTSE futures and seek a number of Jaguar call options that will match 1·771.

The portfolio manager might buy fourteen June 600 Jaguar call options. The number of FTSE futures contracts that would need to be sold in order to hedge the Jaguar options is

$$\frac{\pounds 6{,}300 \times 14 \times \text{Beta} \times \text{Delta}}{\text{Futures contract size}} = \frac{\pounds 6{,}300 \times 14 \times 1{\cdot}25 \times 0{\cdot}82}{\pounds 50{,}962{\cdot}50} = 1{\cdot}774$$

Since the number of FTSE contracts to be sold in order to reduce the portfolio beta to 1 is 0·229, it follows that the total number of FTSE futures contracts to be sold is 0·229 + 1·774 = 2·003, which approximates to two contracts.

In conclusion, one possible strategy would be the purchase of fourteen June 600 Jaguar call options together with the sale of two June FTSE futures contracts. Using synthetics (avoiding writing in-the-money options) would avoid problems of rebalancing as deltas change.

90/10 funds

These funds provide exposure to stock market movements whilst ensuring a degree of capital certainty. They involve most of the portfolio being invested in capital certain assets – for example, three-month deposits – whilst the remainder is used to buy stock (or stock index) call options in order to allow upside capture from market rises.

Despite their generic name, 90/10 funds do not necessarily comprise 90 per cent capital certain assets and 10 per cent stock-related options. The percentages are discretionary and would be determined by factors such as attitude to risk and the confidence with which a bullish view is held. A fund manager might, for example, invest in twelve-month money market securities the proportion of the fund that would yield the original value of the fund from such securities over one year. Having thus secured the capital value of the fund, the remainder could be used to buy call options so as to obtain upside exposure to the stock market.

These funds provide security together with upside exposure. As with other funds, increased profit potential is obtained at the cost of increased risk. The greater the proportion of the fund in options, the lower is the capital certainty. Raising the proportion of the fund that is used to buy options will raise the delta of the fund (the delta being the relationship between changes in the value of the fund and changes in the prices of the stocks that underlie the options). The proportion of the fund in options can be raised either by buying a greater number of options or by buying deeper in-the-money (or less out-of-the-money) options: either way the delta of the fund would be increased.

If the wish is to obtain exposure to the stock market in general rather than specific stocks, then stock index options would be better than options on individual stocks. Such an approach spreads the risk so that adverse developments that are specific to particular stocks can be largely avoided. The avoidance of stock-specific risk reduces option premiums. Volatility is an important determinant of option premiums. Since stock indices avoid the risks that are specific to individual stocks (and bear only the general market risk that is common to all stocks), they tend to be less volatile than individual stock prices. Consequently, option premiums for stock indices tend to be lower than those for individual stocks. This is a good reason for using stock index options rather than individual stock options.

It is preferable to use options with long periods to expiry. Option premiums decline with the passage of time as a result of time value decay. This erosion of option premiums accelerates as the expiry date of the option becomes closer. The rate of time value decay is relatively small for options whose expiry dates are distant. Before time value decay becomes pronounced the options should be sold and replaced with options whose expiry dates are more distant.

The options component of the fund need not consist solely of simple call option positions. For example, under certain circumstances bull spreads might be appropriate. Bull spreads might be used when option premiums are high or when the view taken is that any rise in share prices is likely to be limited in extent. Bull spreads can be constructed by means of buying call options and simultaneously selling call options at a higher strike price.

Suppose that the FTSE 100 is 2045 on 2 March and the June 2050 call is priced at 120 whilst the June 2100 call is 96. The construction of a bull spread is illustrated by Figure 8.6. The cost of the 2050 call option is offset by the proceeds from the sale of the 2100 call option. This reduction in net premium is obtained at the cost of reduced profit potential from the options, which is limited to 26p in the example. The use of bull spreads provides a means of using put options in 90/10 funds since bull spreads can be constructed with put options. The bull spread of Figure 8.6 could be created by means of selling 2100 puts whilst buying 2050 puts.

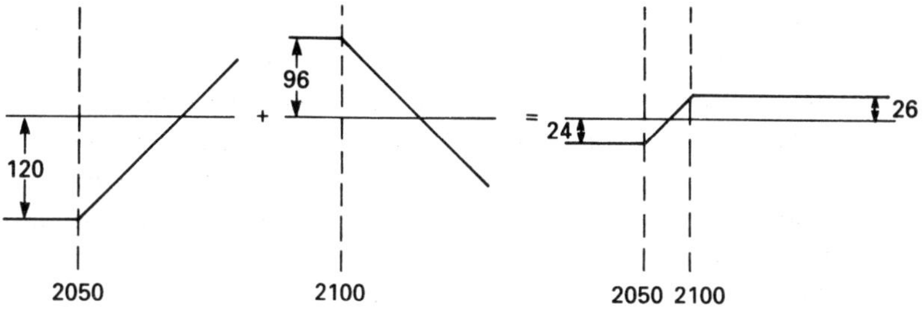

Figure 8.6 Construction of a bull spread

Finally, it might be noted that 90/10 funds provide a means of reducing the currency exposure that normally accompanies exposure to overseas stock markets. A British fund that is 90 per cent invested in sterling deposits and 10 per cent invested in US options has considerably less exposure to the risk of a fall in the value of the US dollar than a fund that is 100 per cent invested in US stocks, although they might have identical exposures to the US stock market.

Exercise 8.7

Question
It is 6 January and the offer price of Courtaulds shares stands at 356p whilst the option prices (deltas in brackets) are as shown in Table 8.14.
A holder of 10,000 shares anticipates a very sharp movement in the stock price but is uncertain as to the direction of change.

(a) Suggest two alternative strategies for limiting risk whilst retaining upside potential.
(b) If, on 6 February, the stock price were (1) 250p and (2) 450p, estimate the investor's profit/loss for both of the strategies. (If it is not possible to provide precise values, suggest and explain plausible figures.)

Answer
(a) (i) Buying puts in a fixed hedge (thereby creating synthetic calls). The shareholder might buy ten April 360 puts.
(ii) A 90/10 strategy. This might entail the investor selling the shares for £35,400 (assuming a bid–offer spread of 2p) of which £3,800 could be used to buy ten April 360 call options whilst the remaining £31,600 is put on deposit.
(b) (i) In case (1) 10,000 shares at 250p are worth £25,000. April 360 puts would have an intrinsic value of 110p. Options that are so far in the

Table 8.14

	Calls		Puts	
Strike price	April	July	April	July
330	55 (0.80)	62 (0.75)	20 (−0.20)	32 (−0.25)
360	38 (0.47)	48 (0.48)	35 (−0.53)	48 (−0.52)
390	28 (0.15)	36 (0.19)	55 (−0.85)	67 (−0.81)

money are likely to have very little time value. A time value of 2p might be assumed. Thus, assuming an option premium of 112p, the ten April 360 puts would be worth £11,200. The investor's net worth on 6 February would therefore be £25,000 + £11,200 = £36,200. This implies a loss of £35,600 + £3,500 − £36,200 = £2,900 (ignoring bid–offer spreads on options).

In case (2) 10,000 shares at 450p are worth £45,000. The 360 puts would be deeply out of the money and would consequently have a very low time value: 3p seems plausible. The ten put options would thus have a value of £300. The investor's net worth would be £45,000 + £300 = £45,300. This implies a profit of £45,300 − £35,600 − £3,500 = £6,200 (ignoring bid–offer spreads on options).

(ii) The investor would have £31,600 (plus accrued interest) in both cases.

In case (1) the options would be deeply out of the money and would possess very little time value. The premium might plausibly be 2p. The total value of the options would thus be £200, giving a net worth of £31,600 + £200 = £31,800 (plus interest accrued on the £31,600). This would imply a loss of £35,600 − £31,800 = £3,800 from which accrued interest should be deducted (ignoring bid–offer spreads on options).

In case (2) the options would have an intrinsic value of 90p. There would also be a small time value, which might plausibly be 3p. The option premium would thus be 93p so that the total value of the options is £9,300. The investor would have a net worth of £31,600 + £9,300 = £40,900 (plus interest accrued on the £31,600). This implies a profit of £40,900 − £35,600 − £5,300 plus accrued interest (ignoring bid–offer spreads on options).

Alternative strategies include volatility trades (straddles, strangles, butterflies) and bull spreads.

A word of warning

Finally, a word of warning about using the financial futures and options markets. The prices of futures and options are determined by the forces of demand and supply in the market. Market participants should be alert to the liquidity of the markets (in the sense of the volumes traded). In an illiquid market the user's purchases or sales could move prices to his disadvantage. So a user of options may need to spread purchases or sales across a number of strike prices and expiry dates so as to avoid an excessive impact on the market for contracts of a particular series. The user may even feel that it is necessary to buy or sell less than the desired number of contracts and hence tolerate a risk reduction which is less than that hoped for.

9

Taxation

Complexities in the tax treatment of transactions in financial futures and options arise as a result of distinctions between revenue and capital transactions and as a result of perceived needs to tax unrealised profits or defer realised losses. The revenue/capital distinction can be particularly problematical, especially when capital taxation applies to assets but not to liabilities. Most countries are free of the revenue/capital distinction and as a result profits from financial futures and options are treated in the same way as other sources of income. The countries that have had the revenue/capital distinction are the United States, the United Kingdom and countries (such as Canada and Singapore) whose taxation systems have been influenced by the UK system. It is therefore appropriate to discuss specifically the US and UK systems, although it might be noted that (at the time of writing) both countries have rates of capital gains tax equal to the corresponding rates of income tax, which could be indicative of intentions to phase out the revenue/capital distinction.

United States

The approach to the taxation of financial futures and options in the United States can be discussed in relation to the pre-1981 situation, the situation existing between 1981 and the implementation of the 1986 Tax Reform Act, and the practices that have followed the implementation of that Act.

PRE-1981

Until 1981 profits on futures transactions were treated as short-term or long-term capital gains depending upon whether the holding period was less than or greater than six months (long-term capital gains were taxed at a lower rate). Long option positions that were sold or lapsed were treated in the same way, but profits/losses on short option positions that were closed out or which lapsed were treated as short term irrespective of the period involved. Also taxes were charged only on realised profits.

This system was subject to abuse. Many traders used spread strategies consisting of matching long and short positions in futures contracts. At the end of the tax year one of the two legs would be showing a loss and the other a profit. Traders would realise the loss but leave the profit unrealised. They would thus have a tax-deductible loss in the present whilst the taxable profit was deferred. This often involved the loss being at the higher short-term capital gains rate and the profit at the lower long-term capital gains rate.

1981–1987

In 1981 a mark-to-market rule was introduced such that certain contracts were treated as sold on the last day of the taxpayer's taxable year even if they continued to be held. Transactions were also rendered subject to a 60/40 rule which treated 60 per cent of the profit/loss as long term and 40 per cent as short term, regardless of the holding period.

The contracts subject to the mark-to-market and 60/40 rules were known as Section 1256 contracts. Section 1256 contracts included futures and non-equity options (although transactions in such instruments were exempt from the rules if they met the Internal Revenue Code definition of hedging). Non-equity options include exchange-traded options on futures, debt instruments, currencies and some stock indices.

POST-1987

The Tax Reform Act of 1986 removed the distinction between short-term and long-term capital gains and rendered all capital gains taxable at the taxpayer's income tax rate. An implication of this was that the 60/40 rule ceased to have any meaning. Section 1256 contracts do, however, remain subject to the mark-to-market rule.

Tax straddles

There are cases in which realised losses are not tax deductible in the tax year in which they occur. These cases arise from straddles. In this context a straddle is a position in which a taxpayer holds assets whose values vary inversely to one another: for example, a treasury bond holding combined with a short treasury bond futures position. The law generally requires the deferment of losses from a position to the extent of unrealised gains from an offsetting position. This prevents taxpayers generating a capital loss to be realised in the current tax year whilst deferring the corresponding gain to a subsequent tax year.

A particular variant of this restriction is known as the Wash Sale Rule, which applies irrespective of whether a straddle exists. According to the rule, if a loss-making position is closed out and replaced by a similar position then the loss must be deferred, for taxation purposes, until the new position (or any subsequent similar position) is closed out. The rule applies when the new position is entered into within thirty days either side of the closing-out date. For the purposes of the application of the rule, a call option on an asset is deemed to be a similar position to that asset. So closing out a loss-making position and replacing it with a corresponding call option would result in the loss being deferred for tax purposes.

Exceptions to the straddle rules

Straddles consisting solely of Section 1256 contracts are not subject to the straddle rule. This is because the mark-to-market requirements prevent matching gains and losses being allocated to different tax years.

If a straddle meets the Internal Revenue Code definition of an identified straddle, its positions are exempt from the loss-deferral rules. For a straddle to be an identified straddle all its positions must be acquired on the same day, all its positions must be closed on the same day and it must be designated in the taxpayer's records as an identified straddle by the end of the day on which the positions were acquired.

In recognition of the frequent use of covered call writing for the protection of investment positions, an exception to the straddle provisions is made for certain call options on stocks. The call options that are treated as qualified for this exemption do not include deep in-the-money options.

Hedging

If a transaction meets the Internal Revenue Code definition of a hedge it will be subject to neither the mark-to-market nor the loss-deferral rules.

For a hedge to meet the code definition it must be entered into in the normal course of the taxpayer's business, and that business must not be an investment business. The purpose of the transaction must be the reduction of the risk of currency fluctuations in relation to the value of assets or receivables or the reduction of the risk arising from currency or interest fluctuations in relation to liabilities of the taxpayer. The taxpayer must identify the transaction as a hedge on the day that it is entered into. Gains/losses from the hedge are treated as ordinary income.

United Kingdom

In July 1988 the Inland Revenue issued a Statement of Practice relating to the tax treatment of transactions in financial futures and options. This brought significant clarification to an area that had previously been fraught with uncertainty, to the extent of deterring many potential users from the derivatives markets.

Prior to the issue of the Statement of Practice, users were guided by case law and the Inland Revenue's interpretation of that case law. The case law involved the *ad hoc* application of often inappropriate tax law to financial futures and options. Although the July 1988 Statement of Practice has helped to provide clearer guidelines to users, it still retains elements that, arguably, are inappropriate to the derivatives markets.

Two elements that continue to cause concern are the Inland Revenue's definition of an investment and the fact that liabilities fall outside the scope of capital gains tax. The Inland Revenue defines an investment as an asset that produces an actual or potential flow of income, such as dividends or coupon yield. This excludes assets whose return takes the form of asset appreciation, and derivatives are instruments whose returns arise from increases in value rather than from dividend or interest flows. So financial futures and options fall outside the Inland Revenue's definition of investments.

The fact that liabilities are outside the scope of capital gains taxation introduces a distorting asymmetry to the tax system. A fall in the value of a liability is just as much a capital gain as a rise in the value of an asset. However, the asymmetric treatment of assets and liabilities means that a loss on a liability cannot be offset against a capital gain on an asset. This has serious consequences for hedging strategies.

In order to understand present tax regulations it is useful to know a little of the history of the development of financial futures and options taxation. So the next step is to consider some of the historical development.

THE CASE OF MARINE MIDLAND (PATTISON V. MARINE MIDLAND LIMITED (1984) AC 362)

This case highlights the issue of liabilities falling outside the scope of capital gains taxation. It also highlights two important distinctions:

between 'capital' and 'revenue' transactions and between 'conversion' and 'translation' as the basis for tax assessment.

Marine Midland borrowed US$15 million redeemable in ten years. This money was then lent on a shorter-term basis. After five years the bank's customers repaid their loans and Marine Midland repaid its debt from the funds received.

Over this five-year period the US dollar strengthened against sterling. So the sterling value of both the bank's assets and liabilities increased. The Inland Revenue took the view that the profit from the effect of the dollar appreciation on Marine Midland's assets was a 'revenue' profit arising from circulating assets and as such was to be assessed for tax under Schedule D, Case I. However, the Inland Revenue considered that the loss arising from the effect of the dollar appreciation on the bank's liability was a 'capital' item. Capital items involve a capital gains tax assessment in the case of assets, but fall outside the scope of any tax assessment in the case of liabilities. As a result the loss on the liabilities could not be offset against the matching profit on the assets, or against any other profit. Marine Midland had remained matched between its dollar assets and dollar liabilities throughout: in other words, it had hedged by avoiding any net foreign exchange exposure. The asymmetric approach of the Inland Revenue undermined the effectiveness of what would normally be a hedging strategy that provides complete protection.

Marine Midland appealed against the Inland Revenue decision and the case went as far as the House of Lords. The House of Lords dismissed the Inland Revenue case on the grounds that there could be no foreign exchange profit or loss when no currency conversion took place. The matter was decided on the basis that there was no realisation of a profit from the appreciation of the dollar. Therefore the only issue actually addressed by the House of Lords' decision was the one deriving from the 'conversion' versus 'translation' distinction. The issues arising from the 'revenue' versus 'capital' distinction and the exclusion of liabilities from the scope of capital gains taxation were not addressed.

Following the Marine Midland case the Inland Revenue published a Provisional Statement of Practice in January 1985. This stated that translation profits were normally still subject to assessment for tax. However, the Provisional Statement of Practice did accept that, when there was a fully matched position and no conversion took place, losses on capital liabilities could be offset against profits on the matching assets.

INLAND REVENUE PROVISIONAL STATEMENT OF PRACTICE, JANUARY 1985

This Provisional Statement of Practice was concerned with the impact of currency fluctuations on the calculation of trading profits. In particular, it addressed the issue of how taxable trading profits should be adjusted when the effect of currency movements on 'capital' assets or liabilities had been included in the profit and loss acount.

The Provisional Statement accepted that cases in which there was complete matching and no conversion would be subject to no tax liability, irrespective of the capital or revenue nature of the foreign currency denominated assets and liabilities. The greater part of the Provisional Statement was concerned with the treatment of unmatched, or incompletely matched, items in relation to the removal of capital profits or losses from the trading results.

If there was a profit on a current item and a smaller loss on a capital item, the difference between them would enter the profit and loss account and would be liable to being taxed as trading profits (vice versa for a current loss and a smaller capital profit, in which case the net loss would be allowable against other trading profits). No adjustment was required in order to eliminate a capital element from the trading results.

An adjustment was required when the capital item was of a greater magnitude than the revenue item. The excess of the capital item over the current item might enter the profit and loss account but would not be taxable as trading profits (or deductible as trading losses). This difference between the current and capital items would need to be removed from the profit and loss account in the computation of taxable trading profits.

Capital items removed from the profit and loss account in the computation of taxable trading profits were to be treated in the usual way under capital gains tax legislation.

INLAND REVENUE STATEMENT OF PRACTICE, FEBRUARY 1987

The Statement of Practice of February 1987 replaced the Provisional Statement of January 1985. It affirmed the contents of the Provisional Statement but considered further cases including that in which there is more than one currency involved and that in which a hedging instrument is employed.

The Inland Revenue expressed the view that where there are transactions in more than one currency each currency should be considered separately. So losses from movements in one currency cannot be matched against profits from another currency.

The Statement of Practice does allow offsetting between cash market instruments and currency futures. So when an asset or liability is matched with futures contracts on the same currency, no tax liability will arise as a result of exchange rate movements. This facilitates hedging with currency futures.

However, the Statement of Practice does not extend the principle of matched positions offsetting each other for tax purposes to cases in which options are used for hedging. The independent treatment of different currencies also reduces the usefulness of currency futures for cross-currency hedging: for example, using Deutschmark futures to hedge a Danish krone exposure on the grounds that the Deutschmark and the krone correlate closely.

THE FINANCE ACT 1985

The Finance Act 1985 transferred many of the cases of derivatives taxation from Schedule D, Case VI to capital gains taxation.

As previously, if a taxpayer uses financial futures or traded options as part of a trade, profits or losses will be assessable for income tax in the case of individuals, or corporation tax under Schedule D, Case I in the case of companies. The definition of what constituted a trade remained unclear. However, relatively infrequent transactions and cases in which the intention was to hedge specific instruments would not be regarded as trades.

The Act, however, did change the tax treatment of transactions that were not deemed to be trades. The Act stipulated that from 6 April 1985 options traded on the London Stock Exchange (LTOM) and the derivatives traded on LIFFE were to be removed from the scope of Schedule D, Case VI and taxed under the capital gains tax legislation. The Inland Revenue has the power to designate any exchange in the world as being recognised for this purpose. A large number of exchanges have now been thus recognised.

As well as being excluded from Schedule D, Case VI, options traded on the recognised exchanges were removed from the scope of the capital gains tax wasting asset rules. These rules would have involved the option premiums being disallowed as a deductible cost to an extent dependent upon the relationship between the period to exercise (or sale) and the period to expiry – such that at expiry the option would have been deemed to have no tax-deductible cost.

The Finance Act 1987 extended the provisions of the Finance Act 1985 with respect to the treatment of financial futures and options to cover many of the over-the-counter derivatives.

THE INLAND REVENUE STATEMENT OF PRACTICE, JULY 1988

The July 1988 Statement of Practice is largely concerned with the question of what transactions are not regarded as 'trades' by the Inland Revenue. Transactions not regarded as trades may fall outside the scope of income tax and corporation tax under Schedule D, Case I.

Paragraph 5 of the statement begins with the sentence, 'If a transaction in financial futures or options is clearly related to an underlying asset or transaction, then the tax treatment of the futures or options contract will follow that of the underlying asset or transaction.' The types of transaction that would be deemed to relate to the underlying instrument and whose tax treatment would therefore reflect that of the underlying instrument could be divided into three categories:

1. The acquisition or disposal of the underlying instrument is intended (e.g. buying call options on shares with the intention of acquiring those shares by exercising the options).
2. The derivatives hedge the underlying instrument.
3. The derivatives are used in the process of asset reallocation.

In category 1 there is flexibility as to the final disposition of the position: for example, the tax treatment of an option does not depend upon whether it is exercised or sold. Also the Inland Revenue accepts that the taxpayer's view may change during the life of a contract and that in consequence the proposed transaction in the underlying instrument might not take place. In the latter case the tax treatment would be the same as if the transaction in the underlying instrument had actually taken place, although the Inland Revenue could regard the derivatives position as a trade if there is a substantial period between the underlying motive disappearing and the derivatives position being terminated.

This category also extends to cases in which a currency future is bought as a first step in the purchase of an asset denominated in that currency.

Category 2, in which the derivatives are used for hedging rather than as part of the process of the transaction, may involve the Inland Revenue requiring evidence of a close correlation between the derivative and the instrument being hedged so that it can be established that the derivative is an effective means of risk reduction.

This category extends to the covered writing of call options, since such a strategy can be regarded as hedging. It does not, however, extend to anticipatory hedging in the sense of hedging possible future purchases in the management of future cash flows. Presumably the essential distinction between anticipatory hedging and the intended purchase of assets (category 1) rests on the matter of whether the hedger has current possession of the liquid funds required for the purchase of the underlying instrument. However, where there is a commitment to a future transaction in the underlying instrument, the use of derivatives might not be regarded as a trade. For example, if a company is committed to making a bond issue in the near future, the use of derivatives to hedge against adverse movements in interest rates prior to that issue would be treated as a hedge rather than a trade.

Category 3 covers cases in which derivatives are used for smoothing or expediting a change in investment strategy. For example, a movement from equities to gilts in a portfolio may involve a short equities derivatives position and a long gilts derivatives position pending the transactions in the underlying instruments. Such use of derivatives would be incidental and temporary in nature.

The Statement of Practice puts emphasis on the intention of the user of derivatives at the time of undertaking a transaction. This requires thorough documentation so that the intention is clear. If the user changes his mind so that the original purpose disappears, the whole of the transaction should be documented so that there is written evidence relating to the original intention and the point at which the intention changed.

The Statement of Practice does not cater for delta hedging. An options position should be directly linked to the size of the underlying instrument. So only fixed hedges fall within the provisions of the statement.

A WORD OF WARNING

Tax law is subject to interpretation and change. This has been one person's interpretation of the situation at a single point in time. Users of financial futures and options should always seek advice from specialist tax advisers before using the instruments.

10

Outlook for the future

In the future there could be significant changes in the types of future and option used. There appears to be an expanding market for long-term options. These are normally referred to as warrants and have expiry dates several years into the future. There has been particular growth in the market for stock index warrants. Although these developments have been in the over-the-counter market, there have been moves to extend maturities in some traded derivatives: for example, the eurodollar futures traded on the Chicago Mercantile Exchange (CME) and the Singapore Monetary Exchange (Simex) now have maturities up to four years (this contract illustrates another interesting development in that contracts may be opened on one of these exchanges and closed out on the other – in other words, CME and Simex have a mutual offset arrangement).

Interest rate differential futures, based on differences between interest rates on different currencies, have been introduced. It seems likely that other interest rate differential derivatives will emerge. The differentials might be between different instruments in the same currency: for example, US treasury bills and eurodollars.

New types of complex option are emerging. These include lookback options. Lookback call options give the right to buy at the lowest price achieved by the underlying instrument between the issue of the option and its expiry date. Lookback put options give the right to sell at the highest price achieved. A straddle of lookback options would give the holder the right to buy at the lowest price and sell at the highest price. Such options are, inevitably, expensive.

Down and out options are means of reducing the cost of using options. A down and out call option ceases to be exercisable if the price of the underlying instrument falls below a particular level. A down and out put option is cancelled if the price of the underlying instrument becomes particularly high.

In many cases ultimate users, such as corporate treasurers and fund managers, prefer to use the tailor-made over-the-counter derivatives. The role of the exchange-traded products then becomes one of providing a means whereby the providers of over-the-counter instruments can hedge the exposures that they acquire. The provision of forward currency and forward rate agreements (FRAs) by banks who then hedge the resulting exposures in the currency and short-term interest rate futures markets is an example of the direction in which the rest of the derivatives markets might go. (FRAs are commitments to compensate for deviations of actual interest rates from predetermined rates. A bank will guarantee an interest rate for a future period and money is exchanged between the bank and the client in respect of deviations of the realised rate from the agreed rate. This is a means of locking in a future interest rate and the compensation payments may be either to or from the client depending upon the direction of deviation.) It is conceivable that forward commitments in relation to bond, stock index or individual equity prices could be provided for clients by banks who then hedge the resulting exposures by means of exchange-traded futures or options contracts. Similarly, a complex array of over-the-counter options could be made available by banks which then hedge the exposures acquired with exchange-traded products.

In respect to stock index products, sector-specific contracts could become much more important. Already there is an over-the-counter provision of sector-specific stock index futures and warrants. There is likely to be an increasing demand for such products from fund managers wishing to take positions on movements in particular sectors relative to the market as a whole.

There are likely to be developments in the way that derivatives are traded. Recently the Chicago Mercantile Exchange has linked up with Reuters to produce the GLOBEX screen-based trading system. Since other markets, including those in Japan, have opted for screen-based trading the question must arise as to whether something like GLOBEX will eventually replace the face-to-face pit trading. However, screen-based trading is, at the time of writing, unproven as an efficient method for high-volume markets.

Screen-based trading opens up the possibility of 24-hour trading. However, there must be some doubt as to whether there would be active trading in derivative products while the market in the underlying instrument is closed. So this might only be useful for derivatives based on instruments that themselves are traded on a 24-hour basis, and this could mean that they are limited to currencies.

Outlook for the future

In the United States there has been a recent movement towards longer trading hours. The Chicago Board of Trade and the Philadelphia Stock Exchange have both introduced evening sessions. However, there must be some doubt as to whether such extensions in trading hours will be successful if the underlying instruments do not trade during those additional periods.

Appendix I The role of stock index futures in the stock market crash of October 1987

The events

Stock markets around the world experienced a dramatic end to a bull market that had begun in the early 1980s and which had intensified in 1987. In the United States the bull market had begun in the summer of 1982 and culminated in a rise of more than 40 per cent in the first nine months of 1987. In the United Kingdom stock prices increased by a multiple of five between early 1980 and the summer of 1987, including a particularly rapid rise in the first half of 1987.

When the market fell the collapse was rapid and substantial. By mid-November stocks in the United States were about 30 per cent below their peak and corresponding figures elsewhere were Japan 17 per cent, the United Kingdom 34 per cent, Australia 43 per cent and Hong Kong 44 per cent. Even so the low point following the crash saw stock prices above those of a year earlier (in New York, London and Tokyo the stock indices for mid-November 1987 were above those for mid-November 1986).

The explanations

There has been an abundant supply of explanations of the crash. Most commentators have taken the view that the market was overbought immediately prior to October 1987. In the United Kingdom the price–earnings ratio increased from about $5\frac{1}{2}$ to $14\frac{1}{2}$ between early 1980 and summer 1987. In the United States blue-chip stocks were at price–earnings ratios in excess of 20 immediately before October 1987. In both countries the rates of return on common stocks (equities) were below the return on government stocks (in the United States the rate of return on common stocks was significantly below the risk-free return on T-bills).

Appendix I

It seems likely that stock prices had been subject to a speculative bubble during 1987. Speculative bubbles are characterised by purchases of assets because of anticipated capital appreciation rather than because of dividend or interest yield. Such behaviour can explain the fall in earnings on common stock below the returns available on risk-free securities. Speculative bubbles always burst eventually. When asset prices cease to rise the attraction of holding the assets is eroded and the desire to buy is replaced by an urge to sell. The resulting fall in prices can be dramatic.

What remains to be explained is the proximate cause of the bursting of the bubble. Interest rates rose strongly through the first nine months of 1987, a phenomenon that would normally entail declining rather than increasing stock prices. This behaviour of interest rates made stocks look even more overvalued. Many analysts must have feared a sharp correction in stock prices.

The scene was set for a fall; all that was required was the trigger. The trigger probably took the form of a combination of factors rather than a single event. The feeling of nervousness was intensified by the large budget and trade deficits in the United States and the apparent lack of resolve on the part of the administration and congress to come to an agreement on how to deal with the budget deficit. The Dow Jones fell by 260 points between Wednesday 14 and Friday 16 October. Market participants in the United States went home for the weekend in a nervous state of mind.

Meanwhile a storm of exceptional intensity hit southern England during the night of 15/16 October. Damage was extensive and the disruption to transport was such that few staff were able to get into the City of London on Friday the 16th.

Over the weekend there was a public disagreement between the American and West German finance ministers over economic policy and the US Treasury Secretary suggested that the dollar might fall in the international money markets.

When the London stock market opened on the morning of Monday 19 October it had two days of falls in the Dow Jones to which to react (being unable to react the previous Friday). Furthermore, there was a fear that insurance companies would sell large amounts of stock in order to meet claims arising from the previous week's storm. The London market declined sharply.

Five and a half hours after the London market opened, trading began in New York. The nervousness of the previous Friday was now heightened by the disagreement between the American and German finance ministers and by the news that the London stock market had fallen sharply that

Monday morning. The Wall Street crash commenced. On Black Monday the Dow Jones Industrial Average fell 508 points; this loss was in excess of 22 per cent of the closing index on the previous trading day. Stock markets around the world quickly followed the downward path.

THE ROLE OF STOCK INDEX FUTURES

A fund manager wishing to reduce his exposure to the stock market may either sell stock or hedge using the derivatives markets. Selling stock is a slow and expensive operation. It is quicker and cheaper to hedge using derivatives. So portfolio insurers sold large numbers of stock index futures contracts on the morning of Monday 19 October. Stock index futures prices fell. The fall in futures prices opened up opportunities for cash-and-carry arbitrage, which was operated by means of program trading. The arbitrage involved buying the (relatively cheap) stock index futures whilst selling the (relatively expensive) stock.

Stock is sold, thereby putting downward pressure on stock prices. The fall in stock prices triggers further selling of futures for the purpose of portfolio insurance and this selling causes futures prices to fall further. More cash-and-carry arbitrage occurs, resulting in more sales of stock. So it would appear that a vicious circle operates with stock index futures and program trading being central to the process.

Futures markets were therefore blamed for the crash by sections of the media and by other interested parties. Heaping blame for the crash on stock index futures seems to be mistaken for a number of reasons. Firstly, stock index futures were sold for portfolio insurance instead of the stocks themselves being sold. The futures market merely rendered the downward pressure on stock prices indirect rather than direct. In fact it might be argued that the problem was inadequate futures trading, that the inability to sell futures caused hedgers to sell stock instead. Locals (those who trade on their own account) on the futures exchanges withdrew from the market in the face of the heavy selling pressure and this made it more difficult for specialists (i.e. market makers in stocks) to cover their positions. The specialists were forced to protect themselves by marking prices down sharply.

The huge imbalance between sell and buy orders forced specialists to halt trading in many of the largest stocks. Many stock openings were delayed for more than an hour, and later in the day program traders found themselves frequently unable to sell the appropriate baskets of stocks. As a result the program trading, much blamed for the crash, largely failed to take place. This is evidenced by the fact that the futures markets traded at a large discount to the stock markets during the opening hour and final three hours on that Monday. Had cash-and-carry arbitrage been operating, the stock and futures markets would have remained in line with each other. Since stock index futures prices were at a substantial discount to stock prices, hedgers resorted to selling stock in preference to the lower price futures. This selling of stock is the behaviour that would have been seen in the absence of futures markets.

It would appear that the vicious circle scenario fails to explain the sharp decline in stock prices on Monday 19 October. It is possible, however, that the futures markets caused the fall to be completed more quickly. Unloading stock can be expensive, administratively cumbersome and time consuming. Selling futures can be done much more quickly. It is possible that a fall that might otherwise have taken weeks occurred in a single trading session. To that extent the final extent of the crash might have been lessened by the futures markets since a prolonged decline could have engendered a deeper bear psychology.

Finally it might be noted that stock index futures and their roles in portfolio insurance and program trading cannot explain the stock market crashes in other countries. In most cases, stock index futures were simply not available. In other cases, program trading based on cash-and-carry arbitrage was not well developed: for example, although stock index futures were traded in London, stamp duty (a tax on transactions in shares) had inhibited the development of cash-and-carry arbitrage.

Appendix II The Black–Scholes option pricing model

The put/call parity relationship gives the opportunity to obtain a further perspective on the Black–Scholes model of option valuation. According to this model the theoretical price of call options is

$$C = PN(d_1) - Se^{-rt}N(d_2)$$

where

C = theoretical price of the call option
P = price of the underlying
S = strike price
r = annualised interest rate
t = time to expiry (in years)

$N(d_1)$ and $N(d_2)$ are values of the cumulative normal distribution, defined by the following:

$$d_1 = \frac{\log (P/S) + (r + 0{\cdot}5\ \sigma^2)t}{\sigma\sqrt{t}}$$

$$\text{i.e. } d_1 = \frac{\log (P/S) + rt}{\sigma\sqrt{t}} + 0{\cdot}5\ \sigma\sqrt{t}$$

$$\text{whilst } d_2 = d_1 - (\sigma\sqrt{t})$$

$$\text{i.e. } d_2 = \frac{\log (P/S) + rt}{\sigma\sqrt{t}} - 0{\cdot}5\ \sigma\sqrt{t}$$

(N.B. The logarithms are natural logarithms.)
The term

$$\frac{\log (P/S)}{\sigma\sqrt{t}} + \frac{rt}{\sigma\sqrt{t}}$$

corresponds to the term $P-Se^{-rt}$. This can be seen by means of equating both terms to zero:

$$P-Se^{-rt}=0$$
$$P=Se^{-rt}$$
$$P/S=e^{-rt}$$
$$\log (P/S)={}^{-}rt$$
$$\log (P/S)+rt=0$$

The magnitude $\log (P/S)+rt$ would form a normal distribution with a mean of zero. This mean occurs when $\log (P/S)=-rt$, which is when $P=Se^{-rt}$. This condition might be interpreted as an at-the-money condition.

d_1 and d_2 are points along the horizontal axis of this normal distribution (when measured in units of $\sigma\sqrt{t}$). When σ is zero, d_1 and d_2 will approach either infinity or minus infinity, depending upon whether $\log (P/S)+rt$ is positive or negative. If P exceeds Se^{-rt} then the term will be positive; if P is less than Se^{-rt} the term will be negative.

If d_1 and d_2 approach infinity, the whole of the area under the normal distribution curve will lie to their left. This means that $N(d_1)$ and $N(d_2)$ will both equal 1 (since $N(x)$ is the area under the normal distribution function to the left of point x on the horizontal axis). If d_1 and d_2 approach minus infinity, $N(d_1)$ and $N(d_2)$ will both be equal to zero since none of the area under the normal distribution curve will lie to their left.

It follows that $C=PN(d_1)-Se^{-rt}N(d_2)$ will equal $P-Se^{-rt}$ if $P>Se^{-rt}$ and zero if $P<Se^{-rt}$. Similar results would ensue from the stipulation that time to expiry (t) is zero.

When $P=Se^{-rt}$, $d_1=0{\cdot}5\ \sigma\sqrt{t}$ and $d_2=-0{\cdot}5\ \sigma\sqrt{t}$. Since $\sigma\sqrt{t}$ is the standard deviation in respect of the time to expiry, $N(d_1)$ is the area under the normal distribution curve to the left of half a standard deviation above the mean (zero) and $N(d_2)$ is the area to the left of a point on the horizontal axis that is half a standard deviation below zero.

The value of the call option at this point (where $P=Se^{-rt}$) might be looked upon as consisting entirely of time value. At this point time value is at its maximum. This peaking of time value can be seen by differentiating $C=PN(d_1)-Se^{-rt}N(d_2)$ with respect to P. This gives

$$\frac{dC}{dP}=N(d_1)$$

which is the option delta and lies between zero and 1. (Although $N(d_1)$ and $N(d_2)$ include P in their expressions, their derivatives with respect to P are infinitely small whereas $N(d_1)$ is finite. Therefore $dC/dP=N(d_1)$.)

A decline in P below Se^{-rt} (which might be regarded as a movement out of the money) will reduce the theoretical value of the call option. Since the value of the option consists entirely of time value when it is out of the money, this implies that time value declines as P falls below Se^{-rt}. As P rises above Se^{-rt} the theoretical value increases by a factor between zero and 1. The value of the option consists of both time and intrinsic value. Intrinsic value has a derivative of 1 with respect to P. It follows that the derivative of time value with respect to P is $N(d_1) - 1$, which would be negative. So time value declines as P deviates from Se^{-rt} in either direction. This implies that time value is at its maximum when $P = Se^{-rt}$.

As P rises above Se^{-rt} the derivative, $N(d_1)$, also rises but at a declining rate. The rate of increase of $N(d_1)$ declines because the normal distribution curve slopes downwards as the mean is deviated from. In other words, the gamma of the option falls as the option moves into the money. A parallel phenomenon occurs as the price of the underlying instrument declines below Se^{-rt}. This involves $N(d_1)$ falling but at a declining rate. Both the delta and the gamma decline.

If the price of the underlying instrument rises to extremely high levels, both $N(d_1)$ and $N(d_2)$ will approximate to 1. In such a situation the theoretical price of the option would approach $P - Se^{-rt}$. This involves a time value of zero ($P - Se^{-rt}$ might be used as a definition of intrinsic value). If the price of the underlying instrument falls to extremely low levels, $N(d_1)$ and $N(d_2)$ would approximate to zero. Consequently, the theoretical price of the option would approach zero. So time value would tend towards zero if the option becomes either very deeply in the money or very deeply out of the money.

It should be realised that option pricing models do not attempt to describe reality. A model is useful if the behaviour of the theoretical price has the same characteristics as the behaviour of real option prices such that the model provides good predictions of the levels of real option prices.

The Black–Scholes model has a number of deficiencies. Firstly, it ignores expected returns on the underlying instrument (e.g. dividends), but the rate of interest used in the equation can be adjusted to reflect such returns. Secondly, it is really only suitable for European-type options, which can be exercised only on the expiry date. Thirdly, it does not reflect any market expectations. A general expectation that the price of the underlying instrument will rise might cause a rise in call option prices and a fall in the prices of put options. The Black–Scholes model also fails to capture other possible price behaviour patterns, such as those arising from the frequent popularity of deep out-of-the-money options. The relative cheapness of such options might attract individuals and the resulting additional demand for them may raise their prices above those predicted by an options pricing model.

The Black–Scholes model treats $P = Se^{-rt}$ rather than $P = S$ as defining the at-the-money condition, and correspondingly intrinsic value is treated as $P - Se^{-rt}$ rather than $P - S$. This reflects the fact that the Black–Scholes model is relevant only to European-type options. American-type call options have an intrinsic value of $P - S$ since intrinsic value is defined as the profit obtained from immediate exercise of the option. European-type options cannot be immediately exercised (except at expiry) and in their case an alternative definition of intrinsic value is appropriate. This definition is the excess of the price of the underlying instrument over the strike price when the two values have been rendered comparable by discounting the strike price to its present value.

Appendix III Delta, gamma and kappa

A relationship of importance is between the price of an option and the volatility of the underlying instrument. This is referred to as kappa, epsilon, omega or vega. It is the change in the price of an option per percentage point change in the volatility of the underlying instrument. Since kappa can, for most purposes, be considered to be proportional to time value, it follows that kappa is also proportional to the square root of time remaining to expiry. Since bid–offer spreads on options often reflect the result on the option price of a particular change in volatility, it follows that the bid–offer spread would tend to be proportional to time value.

Appendix III

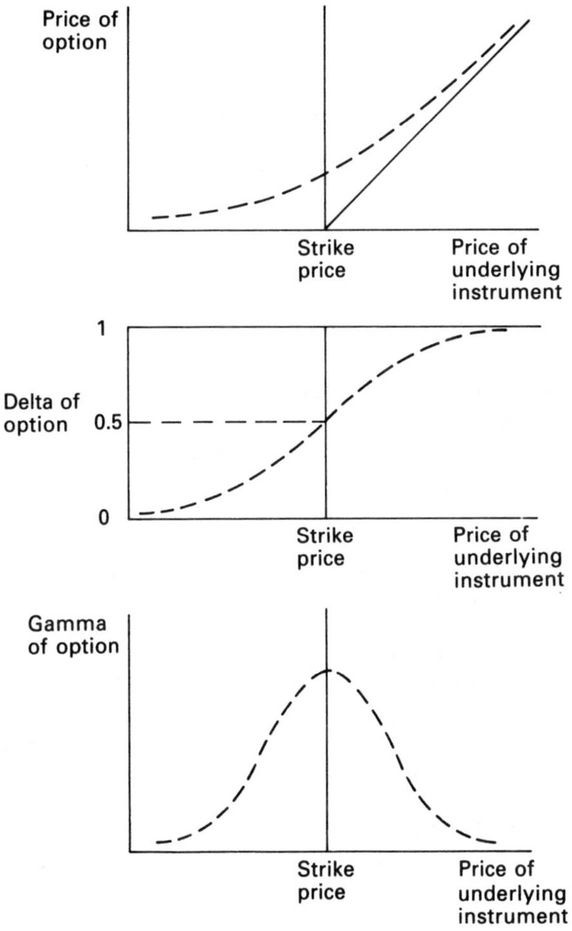

Figure AIII.1 Price, delta and gamma of a call option in relation to the price of the underlying instrument

Glossary

Accrued interest The amount of interest accumulated on a bond since its last coupon payment date.

Actuals The physical or cash financial instrument, as distinguished from a financial futures contract.

Adjusted exercise price The exercise price adjusted to reflect the change when a dividend is paid on a stock subject to a conventional option, or when any capital change such as a stock split occurs to a stock subject to a listed or conventional option.

AFBD Association of Futures Brokers and Dealers. The self-regulatory organisation in the United Kingdom.

All or none order An order to purchase or sell a security or contract in which the broker is instructed to fill the entire order or not fill any of the order.

All or none, same price order An order to purchase or sell a security or contract in which the broker is instructed to fill the entire order at the same price or not fill any of the order.

American option An option that can be exercised at any time before expiration.

Anticipatory hedge A transaction in which a hedger expects to make a transaction in the spot market at a future date and is attempting to protect against a change in the spot price.

Arbitrage The simultaneous purchase and sale of similar financial instruments to benefit from an expected change in relative prices.

Arbitrageur An individual who engages in an arbitrage transaction.

Ask price The price at which a market maker offers to sell. Also known as offer price.

Assignment Notice to an option writer that an option has been exercised by an option holder. An assignment notice is generally issued by the clearing house for exchange-traded options.

At-the-money option An option whose exercise price is equal to the market price of the underlying asset.

Automatic exercise A procedure for exchange-listed options whereby the clearing house automatically exercises in-the-money options at expiration.

Backwardation A condition in financial markets in which the forward or futures price is less than the spot price.

Glossary

Basis The difference between the spot price of a financial instrument and the price of a futures contract on that instrument.

Basis point A measurement of the change in yield levels for fixed-income securities. One basis point equals 0·01 per cent.

Bear A person who believes prices will move lower.

Bear call spread A spread designed to take advantage of falling asset prices by selling a call option with a low exercise price and buying one with a high exercise price.

Bear market A market in which prices are falling.

Bear put spread A spread designed to take advantage of falling asset prices by purchasing a put option with a high exercise price and selling one with a low exercise price.

Beta A measure of the relative volatility of stock price returns and market returns.

Bid An offer to purchase a specified quantity of a financial futures contract at a specified price.

Bid–offer spread The difference between the offer price and the bid price. Also known as the bid–ask spread.

Bid price The price at which a market maker offers to buy a security, option or futures.

Binomial model An option pricing model based on the assumption that at any point in time the price of the underlying asset or futures can change to one of only two possible values.

Black model A pricing model for an option on a forward or futures contract.

Black–Scholes model A pricing model for an option on an asset.

Bond option An option to buy or sell a bond.

Boundary condition A statement specifying the maximum or minimum price or some other limitation on the price of an option.

Box spread A combination of a horizontal, or calendar, call spread and a horizontal put spread. Both spreads have the same expiration dates on their long and short positions.

Break A sudden or rapid fall in asset prices.

Break out Undo a conversion or a reversal to restore the option buyer's original position.

Broker A person paid a fee or commission for acting as an agent in making contracts, sales or purchases. A floor broker is a person who actually executes someone else's trading orders on the trading floor of an exchange.

Bulge A rapid and sharp price advance.

Bull A person who believes prices will move higher.

Bull call spread A spread designed to take advantage of rising asset prices by buying a call option with a low exercise price and selling one with a high exercise price.

Bull market A market in which prices are rising.

Bull put spread A spread designed to take advantage of rising asset prices by selling a put option with a high exercise price and buying one with a low exercise price.

Butterfly spread A combination of a bull and bear spread, either put or call, using three different exercise prices. A volatility trading strategy.

Buy in Obtain assets in the market. Done by an option writer who otherwise holds insufficient assets to deliver to the option buyer at exercise.

Buy on close Buy at the end of a trading session at a price within the closing range.

Buy on opening Buy at the beginning of a trading session at a price within the opening range.

Calendar spread A spread involving the simultaneous sale of an option with a nearby expiration date and the purchase of an option with a more deferred expiration date. Both options have the same exercise price. Also known as a horizontal spread or a time spread.

Call The early retirement of a bond.

Callability A feature associated with many bonds in which the issuer is permitted to pay off the bond prior to its scheduled maturity date.

Call option An option giving the buyer the right to purchase the underlying asset at a fixed exercise price at or before expiration.

Cash and carry A theoretically riskless transaction consisting of a long position in the spot asset and a short position in the futures contract that is designed to be held until the futures contract expires.

Cash commodity The actual commodity or instrument as opposed to futures contracts based upon that commodity.

Cash market The underlying currency, money or capital market in which transactions for the purchase and sale of cash instruments to which futures contracts relate are carried out. Also known as the spot market.

Cash option An option written on an underlying cash instrument rather than a futures contract.

Cash price A price quotation obtained or a price actually received in a cash market.

Cash settlement A procedure for the settlement of a futures contract where, at delivery, instead of the physical transfer of the underlying asset, there is a final marking to market at the existing cash price and the positions are closed.

CBOE Chicago Board Options Exchange.

CBT Chicago Board of Trade.

CFTC Commodity Futures Trading Commission. The federal agency that regulates the futures markets in the United States.

Chart analysis The use of graphs and charts to analyse and predict market behaviour. Also known as technical analysis.

Cheapest to deliver The bond or gilt underlying a futures contract that is the most profitable for the seller to deliver. Also known as the best to deliver.

Class of options All call options or put options on the same underlying asset.

Clean price The price of a bond or gilt exclusive of accrued interest.

Clearing house The organisation which registers, monitors, matches and guarantees trades on a futures or options market, and carries out financial settlement of transactions.

Clearing member A member firm of the clearing house. Each clearing member must also be a member of an exchange, but not all members of an exchange are also members of the clearing house. All trades of a non-clearing member must be registered with, and eventually settled through, a clearing member. Also known as a clearing firm.

Close, the The period at the end of the trading session, officially designated by the exchange, during which all transactions are considered to be made 'at the close'.

Close out Undertake a transaction that cancels an existing position (e.g. a purchase to eliminate a short position).

Closing price The price at which transactions are made at the close on a given day. Frequently there is not just one price, but a range of prices at which transactions were made at the close.

Closing purchase transaction The purchase of an option identical in exercise price and expiration date to an option originally sold to liquidate an open option position.

Closing range The high and low prices at which transactions took place during 'the close'.

CME Chicago Mercantile Exchange.

Combination A position created either by purchasing a put and a call or by writing a put and a call, on the same underlying asset but with different exercise prices and/or expiry dates.

Commercial paper A short-term promissory note issued by a large, creditworthy corporation.

Commission A fee paid by the parties in a transaction to a broker for arranging the transaction.

Commission broker A trader on the floor of an exchange who executes transactions for off-the-floor customers.

Commodity pool An investment arrangement in which individuals combine their funds and the total amount of funds is used to trade futures contracts, with a large cash reserve set aside to meet margin calls. Essentially equivalent to a futures fund.

Commodity pool operator The organiser or manager of a commodity pool.

Commodity trading adviser An individual who specialises in offering advice regarding the trading of futures contracts.

Contango A condition in financial markets in which the forward or futures price is greater than the spot price.

Continuously compounded return A rate of return in which the asset price grows continuously, as opposed to interest being paid at discrete intervals.

Contract A financial futures contract is a binding agreement to make and take delivery at a specified date of a fixed quantity of a specified financial instrument.

Contract grade The type of cash instruments listed in the rules of the exchange that can be used when delivering cash commodities against futures contracts.

Contract month The month in which futures contracts may be satisfied by making or accepting delivery.

Convergence   The movement to equality of spot and futures prices as the delivery date approaches.

Conversion arbitrage   A transaction in which the arbitrageur buys an asset (or futures contract), buys a put option and sells a call option. The options have the same exercise price and expiration date. The purpose is to profit from the excess of the price implied by the synthetic short over the price of the long position.

Conversion factor   A factor used to determine the invoice amount to be paid at delivery for a cash bond delivered against a futures contract. Also known as the price factor.

Cost of carry   The cost involved in holding an asset that consists of interest lost on funds tied up.

Coupon   The interest paid on a bond or gilt.

Cover   To offset a previous futures transaction with an equal and opposite transaction. Short covering is a purchase of futures contracts to offset an earlier sale of an equal number of the same delivery month. Liquidation is the sale of futures contracts to offset an equal number of futures contracts of the same delivery month purchased earlier.

Covered call write   A strategy of writing call options against a long position of the underlying asset.

Covered option   A written option is covered if it is matched by an opposing cash or futures position in the underlying asset, or by an opposing option position.

Covered put write   A strategy of writing put options while simultaneously shorting an identical amount of the underlying asset.

Cross hedging   The hedging with a futures contract of a different, but related, cash instrument.

Cross rates   The exchange rate between two currencies implied by their exchange rates with a third currency, e.g. the £/DM rate implied by the £/$ and DM/$ rates.

Current delivery   The futures contract that will become deliverable during the current month.

Cycle   The set of expiration dates applicable to different classes of option, or delivery months applicable to futures.

Daily price limits   The maximum and minimum prices at which a futures contract can trade. These are established by the clearing house and are expressed in relation to the previous day's settlement price.

Daily settlement   The process in a futures market in which the daily price changes are paid by the parties incurring losses to the parties making profits.

Day order   An order that is placed for execution, if possible, during only one trading session. If the order cannot be exercised that day, it is automatically cancelled.

Day trading   Refers to establishing and liquidating the same futures position or positions within one day's trading.

Dealer   A person who or firm which assists in a transaction by purchasing the security or contract from a seller and selling it to a buyer.

Deferred futures The more distant delivery months in which futures trading is taking place.

Deliverable names Financial instruments, specified in the rules of the exchange, which may be offered when making delivery of an actual instrument in satisfaction of a futures contract.

Delivery The tender and receipt of an actual financial instrument or cash in settlement of a futures contract.

Delivery month A calendar month during which delivery against a futures contract can be made.

Delivery notice The written notice given by the seller of his intention to make delivery against an open, short futures position on a particular date.

Delivery points Those locations and facilities designated by futures exchanges at which the financial instruments covered by a futures contract may be delivered in fulfilment of such a contract.

Delivery price The price fixed by the clearing house at which deliveries on futures contracts are invoiced.

Delta A measure of the amount the option price will change for a one-unit change in the underlying asset (the derivative of the option price with respect to the asset price).

Delta hedge An options hedge in which the number of contracts is ratioed up by the reciprocal of the option delta in order to achieve complete cover for the hedged position.

Delta spread A ratio spread of options established as a neutral position by using the deltas of the options concerned to determine the hedge ratio.

Diagonal bear spread The purchase of a longer maturity option and the sale of a shorter maturity, lower exercise price option. The options can be either puts or calls.

Diagonal bull spread The sale of a shorter maturity option and the purchase of a longer maturity, lower exercise price option. The options can be either puts or calls.

Diagonal spread A spread in which the options differ with respect to both strike price and expiry date.

Difference account In the United Kingdom, an account given to a client by a broker when a position is closed.

Discount An option is trading at a discount if it is trading for less than its intrinsic value.

Discretionary account An account over which any individual or organisation, other than the person in whose name the account is carried, exercises trading authority or control.

Dividend protection A feature associated with over-the-counter options in which the exercise price is reduced by the amount of any dividend paid on the underlying stock.

Dividend yield The ratio of the dividend to the stock price.

Double option An option to buy or sell but not both. Exercise of the right to buy causes the right to sell to expire and vice versa.

Down-and-out call A call option that expires if the asset price falls below a predetermined level.

Duration The sensitivity of a bond's price to a change in its yield.

Dynamic hedge An investment strategy, often associated with portfolio insurance, in which a stock is hedged by selling futures in such a manner that the position is adjusted frequently and simulates a protective put.

Early exercise Exercise of an option before its expiration date.

Efficient market A market in which the prices of assets reflect all the available relevant information.

Elasticity The responsiveness of one variable to a change in another variable. It is computed as the percentage change in one variable divided by the percentage change in the other.

Eligible margin The cash or other collateral which the exchange specifies that members may accept from their customers to satisfy initial and variation margin requirements.

Epsilon The change in the price of an option associated with a 1 per cent change in implied volatility (the derivative of the option price with respect to volatility). Also referred to as eta, vega, omega and kappa.

Equity option An option on a stock.

Eurodollar A dollar deposited in a bank outside the United States.

European currency unit A combination of major European currencies.

European option A call or put option that can be exercised only on the expiration date.

Evening up Buying or selling to offset an existing market position.

Exchange The market in which the purchase or sale of financial futures or options contracts takes place, generally through open outcry.

Exchange of cash for futures The exchange of a specified quantity of the cash instrument for the equivalent quantity in futures.

Exchange rate The rate at which a given amount of one currency converts to another currency.

Ex-dividend date A date after which an investor purchasing a stock does not receive the upcoming dividend.

Exercise The action taken by the holder of an option contract to exercise his right. When a call is exercised, the holder acquires the underlying asset at the option exercise price. When a put is exercised, the holder sells the underlying asset at the option exercise price.

Exercise limit A limit on the number of option contracts a holder may exercise within a specific period.

Exercise price The price at which the option holder may buy or sell the underlying asset, as defined in the option contract. Also known as strike, or striking, price.

Expiration date The date after which an option can no longer be exercised.

Face value The principal amount borrowed on a loan.

Fair value The option value derived from an option valuation model. The theoretical futures price (the price that would offer no arbitrage opportunities).

Fill or kill order An order at a specified price which must be offered or bid three times. If not filled, it is cancelled immediately.

Financial instrument The actual currency, fixed-interest security or deposit which is specified in a financial futures contract.

First notice day The first day on which notices of intention to deliver actual financial instruments in fulfilment of a given month's financial futures contracts are authorised.

Fixed hedge A hedge in which the quantity being hedged is matched by the quantity that the options give the right to buy or sell.

Floor broker A trader on the floor of an exchange who executes trades for others who are off the floor.

Floor trader An exchange member who executes his own trades by being personally present in the pit or place provided for futures trading.

Forward contract An agreement between two parties, a buyer and a seller, to buy an asset or currency at a later date at a fixed price.

Forward/forward rate The rate agreed upon in a forward contract for a loan or the rate implied by the relationship between interest rates for different maturities.

Forward market A market in which forward contracts are constructed.

Forward months Futures contracts calling for a deferred delivery.

Fundamental analysis The prediction of market behaviour and price trends by analysis of underlying factors of demand and supply (contrasted with technical analysis).

Futures commission merchant A firm in the business of executing futures transactions for the public (United States).

Futures contract A contract traded on a futures exchange for the delivery of a specified quantity of a specified commodity or financial instrument at a future time.

Futures fund A mutual fund that specialises in trading futures contracts.

Futures option An option written on a futures contract rather than a cash or spot instrument.

Gamma The amount by which the delta of an option changes for a one-unit change in the price of the underlying asset (the second derivative of the option price with respect to the asset price).

Gilt Gilt-edged security. A British government bond.

Give-up At the request of the customer, a brokerage house which has not performed the service is credited with the execution of an order.

GNMA Government National Mortgage Association. A US government agency that approves the issue of mortgage-backed securities with repayment of principal and interest fully guaranteed by the US Treasury.

GTC Good till cancelled. Open orders to buy or sell at a fixed price that remain effective until executed or cancelled.

Heavy A market in which there is a large number of selling orders overhanging the market without a corresponding number of buying orders.

Hedge A transaction in which an investor seeks to protect a position or anticipated position in the spot market by using an opposite position in options or futures.

Hedge portfolio A portfolio being hedged, often used in the context of a long stock, short call or long stock, long put in which the hedge ratio is continuously adjusted to produce a risk-free portfolio.

Hedger A person who hedges.

Hedge ratio The ratio of options or futures to a spot position that achieves an objective such as minimising or eliminating risk.

Historical volatility The standard deviation of a security, futures or currency obtained by estimating it from historical data over a recent time period.

Holder Buyer.

Holding period The time period over which an investment is held.

Horizontal spread See calendar spread.

ICCH International Commodities Clearing House. The clearing house for LIFFE contracts and LTOM currency options.

Implied repo rate The difference between the current cash price and a futures price expressed as an interest rate.

Implied volatility The value of asset price volatility that will equate the fair value of an option with the market price of that option.

Index option An option written on an underlying stock index as opposed to a specific asset.

Initial margin The deposit a customer must make on purchasing or selling a futures contract.

Intercontract spread A futures transaction involving a long position in a futures on one instrument and a short position in a futures on another instrument.

Interest rate parity The equality of the forward (or futures) premium/discount between two currencies and the interest rate differential between those currencies.

In-the-money option An option which has intrinsic value. A call is in the money if the asset price is above the exercise price; a put is in the money if the asset price is below the exercise price.

Intracontract spread A futures transaction consisting of a long position in a futures expiring in one month and a short position in an otherwise identical futures expiring in another month.

Intrinsic value The amount of profit that would be realised if the option were immediately exercised. Also known as parity value.

Introducing broker A broker who arranges futures transactions for customers but contracts with another firm or individual for the execution of the trade.

Inverted market A futures market in which the nearer months are selling at a premium to the more distant months.

Invoice amount The cash amount paid and received upon delivery against a government bond futures contract.

Kerb trading The execution of transactions after the close of the official market.

Last trading day The final day during which trading may take place in a particular delivery month. Futures contracts outstanding at the end of the last trading day must be settled by delivery of the specified financial instrument, or settlement may be made in cash in certain contracts.

Life of contract Period between the beginning of trading in a particular future and expiration of trading in the delivery month.

Limit down An occurrence in which the futures price moves down to the lower daily price limit.

Limit move An occurrence in which the futures price hits the upper or lower daily price limit.

Limit order A request to purchase or sell a security, option or futures that specifies the maximum price to pay or the minimum price to accept.

Limit up An occurrence in which the futures price moves up to the upper daily price limit.

Liquidation Any transaction that offsets or closes out a position.

Liquid market A market where buying and selling can be accomplished with ease, due to the presence of a large number of interested buyers and sellers prepared to trade substantial quantities at small price differences.

Local A trader on the floor of the futures exchange who executes trades for his or her personal account.

London Interbank Offer Rate (LIBOR) The interest rate at which London banks will lend to one another.

Long The position which is established by the purchase of an asset or option if there is no offsetting position.

Long hedge The purchase of a futures contract in anticipation of actual purchases in the cash market.

Long of the basis The position of a person who has purchased the cash instrument and hedged it with sales of the corresponding futures contract.

LTOM London Traded Options Market.

Macro hedging A strategy in which a firm hedges the combined exposure of all of its assets and liabilities.

Maintenance margin The minimum margin which a customer must keep on deposit with a member at all times.

Margin calls Additional funds which a person with a position may be called upon to deposit if there is an adverse price change or if margin requirements alter.

Market order An order to buy or sell a contract that is to be executed at the best possible price and as soon as possible.

Mark to market The process by which daily price changes are reflected in payments by parties incurring losses to parties making profits. Also known as daily settlement.

Maximum price fluctuation The maximum amount the contract price can change, up or down, during one trading session, as defined by exchange rules.

Micro hedging A strategy in which a firm hedges only specific assets, liabilities or transactions as opposed to hedging the aggregate net exposure.

Minimum price fluctuation The smallest increment of price movement possible in trading a given contract. Also known as a tick.

Money market The market for short-term securities.

Money spread An option transaction that involves a long position in one option and a short position in an otherwise identical option with a different exercise price. Also known as a vertical spread.

Naked call writing Writing a call on an underlying asset which is not owned by the writer.

National Futures Association An organisation of firms engaged in the futures business that serves as the industry's self-regulatory body in the United States.

Nearby The nearest trading month.

Net position The number of contracts bought or sold which have not been offset by opposite transactions.

Nominal price Price quotation on a futures contract for a period in which no actual trading took place.

Notice day A day on which notices of intent to deliver, pertaining to a specified delivery month, may be issued.

OCC Options Clearing Corporation.

Offer Indicates a willingness to sell at a given price.

Offer price The price at which a market maker offers to sell.

Offset The liquidation of a purchase of futures through the sale of an equal number of contracts of the same delivery month, or the covering of a short sale of futures through the purchase of an equal number of contracts of the same delivery month.

Omnibus account An account carried by one futures commission merchant or broker with another in which the transactions of two or more persons are combined rather than designated separately.

On opening The specification of execution of an order during the opening or as soon thereafter as possible.

Open contracts Contracts which have been bought or sold without the transactions having been completed or offset by subsequent sale or purchase, or actual delivery or receipt of the underlying financial instrument.

Opening The period at the beginning of the trading session officially designated by the exchange during which all transactions are considered to be made 'at the opening'.

Opening price (or range) The price or price range of transactions recorded during the period designated by the exchange as the official opening.

Opening transaction The purchase or writing of a put or call option which establishes a new position.

Open interest The net total of outstanding contracts for a particular options or futures class.

Open order An order which is good until cancelled or executed.

Open outcry Method of dealing on futures and options markets involving verbal bids and offers which are audible to all other market participants on the trading floor or pit.

Option The right to buy or sell a specific quantity of a specific asset at a fixed price at or before a future date.

Original margin The initial deposit of margin money required to cover a specific new futures position.

Out-of-the-money option An option that has no intrinsic value – because for a call the exercise price is above the asset price, and for a put the exercise price is below the asset price.

Overbought A condition under which heavy liquidation of weakly held long futures positions appears imminent.

Oversold A condition under which heavy covering of weakly held short futures positions appears imminent.

Over-the-counter option An option traded over the counter as opposed to on a listed exchange. There is a direct link between buyer and seller, and no standardisation of striking prices and expiration dates.

P+S A purchase and sale statement sent by a broker to a customer when his futures position has changed, showing the number of contracts involved, the contract prices, the gross profit and loss, commission charges, and the net profit and loss on the transactions.

Paper profit The profit that would be realised if open futures contracts were liquidated as of a certain time or at a certain price.

Perfect hedge A hedge in which the change in the futures price is identical to the change in the cash market price.

Perturbation A measure of volatility based upon the change in the price of a bond in response to a specific change in the relevant interest rate.

Pit An octagonal area on the trading floor of an exchange, surrounded by a tier of steps upon which traders and brokers stand while executing futures trades.

Point The smallest increment of price movement possible in trading a given futures contract, equivalent to the minimum price fluctuation. Also known as a tick.

Portfolio insurance An investment strategy employing combinations of securities, options or futures that is designed to provide a minimum or floor value of the portfolio at a future date.

Position An interest in the market, either long or short, in terms of open contracts.

Position limit The maximum number of puts and calls on the same side of the market (e.g. long calls and short puts) that can be held in a single account.

Position trading A type of trading involving the holding of open futures contracts for an extended period of time.

Premium The price of an option – the sum of money which the option buyer pays and the option writer receives for the rights granted by the option.

Price limits The maximum price advance or decline from the previous day's settlement price permitted for a contract in one trading session by the regulations of the exchange.

Price sensitivity hedge ratio The number of futures contracts used in a hedge that leaves the value of a portfolio unaffected by a change in an underlying variable, such as an interest rate.

Primary market The principal underlying market for a financial instrument.

Profit graph A graphical representation of the profits to a given options strategy for different underlying asset prices.

Program trading The use of computers to detect and trade upon mispricing in the relationship between the prices of stocks and stock index futures.

Protective put An investment strategy involving the use of a long position in a put and a stock to provide a minimum selling price for the stock.

Pure discount bond A bond, such as a Treasury bill, that pays no coupon but sells for a discount from par value.

Put/call parity A relationship between put and call prices that implies an absence of arbitrage opportunities.

Put option An option which gives the buyer the right to sell the underlying asset at a fixed price at or before the expiration date.

Pyramiding The practice of margining additional futures trades using accrued profits to previous futures transactions.

Rally An upward movement in prices following a decline.

Range The high and low prices, or high and low bids and offers, recorded during a specified period.

Ratio calendar spread Selling more near-term options than longer maturity options at the same strike price.

Ratio spread A spread in which the component options are not equal in number.

Ratio write Buying stock and selling options on a larger amount of stock.

Reaction A decline in prices following an advance.

Recovery A price advance following a decline.

Registered representative An individual registered with the exchange and the regulatory authorities to solicit customer business for his firm (United Kingdom).

Repurchase agreement The selling of a security by one party to another at the same time that the other party enters into an agreement to resell the securities to the first party at a predetermined price and date. Also known as repo.

Reversal A synthetic long position combined with a short position in the underlying instrument.

Risk aversion The characteristic of an investor who dislikes risk and will not assume more risk without an additional return.

Risk premium The additional return risk-averse investors expect for assuming risk.

Risk–return trade-off The concept in which additional risk must be accepted to increase the expected return.

Roll A futures hedging strategy that constantly uses only contracts with the nearest delivery month.

Roll-over Substitute a futures or options contract with a more distant expiry/delivery date for a previously established position.

Round turn A complete futures transaction in which an individual long or short position is closed out by an opposite futures transaction, or by making or taking delivery. Also known as a round trip.

Sandwich spread See butterfly spread.

Scalp Trade for small gains. Scalping usually involves establishing and liquidating a position quickly, always within the same trading day.

Seat A membership of a futures or options exchange.

SEC Securities and Exchange Commission. The federal agency responsible for regulating the securities and options markets in the United States.

Secondary market The market for assets that were issued previously and are now trading among investors.

Seller Equivalent to an option writer.

Series All options of the same class having the same exercise price and expiration date.

Settlement price The daily price at which the clearing house clears all trades. The settlement price is determined by reference to the closing range, and is used to determine margin calls and invoice prices for deliveries.

Short The position created by the sale of an asset or option if there is no offsetting position.

Short hedge The sale of a futures contract to lock in the current price and thereby eliminate or lessen the possible decline in value of ownership of an approximately equal amount of an actual financial instrument.

Short of the basis The position of a person who has sold the cash financial instrument and hedged it with a purchase of financial futures contracts.

Short sale An investment transaction in which securities are borrowed from a broker and sold to a buyer.

Short squeeze A situation in which a lack of supply tends to force prices upwards to the disadvantage of those who are short.

Simple return A rate of return that is not compounded.

Specialist A trader on the floor of an exchange who is responsible for making a market in certain securities or options (United States).

Speculator A person who buys or sells futures contracts in the hope of profiting from subsequent price movements.

Spot market The market for assets that involves the immediate sale and delivery of the asset.

Spot price The price of an asset on the spot market.

Spread An option or futures transaction consisting of a long position in one contract and a short position in another, similar contract.

Spread delta A measure of the sensitivity of a spread to a change in the price of the underlying asset, currency or futures.

Standard deviation A measure of the dispersion of a variable around its mean, equal to the square root of the variance.

Stock index An indicator of the general level of stock prices.

Stop loss order An order to sell at the market when a definite price is reached. Usually used as a method of limiting losses by traders with open positions.

Straddle A combination of a long put and a long call (or a short put and a short call) on the same underlying asset, each with the same exercise price and expiration date. An intracontract futures spread.

Strap A combination of two calls and one put, with the same exercise price and expiration date.

Strike price See exercise price.

Strip A combination of two puts and one call, with the same exercise price and expiration date. A strip hedge uses futures contracts of differing maturities in order to approximate the maturities of the exposures being hedged.

Switching Liquidating an existing futures position and simultaneously reinstating that position in a different maturity future on the same financial instrument.

Synthetic call A combination of a long put and long asset, futures or currency that replicates the behaviour of a call.

Synthetic put A combination of a long call and short asset, currency or futures that replicates the behaviour of a put.

Synthetic stock A combination of a put and a call option which is equivalent to the stock.

Systematic risk The risk associated with the market as a whole. As opposed to non-systematic risk which characterises specific sectors or stocks.

Tender Delivery against futures.

Term structure of interest rates The relationship between interest rates and maturities of money market instruments and bonds.

Theta The change in the price of the option associated with a one-period reduction in the time to expiration (the derivative of the option price with respect to time).

Tick The minimum possible change in price, either up or down.

Time value The amount by which an option's premium exceeds its intrinsic value.

Time value decay The erosion of an option's time value as expiration approaches.

Traded option An option that can be bought and sold on the floor of an exchange.

Treasury bond A coupon-bearing bond issued by the US government with an original maturity of at least ten years.

Treasury note A coupon-bearing bond issued by the US government with an original maturity of one to ten years.

Trend The general direction of market prices.

Underlying instrument The instrument to which an option relates.

Upside capture The percentage of the increase in market value of an uninsured portfolio earned by an insured portfolio in a bull market.

Valuation trading The purchase of undervalued and simultaneous sale of overvalued options.

Value basis The difference between the theoretical and actual futures prices.

Variable limits   A system on some futures exchanges which allows for larger than normally allowable price movements under certain circumstances.

Variation margin   The gains or losses on open positions which are calculated by marking to market at the end of each trading day, and credited or debited by the clearing house to each clearing member's account, and by members to their customers' accounts.

Vertical bear spread   The purchase of an option with a high exercise price and the sale of an option with a lower exercise price. Both options will have the same expiration date and could be puts or calls.

Vertical bull spread   The sale of an option with a high exercise price and the purchase of an option with a lower exercise price. Both options will have the same expiration date and could be puts or calls.

Volatility   A measure of the amount by which an asset price is expected to fluctuate over a given period. Normally measured by the annual standard deviation of daily price changes.

Volume   The number of transactions in a contract made during a specified period of time.

Wash sale   A transaction in which a stock is sold at a loss and an essentially identical stock, or a call option on the stock, is purchased within a 61-day period surrounding the sale. Tax laws prohibit deducting the loss on the sale (United States).

Wild card   An arbitrage transaction associated with the Chicago Board of Trade's treasury bond futures contract that exists because of differences in the closing times of the spot and futures markets.

Writer   The seller of a call or a put option in an opening transaction.

Yield curve   The relationship between yields on money market instruments and bonds and their maturities.

Yield to maturity   The rate of discount that equates the future coupons and principal repayment with the current price of a bond or gilt. Also known as the (gross) redemption yield.

Index

Index

Index

Index